HAMPSHIRE

COUNTY CRICKET CLUB 1946-2006

ENTERTAIN OR PERISH

DAVE ALLEN

PHILLIMORE

2007

Published by
PHILLIMORE & CO. LTD
Shopwyke Manor Barn, Chichester, West Sussex, England
www.phillimore.co.uk

ISBN 978-1-86077-448-5

Printed and bound in Great Britain

HAMPSHIRE

COUNTY CRICKET CLUB 1946-2006

ENTERTAIN OR PERISH

The Rose Bowl pavilion: Warne bowling.

CONTENTS

ACKNOWLEDGEMENTS

MY FIRST and greatest gratitude is to all the Hampshire cricketers who have contributed to this project. I am also grateful to fellow supporters, committee members, vice-presidents and officers of the club who helped in any way.

The players who shared thoughts and memories with me in various ways were:

Jon Ayling, Adi Aymes, Dennis Baldry, Mike Barnard, David Blake, Vic Cannings, Alan Castell, Cardigan Connor, John Crawley, Richard Gilliat, Jimmy Gray, Bernard Harrison, Leo Harrison, Peter Haslop, Malcolm Heath, Bob Herman, Gerry Hill, Arthur Holt, Colin Ingleby-Mackenzie, Kevan James, Will Kendall, Derek Kenway, Charlie Knott, John Manners, Raj Maru, Dimitri Mascarenhas, Neil McCorkell, Richard McIlwaine, Tony Middleton, Bobby Parks, Lawrie Prittipaul, Nic Pothas, Alan Rayment, Barry Reed, John Rice, Neville Rogers, Peter Sainsbury, Lee Savident, Derek Shackleton, Robin Smith, Bob Stephenson, Mike Taylor, Bryan Timms, David Turner, Tim Tremlett, Shaun Udal, Alan Wassell, Keith Wheatley, Paul Whitaker, 'Butch' White.

I wish to acknowledge the enormous influence of Hampshire's many fine historians and cricket writers. From the past, the key names include John Nyren jnr, Harry Altham, Desmond Eagar and, of course John Arlott. Among my friends and contemporaries I am very grateful for the kindness, support and interest over some years of Neil Jenkinson, Andrew Renshaw, Ashley Mote, Stephen Saunders, Vic Isaacs and Alan Edwards. The family of the late Richard Humphries donated many wonderful scrapbooks covering the period, which contributed significantly to some aspects of the work and Peter Marshall loaned a number of scrapbooks that had been organised by Desmond Eagar.

Many of the photographs are mine and a few historical images come from the club's archive. Elsewhere they generally and rightly enjoy a Hampshire 'heritage'. Patrick Eagar, son of Desmond, has provided a number of delightful images, including one or two from the 1970s that I believe have not appeared before. Another professional photographer and Hampshire member, Innes Marlow, has also provided a number of images as has his mother Susanne and my thanks go to Hampshire member Dave Lloyd, Mike Adams (father of Jimmy) and to the *Daily Echo* in Southampton for their generosity in making pictures available.

Finally, I am grateful for the companionship and joint purpose of my colleagues on the Heritage Group at Hampshire Cricket. All the profits from the sale of this book will support our future activities and enable us to extend our tributes to Hampshire cricketers past, present and future.

DAVE ALLEN
Old Portsmouth
Autumn 2006

Preface

The real cricket history is not in the scoresheets but lives absolutely untarnished through being told by succeeding generations of cricketers.

John Arlott, Hampshire Handbook, 1951

IN THE INTRODUCTION to this book I point out that while the Hampshire village of Hambledon is often popularly thought to be the birthplace of cricket, the game's historians know that it was no such thing, although in the second half of the 18th century it was the most important centre of English cricket before it handed over control to London, Lord's and the MCC.

Nonetheless there is one reasonable claim to be made on behalf of the old Hambledon men that is particularly relevant to this book. Some years after the English cricket centre moved to the capital, John Nyren, son of the great player Richard Nyren, sat down with Cowden Clarke to tell the story of those days and the subsequent publication *Cricketers of My Time* became a true classic of cricketing literature. In particular it can claim to be the first classic cricketer's tale telling of the cricket, and that has become a familiar approach, not least in Hampshire.

There have been various books about the history of Hampshire cricket. The first, by the eminent cricket historian F.S. Ashley-Cooper, was published in 1924 and traced a history of Hampshire cricket since the 1780s when Hambledon sides sometimes adopted the county name. The first 'official history' was written by three of its participants, Harry Altham, John Arlott and Desmond Eagar, and published in 1957.

Thirty-one years later, Peter Wynne-Thomas repeated the season-by-season story and brought it up-to-date but to the point just before Hampshire's first Lord's cup final in 1988. In 2000 the three cup triumphs were included in an illustrated history of the county cricket club compiled by Neil Jenkinson, Andrew Renshaw and me. By then Norman Gannaway (1990) had also written *A History of Cricket in Hampshire* that considered 'all levels of the game' in the county over a period of 300 years, not merely the first-class game. In the past 50 years there have also been a number of important statistical histories published by Norman Drake, Roy Webber and Vic Isaacs.

Wynne-Thomas's history was one of a series on the counties. The series editor had wanted John Arlott but he was too elderly to offer more than a personal perspective, which opened the book. Wynne-Thomas is one of England's leading cricket historians but it is largely a book culled from the record pages, although this perhaps made his history 'objective'. By contrast Altham, Arlott and Eagar had all appeared on the field with Hampshire sides and Eagar wrote specifically about the post-war period when he was both captain and secretary. In a paragraph preceding this third part of the book Altham wrote that 'inevitably' the authorship could not 'reflect' Desmond Eagar's significant contribution to Hampshire cricket and the county cricket club during the period.

The process by which Nyren recounted his stories was always an influence in the writing of this book. A key source and major influence was, of course, the writing of John Arlott, in particular the extent to which his work always drew upon his conversations with the cricketers of whom he was so fond. I remember once commenting to Neville Rogers and Leo Harrison that, for a 'non-player', Arlott was a good judge. The three men had been great pals so Neville's chuckle was a kindly one as he replied that among Arlott's attributes were a sense of the right question at the right time and a good retentive memory when replies were forthcoming.

My first significant conversation with a Hampshire cricketer occurred at a 2nd XI match when I asked Hampshire's former batsman and first major coach Arthur Holt to autograph a picture in a book of Hampshire biographies. He complied willingly but not for about half-an-hour, during which time he read many of the entries and embellished the accounts with tales of his own. It encouraged me to seek out other players who had played for Hampshire and I carried out formal public and private interviews, informal conversations and correspondences with many of them. In many cases these dialogues are obvious in the text that follows, although in some cases I have paraphrased or generalised from a number of similar views.

It is for others to decide whether the approach works but I wish to record my enormous gratitude to the men – many of them lifelong heroes – who have shared minutes or hours with me. I am also grateful to colleagues on the committee in the county's administration or fellow vice-presidents and club historians who have been able to furnish me with information and memories from the past in the construction of this tale.

I hope that the book stands as a tribute to all those who have contributed to Hampshire cricket but of course I accept full responsibility for any errors or misrepresentation herein. The matter of my own involvement in the recounting of this story is a complex one. I have written this book about a period in Hampshire cricket, most of which I have followed as a county member and committed supporter, and the account incorporates many conversations and comments from others who have been involved. One section tells of the period from the mid-1990s when the club took a radically new direction on and off the field. During that period I was variously an Executive Committee member, a vice-president, Chairman of Portsmouth Area Committee and Hon. Curator of the Heritage Group. As a consequence, there will be passages in what follows where the voice you hear is clearly mine, just as I hope that elsewhere it was clearly Peter Sainsbury perhaps, or Cardigan Connor. I suspect that others might occasionally tell parts of this tale differently but on the whole it is derived as much from the full range of available documents as from any idiosyncratic or merely personal memory. It is more than anything a record of thanks that I have been privileged to witness and lately be involved in the most exciting years in the history of county cricket in Hampshire.

FOREWORD

SHAUN UDAL

I GREW UP in a cricketing family in north Hampshire where my father was a very good club cricketer. His father had played for Leicestershire and Middlesex and my great-great-grandfather played first-class cricket in the 1870s.

As a teenager in the 1980s I played for Hampshire's junior representative sides and then in 1987 I made my 2nd XI debut at The Oval and took seven Surrey wickets in the match. During this period I worked with a number of coaches who had played cricket for Hampshire including Barry Reed, John Rice and Peter Sainsbury. Two years later I made my county debut in Mark Nicholas's side, thrilled to be playing alongside Test cricketers like Malcolm Marshall, Robin and Chris Smith and Paul Terry. I was very proud to be presented with my county cap in 1992.

There was also the great excitement of two winners' medals in the cup finals of 1991 and 1992 and a couple of years later I found myself in England's Test and one-day squads. I made a number of limited-overs international appearances and dreamed of a full Test match. Sadly for a few seasons my career did not develop as I hoped and Hampshire also struggled as the fine side of the 1980s broke up. Nonetheless there were still good moments – in 1997 I made my highest first-class score (117*) and my best limited-overs score of 78. I have always enjoyed batting and there have been some good days.

From 2001, I have been very excited to be involved in the Hampshire 'revolution'. On the field, Shane Warne has been a brilliant captain as well as the world's greatest spin bowler and on occasions I have been proud to act as his deputy – never more so than when I became the first Hampshire-born captain to lift a trophy, at Lord's in 2005. Although we have been near-yet-far from the Championship in the past couple of years there is still time for Shane's side to win that trophy.

Off the field, Rod Bransgrove has taken the whole club to a new, hardly imaginable level. We have a magnificent ground and practice facilities and the future is very bright as long as we are encouraged to develop the ground as an international venue.

Talking of internationals, for some time I thought my England career was over but in the winter of 2005-6 came the call that culminated in that magical day in Mumbai when my 4-14 helped England to victory.

Cricketers can never plan too far ahead for we cannot know what the future may bring. For myself, I am proud to have enjoyed a 20-year career with my home county and delighted that this book records that period and the years leading up to it in detail.

SHAUN UDAL
Hampshire and England

INTRODUCTION
SEPTEMBER SONGS

AT AROUND TEATIME on 1 September 1961, Peter Sainsbury from Southampton bowled a ball to the young Derbyshire wicketkeeper Bob Taylor, who hit it long towards the boundary where Danny Livingstone held the catch. The Bournemouth crowd spilled onto the ground to cheer Hampshire's first County Champions and within twenty minutes the glamorous Hampshire captain Colin Ingleby-Mackenzie was addressing the crowd from the balcony of the old Dean Park pavilion.

Outside the frequently grumpy swathes of Yorkshire's cricket empire, Hampshire's success – and particularly the captain's – was popular throughout the world of English cricket. On the following morning, Brian Chapman in the *Daily Mirror* summed up the general view:

> A mighty fine thing happened on a golden afternoon here today. If you are sentimental, you may, by permission, rhapsodise a little and call it a moving and many splendoured thing. The greatest prize in England cricket's gallery, the County Championship, came home to its own heart and birthplace.

We know of course that his last point makes reference to the famous 18th-century Hambledon club and equally that while Hambledon took English cricket towards professional maturity it was not actually the birthplace of cricket – not even the first location of cricket in the county. But, swept up in the excitement

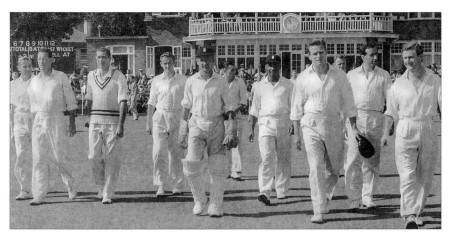

1   *Colin Ingleby-Mackenzie with his Champions at Bournemouth 1961.*

2 *Hampshire's Australians Watson and Bichel hold the C&G Trophy in 2006 watched by Southern Africans Latouf, Ervine and McLean and applauded by home-grown Tremlett.*

and sentiment of the moment, we may endorse Chapman's poetic licence and E.W. Swanton's more measured view in the *Daily Telegraph* that the victory was 'to a considerable extent a triumph' for Hampshire's dashing young captain.

Almost exactly 44 years to the day after that triumph the dashing captain – no longer quite so young but as charismatic as ever – was at Lord's as the great English season of 2005 drew to a close. He was there in his official capacity as the President of his beloved county, as he and thousands of Hampshire fans descended on Lord's for the last of the traditional knock-out cup finals that had begun in 1963 when Ingleby-Mackenzie still captained Hampshire. By the end of that Saturday in 2005 he was applauding his county as they won the ninth of their major domestic titles, which had begun with his triumph in 1961. Before the start of the following season, Ingleby-Mackenzie was dead. His connection with Hampshire stretches from his appearance in the schoolboy nets at the start of the first post-war season in 1946 to the most recent of those triumphs in September 2005 and into 2006. This book tells the story of those 60 years in the history of Hampshire cricket, partly in the broader context of dramatic changes in the domestic, national and international game.

One of the changes for Hampshire was that the popular acclaim of 1961 was less evident outside the county in 2005. Whereas Chapman, Swanton and the press had welcomed Hampshire's 'fairy tale' success of 1961, the reaction to their triumph of 2005 was very different – this time the national press did not compete to find superlatives and sentiment to salute Hampshire's triumph. Although Shaun Udal became the first Hampshire-born Hampshire captain to claim a trophy for his home side in 2005, the press were generally heavily critical of Hampshire's approach to team-building in pursuit of success.

In 1961 Hampshire did what they had generally done since their earliest years in the Championship when they blended local men like Newman, Stone and Hill with English imports like Mead and overseas players such as Llewellyn. In 1961 they had done much the same with a number of local men, a couple of West Indians plus Horton and Baldry who had previously played for other counties. But, by 2005, the press and television broadcasters tended to suggest that Hampshire had succumbed to all the temptations of 'Kolpak', EU employment laws and the maximum permitted overseas players in their single-minded pursuit of success.

The reality was more complex but there is no question that Hampshire's new-style chairman Rod Bransgrove had not invested in his 'dream team' of coach Paul Terry and captain Shane Warne merely to provide some pleasant entertainment on sunny afternoons for the members of the club. That may have been the expectation at Northlands Road 60 years earlier when only the bigger clubs like Surrey, Yorkshire and Middlesex could anticipate regular success in English cricket, but it is no longer the case and Bransgrove is an ambitious man – for himself and his club.

2005 was also 13 years since Hampshire's last success, and that was the longest period without a trophy since Ingleby-Mackenzie's first triumph in 1961. Indeed, Hampshire had subsequently won eight trophies in 32 years and seven in 20, so the supporters were used to success and less patient for the lack of it after 1992. Hampshire's previous success had come when Mark Nicholas's team had won the old Benson & Hedges Cup at Lord's in 1992. That was the season in

which Durham had increased the number of first-class counties to 18 and through the 1990s both Durham and Hampshire had struggled. At the end of the decade, *Wisden* produced their usual aggregate Championship table for the preceding ten years, placing Durham at the bottom and Hampshire next to them in 17th place. In their first dozen years, Durham never came close to winning anything and, while Hampshire reached a couple of cup semi-finals, they never really looked likely to win any trophies either.

In that period, the only other counties who failed to win a major trophy were Nottinghamshire and Northamptonshire, although both won the new Second Division of the County Championship in the interim period. As Hampshire were winning the C&G Trophy in 2005, Nottinghamshire were securing the County Championship before coming to the Rose Bowl, where they were hammered by a Hampshire side recording their record first-class score. Meanwhile, Durham achieved promotion in both the Championship and the Totesport National League and provided two home-grown members of England's Ashes side, Harmison and Collingwood – plus Plunkett during the winter. Hampshire's victory over Nottinghamshire assured them of the runners-up spot, which they had enjoyed for the first time in Colin Ingleby-Mackenzie's first

3 *Beginnings and endings: Rod Bransgrove, the mastermind of the Rose Bowl, at the historic Broadhalfpenny Down with Ashley Mote, President of the Hambledon Club, which was founded 250 years ago and revived in 1998.*

season as captain in 1958. At the time none of us knew that there would be a tragic symmetry between his first year in charge and his final year as President. By Christmas he was poorly and, on a bitter March day in 2006, Colin Ingleby-Mackenzie died.

In his first season as captain only a disappointing run-in prevented Hampshire from clinching the title. In the event, Surrey won for the seventh consecutive year. Then Yorkshire won the title in 1959 and 1960 before Ingleby-Mackenzie's great year when Yorkshire were second, but overall Surrey and Yorkshire were the dominant sides in post-war cricket as they had been generally in the earlier decades.

By 2005, however, Surrey and Middlesex were struggling to avoid relegation from the First Division and Yorkshire and Lancashire were members of the Second Division in both leagues, so there was a sense of the old order changing in English county cricket just as England were challenging years of Australian supremacy. But these changes were not merely reflected in the list of winners and losers – they were also apparent in the ways in which Durham and Hampshire had turned away from the traditional model of the members' county cricket club towards a more 'modern' business-oriented approach. Indeed, when the Lord's video screen welcomed 'Hampshire CCC' at the start of the day it was not strictly correct. The old county cricket club, formed at the end of the 1863 season, is now known as Rose Bowl plc and Hampshire Cricket and Colin Ingleby-Mackenzie was the first President of the new organisation.

This book will celebrate the period between Colin Ingleby-Mackenzie's introduction to Hampshire County Cricket Club and his final year as President of Hampshire Cricket. But alongside the celebration will run a broader examination of those changing times and their implications for the future of English cricket. It will focus upon the transformation of Hampshire from a traditional, fairly parochial 'shire' county cricket club playing on a number of Victorian cricket grounds to Hampshire Cricket, with an entrepreneurial Chairman and a brand new ground on the motorway corridor between the county's two major cities. In 2005 that ground played host to Hampshire's Championship side, just as Northlands Road had done in the 1950s. But now there were also limited-overs county matches, while the ground attracted its biggest gates for the inaugural Twenty20 International between England and Australia and for a performance by the 'Britpop' group Oasis.

In that year, Colin Ingleby-Mackenzie was a highly visible and greatly loved President who provided a nostalgic link to a great past without inhibiting any sense of vision or ambition. But when Hampshire won the C&G Trophy at Lord's, it was the Chairman who was seen in the celebratory photographs, the headlines and news reports. On the morning of the match Richard Hobson (*The Times*) suggested under Rod Bransgrove Hampshire 'have clearly entered a new era'. Reporting their victory, John Stern in *The Sunday Times* observed that Bransgrove and his captain Shane Warne had 'set (their) sights high for Hampshire' and the C&G represented 'the first reward of the new era' following the 'establishment of [the] swanky Rose Bowl as an international venue'. On the following day *The Times'* headline read 'Hampshire revel in fulfilment of chairman's vision'. The Southampton *Echo* carried four photographs on the front of their Monday sport supplement, three of them featuring Bransgrove, while the Portsmouth *News* quoted Hampshire's captain Shaun Udal saying if Bransgrove 'hadn't come in when he did, the club might not be alive, it's as simple as that'.

Indeed, it was as simple as that. Bransgrove had been the most recent addition to the old committee a few years earlier when the ambition of the new ground outweighed the resources available to such an extent that the club was literally days from bankruptcy. At that point, Bransgrove's personal fortune rescued Hampshire but it also transformed them into the first truly modern (21st-century) English first-class club, with all the consequences of that major change.

One of those consequences was that Bransgrove ignored the old committee structures and many of the assumptions and beliefs about players that came with that. He inherited a side that had been in decline for a decade, drew heavily upon the advice of a few major figures in recent Hampshire cricket, including Robin Smith and Mark Nicholas, and, after some brief frustrations, assembled his team of manager/coach Paul Terry and captain Shane Warne. He invested in them and Tim Tremlett (Director of Cricket) the authority to assemble a squad capable of becoming a force in English county cricket and (publicly at least) he announced a five-year plan whose term was up at about the time they won the C&G and confirmed their place in the top division of the Championship.

However, their success was not universally welcomed by English journalists who had spent years honing their critical skills and were suddenly struggling to locate appropriate targets upon which to use them, given the national side's welcome success. Despite the Ashes triumph, the issues raised in various accounts of Hampshire's C&G success indicate a certain view of the future health of English cricket. This is of course *principally* dependent on the success, economic and otherwise, of the Test team but this success is not possible or meaningful without the support of the best possible county system. This system must produce a regular supply of top-quality cricketers while also nurturing and satisfying generations of cricket supporters across the whole country.

In respect of the latter point, one surprising observation on the C&G triumph came from Stephen Fay (*Independent on Sunday*) who suggested that the final 'promised rather more than it delivered'. What it delivered was a result in doubt from 10.45 am until at least 6.15pm, 562 runs, two centuries and 20 wickets in front of a large crowd on a sunlit day. I doubt whether any match between two first-class sides can ever have produced as much before the introduction of limited-overs cricket in 1963 and not that many since. Fay's ungenerous comment may serve as a warning against complacency or saturation if it is really possible to find such a match disappointing.

More common in the reports on the match were the critical references to the number of non-English players taking part and the implications of this for English cricket. Some of the 'foreigners', like Trott, Ntini and Carter were on the Warwickshire side but the main concerns were about Hampshire. For example, Vic Marks (*The Observer*) wrote of 'the continuing influx of talented cricketers' not qualified to play for England. He continued

> Adopting such a policy is so tempting for clubs seeking immediate success
> and none is currently more ambitious than Hampshire ... Maybe
> Hampshire can be lauded for ... assembling one of the more successful
> sides in their history. But in the long term their strategy is not doing the
> English game many favours.

Fay meanwhile offered us a headcount and a suggestion that Hampshire might
be renamed 'Hampshire International Select'. He added that

> Only three of the team are English – four if you include Dimitri
> Mascarenhas who was born in London but grew up in Australia. Five
> were born in southern Africa ... Either two or three are from Australia
> depending on Mascarenhas. For most, the Rose Bowl could be anywhere
> that offered a contract.

We might make two observations about Fay's comments. Firstly, his sums about
birthplace are entirely correct but somewhat pedantic, for they beg the question of
how we define 'English' in the contemporary world. Secondly, the final sentence
does not follow inevitably from the statistical count. It may be that at least some
of these players have become committed to 'their' county more than they might
be to another. This is speculative but no more than Fay's implication that outsiders
are *necessarily* mere mercenaries.

A statistic that Fay and some of his colleagues chose to ignore is that, whereas
only four of the Hampshire team were born in England, six members of the
side had represented England at various levels. They were Shaun Udal, the first
Hampshire-born captain to secure a trophy, John Crawley, Chris Tremlett, who
had played for England's limited-overs side earlier in the season and Dimitri
Mascarenhas, who played in the Hong Kong tournament in the previous autumn
and was clearly in the thoughts of the limited-overs selectors. Most significantly
there was Kevin Pietersen, in the eyes of most reporters a foreigner in the
C&G Trophy Final. Nine days later the same newspapers would laud him as the
English hero for his innings of 158 at The Oval that won him Man of the Match
as England secured the Ashes. Indeed *The Independent* (13 September) ran the
headline 'Fearless Pietersen tames Warne to win back Ashes for England' alongside
a photograph of 'our' new English hero!

In addition Kevin Latouf, the promising 19-year-old, was born abroad but
had moved to England with his parents to escape Robert Mugabe's monstrous
regime. In Hampshire he played through the various colts sides and his promise
was mentioned four years earlier in the *Hampshire Handbook*. In 2005 he followed
Hampshire's David Griffiths and Mitchell Stokes into the England Under-19 side
so it is difficult to see why – in the modern sense – he is not at least as English
as players like Strauss, Lamb, Hick, Malcolm, DeFreitas, Robin Smith or Geraint
Jones, all of whom were born abroad.

So let us revise Fay's calculations and suggest that Udal, Crawley, Tremlett,
Pietersen, Mascarenhas and Latouf are all England (and therefore 'English'?)
cricketers.

This is not to excuse Hampshire's general failure to develop their own cricketers
over the previous 15 years, which will be a key theme of this book, but rather

it is intended to ask how exactly county sides are expected to contribute to England and English cricket. For, in addition, the simple fact is that Hampshire's ready acquisition of players like Nic Pothas or Sean Ervine has not suddenly terminated a smooth-running conveyor belt carrying Hampshire's cricketers into the England side. Indeed, while three Hampshire-born players, Trevor Jesty, Udal and Tremlett, had played in limited overs internationals for England since 1980, no Hampshire-born Hampshire cricketer played for England throughout the whole of the 20th century so the problem is not a new one. Hampshire's Championship success of 1961 would have been impossible without a strong top order in which two of the first four – Roy Marshall and Danny Livingstone – were West Indians. Hampshire's 2005 success was their first without at least one Caribbean contribution (Greenidge, Roberts, Connor and Malcolm Marshall having featured previously).

Furthermore, the C&G Trophy triumph was the only one of the nine trophies to be secured by a Hampshire-born captain, Shaun Udal, and, by the end of that calendar year at the age of 36, he had become the first 'home' Hampshire player to represent England since A.J.L. Hill on the tour of South Africa in 1896. Hill played in four Tests, in which he averaged 62.75 and took four wickets for eight runs, but he never played again. This is because most senior England players (including W.G. Grace) had chosen not to participate in a tour that was only subsequently defined as Test standard. The senior players returned for the following home series. Since Hill was therefore not a first-choice England player, we might argue that Hampshire never produced a genuine Hampshire-born, home-grown international player until Udal, who also played in four Tests during the winter of 2005–6. Incidentally, if we think that cricketers of convenience are a new phenomenon we might note also that Hampshire's amateur batsman Brigadier General R.M. Poore, born in Ireland, represented South Africa in that ancient series simply because he was stationed there with the British Army.

Vic Marks suggested that Hampshire's acquisition of various 'outsiders' had enabled them to assemble one of their most successful sides. He may eventually be correct but in 2005 they won only the single trophy – and no more in 2006 – so it is not yet as consistently successful as at least three of its predecessors. The first of these were the teams of 1955–61, which for the first time took Hampshire to third (1955), second (1958) and then first in 1961. The second was Richard Gilliat's side of the mid-1970s, which won one Championship, should have won two and might have won three as well as their two Sunday League titles. The third side was Mark Nicholas's team from 1985–92, which won four limited-overs trophies and twice challenged for the Championship.

In addition, it might be argued that Lionel Tennyson's team of the 1920s was a consistently good side with some major professional cricketers including Mead, Kennedy, Brown, Newman, Livsey and Bowell. They relied on too many occasional amateurs and lacked a regular fast bowler but, while they never challenged for the title, they enjoyed more consistent success than any Hampshire side since the great Hambledon club of 150 years earlier. The key players in those four Hampshire sides included:

1920s	1950–60s	1970s	1980–90s
Tennyson (c)	I-Mackenzie (c)	Gilliat (c)	Nicholas (c)
Bowell	R. Marshall	Richards	Terry
Day	Gray	Greenidge	C. Smith
Mead	Horton	Turner	R Smith
Brown	Livingstone	Jesty	Gower
Harfield	Sainsbury	Sainsbury	James
Jameson	Barnard	Taylor	Ayling
Livsey (wk)	Harrison (wk)	Stephenson (wk)	Parks (wk)
Boyes	Burden	Cowley	Udal
Newman	Shackleton	Herman	M. Marshall
Kennedy	White	Roberts	Connor

In truth, Day, Harfield and Jameson were intermittent players in the first side, emphasising that the great professionals lacked consistent support, largely because Hampshire, like other poorer counties, could not afford a full complement of professional cricketers. In the later sides there were other important regular players like Baldry, Heath, Burden, Mottram, O'Sullivan, Aymes, Maru, Tim Tremlett, Middleton and Jefferies.

It is indicative of the general changes in English cricket (and of course English society) to note that Tennyson's side were all English cricketers and the captain, plus Brown, Kennedy and Mead, represented England – although in a total of only 38 Test matches. This was perhaps most surprising in the case of Mead and suggests that it has always been difficult for Hampshire players to impress the selectors. Mead scored more runs for his county than any player has ever scored for *any* one first-class side and his Test batting average was almost fifty per innings, including in 1921 the highest score to that date by an England batsman against Australia. And yet he played in only 17 Test matches. Newman was another interesting case, a man who could open the batting and bowling but was perhaps most effective as an off spin bowler. Newman, Dennett of Gloucestershire and Don Shepherd (Glamorgan) are the only players to take 2,000 first-class wickets without being selected for Test cricket and Newman was easily the best batsman of the three.

The decade before the Second World War was not successful for Hampshire, although they featured some good cricketers – again all of them English. But, shortly after the war, this began to change. In 1953 they signed Roy Marshall, who had played in four Tests for his native West Indies but turned his back on a Test career to play county cricket. A few years later Danny Livingstone, an Antiguan who had arrived in England in the migration of the 1950s, joined the county. Following the instant registration of overseas cricketers in 1968, Hampshire welcomed Richards, Roberts and O'Sullivan in their successes of the 1970s, although Greenidge had learned his cricket in Berkshire and on the Hampshire groundstaff – indeed he might have played for England and is perhaps the one genuine *international* product of Hampshire's junior sides.

Mark Nicholas's teams in the 1980s featured Chris and Robin Smith, South Africans who played for England, and Marshall and Connor, who were the last of a run of West Indians to make a significant contribution to the Hampshire side. Of the 54 players listed above, eight (Marshall, Livingstone, Richards, Greenidge, Roberts, O'Sullivan, Marshall and Connor) were 'overseas' players. In addition to the four England cricketers from the 1920s, Shackleton (seven Tests), White (two), Terry (two), Chris Smith (eight), Robin Smith (62), and Gower represented England, while Jesty and Udal played in limited-overs internationals until Udal's Test matches in 2005–6. Of course, most of Gower's matches were while he was with Leicestershire, while Bob Cottam played for England in 1968–9.

The point is then that even when Hampshire were enjoying their greatest successes they were not producing many Test cricketers and particularly not many who made a major impact for England, so the observation that the Hampshire side of 2005 was not contributing to England's cause is hardly unusual. But there are a number of other points that may be made about this issue.

Firstly, there is no clear evidence that Hampshire set out in 2005 to field a side bereft of English cricketers. They began the season with 24 contracted professionals. We have noted the unusual case of Mascarenhas, who did at least come through the Hampshire 2nd XI. Two men, Warne and Katich, were overseas players. When they left to play for Australia they were replaced at various times by MacMillan, Watson and Bichel. Then there were the Southern Africans – mostly in various stages of pursuing an English residential qualification and declaring themselves keen to represent their new country. They were Ervine, Lamb, McLean and Pothas. Six English players, Brown, Crawley, Logan, Mullally, Pietersen and Hampshire-born Billy Taylor had joined (or in Mullally's case, rejoined) from other counties. This left Adams, Benham, Bruce, Burrows, Griffiths, Kenway, Latouf, Prittipaul, Tomlinson, Tremlett and Udal who had been born in the county or at least been raised as Hampshire cricketers through their junior sides. Nine of those 11 local players played for the first team in 2005 while Griffiths and Tomlinson both spent most of the season in the physiotherapist's room. In addition Mitchell Stokes, a Hampshire Academy player who has represented his England age group, made his Hampshire debut in the 2005 Twenty20 competition.

In reality only three of the local men, Udal, Tremlett and Adams, played in the first team with any regularity whereas in 1961 eight of the players who appeared in first-class cricket for Hampshire were locals: Gray, Sainsbury, Leo Harrison, Barnard, Wassell, Heath, Burden and Timms the reserve wicketkeeper. While a staff of 28 in 2005 was perhaps too large, it did at least offer a chance to a number of local players and at least twenty of those players were eligible to represent England. Many of them languished in Hampshire's reserve side, either because they are still a little too young or because it seemed they could not compete with their overseas peers. This was particularly the case with Ervine from Zimbabwe who, at 22, outperformed older 'promising' Englishmen like Adams, Bruce, Kenway, Logan, Prittipaul and Taylor.

English domestic cricket in the 21st century has a cosmopolitan approach to team building although it does not seem to be harming the development of the Test side, which is more successful than it has been for decades. While some commentators express an understandable desire to see more 'home-grown' cricketers in the county game we cannot be sure that this would improve standards throughout English cricket.

One of Hampshire's young players, Chris Tremlett, did move up from county to international cricket in 2005. Sadly, after an exciting start in the limited-overs internationals, it was not a particularly happy experience for the young man. He was 12th Man in the first four Test matches and when his chance came with Simon Jones's injury at The Oval he had lost form and was overlooked. In interviews he suggested that he had found it hard to adjust to a life where he was not bowling regularly but instead travelling up and down motorways, joining county matches late. But Tremlett was not the first Hampshire player in recent years to suffer from the elevation to England level. As a youngster one of his coaches was Tony Middleton. In the winter of 1992–3 Middleton went to Australia with England 'A' when not yet 30 and he looked set to be Hampshire's opener for the 1990s.

During the winter his 'A' tour was unsuccessful. By his own admission he tried to increase his range of strokes and this did not work. Evidently he was allowed to do this. In the following English season he scored 377 runs at 20.94 and was dropped. In 1994, he managed just 422 at 22.21, and in 1995 he played in his last match and became Hampshire's 2nd XI and Academy coach.

By then, Shaun Udal was impressing Ray Illingworth, the Chairman of Selectors, with his off spin and batting potential. He played nine first-class matches in three seasons following his debut in 1989, then in 1992 took 58 wickets at 34.69 and, in 1993, 74 wickets at 30.16. In 1994 his 62 wickets cost just 28.30 and he was selected for 10 limited-overs internationals in that summer and the Australian tour of 1994–5.

When he returned from Australia, his wicket haul in 1995 fell to 53 at a higher average. He went to Pakistan with England 'A' in the winter but in 1996 he dropped to the foot of the county's averages with just 34 wickets at 46.52. The same number of wickets cost him 53.23 in 1997 and in 1998 he took just 16 wickets. By then, Udal seemed to have been forgotten by England although his wicket-taking and average subsequently improved consistently, but those three seasons in his mid-twenties, when the wickets dried up, deprived England and Hampshire of a useful off-spinning all-rounder. Then came the unexpected call up for the tours of Pakistan and India. Udal has always admitted that he lost his way during those heady mid-1990s days but one wonders whether better advice might have produced a good Test player for a number of years.

Meanwhile, Hampshire were investing heavily in the development of young players in the 1990s and one of the first to establish himself in the county side was the batsman and occasional wicketkeeper Derek Kenway. He was born in Fareham, had family connections with the famous Hambledon club and showed considerable promise in Hampshire's colts sides. He made his debut in 1997 and passed 1,000 runs in his first full season two years later. He slipped slightly in the notoriously 'difficult' second season but made 932 runs at 34.51 in 2001 and was rewarded with a place at the first England Academy under Rod Marsh the following winter. He returned looking fitter but scored just 238 runs at less than twenty per innings in the following summer, never came close to 1,000 runs again and his contract was not renewed at the end of 2005.

One key characteristic of Middleton, Udal, Kenway and Tremlett is that all four were born in Hampshire and came through the county's junior ranks. A fifth, Adrian Aymes, came close to tour selection on a couple of occasions while Jon Ayling from Portsmouth also showed considerable promise in the late 1980s and joined England training sessions until his career was curtailed by a serious knee injury. Had Hampshire provided England with six locally born Test players between (say) 1995 and 2005 they would have exceeded most counties' realistic obligations to their national side and far exceeded anything achieved by the county throughout its history.

One advantage of an improved relationship between the counties and England would be English county cricketers performing at a consistently higher level and having a sense of what is needed to become a Test player. Had this happened with Middleton and Kenway, even if they had not become Test players, they might have occupied a position of strength within the county side, able to pass to the younger English players in their side a sense of what is needed to

4   *Colin Ingleby-Mackenzie.*

make the transition from county to international cricket. Instead, they will be remembered as opening batsmen who showed promise without sustaining a complete county career.

In the debate about developing young players, the media's attention is almost always on England's needs rather than the counties. But there is an implicit assumption in much of what they write that the 18 counties should field eight or nine 'English' players for the sake of the England side. This of course is generally in addition to England's centrally contracted players who rarely appear in county cricket.

This begs the question of how many players are needed by England? If, say, 200 Englishmen play against each other through a first-class season and 50 per cent of them are not as good as the players (including those from overseas) currently playing county cricket, how will that improve England? Michael Vaughan, England's recent captain, wears number 600 on his shirt – that is 600 players in around one hundred and twenty-five years. Some were not very good at Test level and, in the crowded schedule of 2005, England needed fewer than twenty players. Why do they need 200 in any given season or even a decade?

But all these questions are far from the old Northlands Road ground at the Easter of 1946 when the cricketers were coming back from war to resume their games. During those school holidays a young prep school lad arrived and played a few decent left-handed shots against the bowling of the kindly old professional Jim Bailey. Harry Altham and Desmond Eagar were impressed witnesses and the young Colin Ingleby-Mackenzie set out on a journey that would eventually mean so much to so many people.

This book is a record of what happened to him, to his county club and more broadly to English county cricket over the next 60 seasons. It is a story of crises and triumphs, dangers, disappointments and opportunities. The tale is not finished but it will eventually cease where it has begun – with the C&G Trophy Final of 2005, the death of Colin Ingleby-Mackenzie a few months later and that season of 2006. As such, it stands as a special tribute to that fine man but it is more than that, a record of appreciation to everyone – player, official and supporter – who has ever cared about and in caring contributed to Hampshire cricket.

1

1945–1955

We never thought of ourselves as a great side, we were just happy to play cricket and do our best.

Vic Cannings

THE SUMMER OF 2005 was not simply one of celebration for England's triumphant Ashes side or Hampshire's C&G Trophy winners. In mid-summer the nation, especially around Hampshire's Solent waters, paid tribute to Admiral Lord Nelson and the British Navy's exploits at the Battle of Trafalgar. And, after some years of marking anniversaries of events in the Second World War, Europe shared memories for probably the last time with the remaining heroes who had liberated the world 60 years earlier.

For English cricketers, the summer of 1945 was largely barren of first-class cricket but, as the realisation of peace grew in the late summer, a few cricket grounds welcomed those players able to free themselves from their duties to take up again the game that they loved.

Some of the matches brought together the oldest of Test rivals as an Australian Services XI met a variety of English sides. Then, in late August, members of that side joined others in a Dominions XI that met 'England' in a first-class match at Lord's. The thought of such a contest marking a return to the old freedoms is highly evocative today. For the Dominions, Martin Donnelly and Keith Miller scored centuries while Wally Hammond replied with one in each innings for England. And the expression of freedom was perhaps nowhere more apparent than in the 10 wickets secured in the match by the imaginative leg spin of Doug Wright. Elsewhere, Yorkshire drew with Lancashire in Bradford and also met the RAF at Scarborough as autumn approached. And finally, at Lord's, the 27-year-old Desmond Eagar played for an Over-33 side against an Under-33 side, which included the Hampshire amateur John Bridger, just two years his junior.

Hampshire did not play any first-class cricket in that first summer after victory was declared in Europe in mid-May, but they did arrange some matches fairly quickly on the county ground in Southampton. This was possible partly because they had maintained a skeleton administrative staff throughout the war, supported by the subscriptions of 550 members who saw no first-class cricket from 1940 until it resumed in the 1946 season.

In mid-summer a Hampshire side entertained and beat teams from Sussex and Northamptonshire and they played other matches too. Among the cricketers who represented them in these friendly matches were Charlie Knott, David Blake, John Arnold, Jim Bailey, 'Lofty' Herman, Neil McCorkell, Arthur Holt and Leo Harrison. A number of other pre-war players were not yet demobbed, some did not return to first-class cricket and two, Donald 'Hooky' Walker and John Blake (David's brother), had been killed on active service.

The pleasure in playing these matches was less important than the task of rebuilding a county club capable of playing a full year of Championship cricket. Crucially there was no captain at a time when those men were principally responsible for the organisation and leadership of the county sides. The problem for Hampshire was that, like most counties, they had a tradition that was equally a statement of faith, that the captain should be an amateur – a disinterested leader of professional players, able to make the best judgements in the interests of the game and the club.

Between the wars, Hampshire's great amateur captain had been the Hon. (later Lord) Tennyson. But it was a sign of the changing times that by the mid-1930s his family fortune was disappearing and he found employment in the media, which precipitated a change of leader. In 1895, Hampshire's first year in the Championship, their great benefactor Russell Bencraft led the side. Subsequently, in over twenty years as a first-class county Hampshire had appointed just four amateur captains, E.G. Wynyard, C. Robson, E.M. Sprot and Tennyson. But when the latter stood down after 1933, W.G. Lowndes, R.H. Moore, C.G.A. Paris and G.R. Taylor each took a turn over just six years. Of those four, only Moore was indisputably a first-class cricketer – he still holds the record highest score for the county – while G.R. Taylor in 1939 was simply never good enough. In 37 innings he scored just 306 runs with a highest score of 41 and he took one wicket, but he *was* an amateur.

Hampshire found a pragmatic solution to their post-war problem, advertising in the *Cricketer* for a secretary-captain. They would then pay the successful applicant for his administrative and marketing efforts but not for his work as a cricketer or a captain. Elsewhere, Wilfred Wooller at Glamorgan and Trevor Bailey at Essex would fulfil a similar role in the post-war years.

The county interviewed a number of applicants in the autumn of 1945 and offered the post to Freddy Brown (Cambridge University, Surrey and England) but he declined, moving eventually to Northamptonshire. Instead they turned to Desmond Eagar, who, before the war, had played for Oxford University and Gloucestershire. He was a middle-order batsman and a fine close fielder and he would transform Hampshire's fortunes in the decades after the war with a clear vision of how to create a successful side at an impoverished and unfashionable 'shire' county.

Hampshire had first entered the expanded Championship in 1895 with a side that included a number of professionals, particularly the bowlers, but was heavily reliant upon amateur batsmen. This was not simply a class issue, although there was always a sense in which most county sides would create opportunities for young men who wished to play at a higher level without committing themselves to cricket as a profession. The two exceptions were Yorkshire and Surrey. While they also appointed amateur captains they would frequently field nine or 10 professionals and it is perhaps unsurprising that they enjoyed the most success. In Hampshire's first decade in the County Championship, Surrey won two titles and Yorkshire five.

Meanwhile Hampshire, after a modest start, finished bottom in 1900 and from 1902–5. To a large extent there were two reasons: their key professional bowlers Baldwin and Soar were both over 35 by 1900 and they had no settled side. For example, 41 players appeared in 1900 and that was largely because so many of the amateurs could only play occasionally, but Hampshire could not afford more professionals. A major reason for the absent amateurs was that, in Hampshire, many of them were recruited from the services and Britain had need of them during the period of the Boer War.

Another measure is that in the six seasons of 1900–5 when Hampshire were the weakest side in England, they gave debuts to 62 players, of whom 40 played less than 10 matches – and most of them less than five. Compare this, for example, with three similar but successful periods in their history. From 1955–60 and 1974–9 just 12 players began their careers over six seasons and from 1986–91 the figure was 14.

It is not surprising that a relatively impoverished club was unable to employ a squad of top professionals or that the consequence of these limitations was a struggling side. However, those who ran the club were blessed with the foresight and good fortune to discover and develop a group of fine professionals in the period running up to the First World War. These players included Mead, Kennedy, Newman, Brown, Livsey and Bowell and they helped Hampshire to places in the top half of the table in 1906, 1908, 1909, 1910, 1912 and 1914.

When cricket resumed in 1919, these players came under the captaincy of the Hon. Lionel Tennyson and Brown and Mead also enjoyed some success under his leadership in the 1921 Ashes series.

From 1919–26 Hampshire again finished in the top half in six of the eight seasons although they were never strong enough to challenge the Champions, variously Lancashire, Middlesex and Yorkshire – nor Surrey and Kent who were always in the top six throughout the first post-war decade without winning the title. Their weakness was still largely economic. Although they added the fine slow left-arm bowler Stuart Boyes, they were still short of sufficient hardened professionals to beat the best sides but they were consistently stronger than sides like Derbyshire, Glamorgan, Leicestershire, Northamptonshire, Somerset, Warwickshire and Worcestershire. Indeed, it might be argued that there were three natural 'groups' in that period with Hampshire fairly pleased to be among the middle achievers alongside Nottinghamshire and Sussex and just ahead of Essex and Gloucestershire.

Hampshire's best positions were fifth in 1914 and sixth in 1909, 1913, 1921 and 1922. However, by 1927 those great players were ageing and they finished 13th. As sides like Essex, Nottinghamshire and Sussex improved, Hampshire declined. Between 1927 and 1954 they were only once in the top half of the table, when in 1932 they came eighth. They had good players to replace the first set of professionals but the side was never consistently strong enough to pull away from the lower positions, although they were never bottom.

In the last pre-war summer under the captaincy of G.R. Taylor they finished in the bottom four for the sixth time in seven years. Of the main eleven from that year Neil McCorkell, Jim Bailey, John Arnold, Gerry Hill and George

Heath would return from war to make a significant contribution to Hampshire's rebirth. John Arlott also noted the promise of the young batsman Leo Harrison – considered by cricket writer Charles Bray as the 'new Bradman' – and the two spin bowlers, Charlie Knott and Tom Dean.

In that final pre-war summer, the young Neville Rogers had travelled from Oxford to Southampton to pursue a career as a professional county cricketer but, under the rules of the time, he could not play first-class cricket until he had spent that season qualifying by residence – despite the fact that his native Oxfordshire was not a first-class county. His father 'Brusher' had played and coached professionally in Oxfordshire's clubs and minor counties side but his son aimed higher.

Rogers was not the first Oxfordshire man to make an impact at Hampshire. That was the 22-year-old Horace Alexander William ('Alec') Bowell, who made his debut in 1902. Over the next few decades he was followed by a number of important Hampshire cricketers who journeyed south from the university city to make their impact in Hampshire as *professional* cricketers. That emphasis is important since, in addition to these professionals, more than 30 players have come down with an Oxford 'blue' but only the most recent of those, Will Kendall, became a professional player.

After Bowell (1902–27) came the great all-rounder George Brown (1908–33), Alec's son Norman (1924), double-international John Arnold (1929–50), 'Lofty' Herman (1929–48), 'Jack' Godfrey (1939–47) and, in 1939, Neville Hamilton Rogers. He remained until 1955 and was almost the last of a productive line. Since the war only Alan Castell (1961–71) has made the same journey. It is interesting too to reflect that, in the past half century, few players have come into the professional game from the southern minor counties like Oxfordshire, Wiltshire and Dorset.

Brown and Arnold both represented England in Test cricket while Neville Rogers came as close as a Test trial and the duties of England's 12th Man. In the early 1950s any aspiring opening batsman had to fight his way past such players as Bill Edrich, Watson, Robertson, Simpson and Kenyon only to find the top places occupied by Hutton and Washbrook. As if this was not enough, Rogers had the additional burden of starting his first-class career at the age of twenty-eight. Nonetheless, John Arlott suggested that Rogers was the best player of his generation never to represent his country.

Neville Rogers was born in Oxford in March 1918 and as a young man he played most of his cricket in the city. He believes that so many good cricketers came from Oxford in the first half of the 20th century because

> The facilities were so good. There were roughly twenty colleges at that time, all with sports grounds. The groundsmen were very proud men and all produced good wickets. Most clubs were roving until the end of June but once the term finished we moved onto the college ground. We played at Merton which was a beautiful old marl wicket and great for batting.

This was why most of the leading Oxford cricketers were batters. The exception was 'Lofty' Herman but 'he was a tall bloke with a natural action so when he arrived at Southampton they looked at him and said "we like that kind of action".'

As a young man in Oxfordshire, Neville top-scored in 'a couple of trials' for the minor county side and played in one friendly against the university, but he never represented them in their championship. He played for Oxford City alongside Norman Bowell and this led to Alec Bowell recommending Neville to Hampshire. The pace bowler 'Jack' Godfrey, who played for the Morris Motors side, accompanied Neville for a one-month trial at Southampton in April 1939. They worked under the coach Sam Staples and were paid £2 per week, of which 25s. went to their digs. Nothing was said to them for three months, at which point Neville approached the Chairman who replied 'You're still here aren't you?' He remembers that first season mainly for its 'good times'.

> I can honestly say that the year I enjoyed most of all was the summer of 1939. It was brilliant, absolutely brilliant. I was away from home for the first time, I was mixed-up with a crowd of very genuine people and we got on splendidly together. I had a very good time, really enjoyed it.

Among Neville's pals were Tom Dean, Alec Mackenzie, Leo Harrison, Jack Godfrey and John Taylor. Alec was prone to terrible car-sickness so that even a trip to Romsey would entail a couple of stops yet, when the war started

> He said 'I'm going into the R.A.F.' and everyone laughed him down. He went in and was decorated twice, flying planes over the continent. He went into flying after the War ended – he couldn't afford not to he was offered so many good jobs.

Leg spinner Tom Dean was one of the very few genuine wrist spinners to play for Hampshire in the 20th century. He took a hat-trick (and four in five balls) at the age of 18 in his second match against Worcestershire at Bournemouth in 1939 and in the next, against Yorkshire, a spell of 5-8 twice included two in two balls. Tom was brought up in South Africa but was actually born in Gosport. He returned to Hampshire after the Second World War

> But he was a different man. We used to call him split-pin in 1939 because he was so thin and wristy. When he came back, he must have weighed 17 stones and he seemed to be rolling it more, not getting a proper flick.

He was not alone. Bernie Constable at Surrey departed for the war as a promising leg spinner but returned in 1946 having lost the art and turned himself into an effective batsman. Dean was less fortunate and also had the problem of competing for his spin-bowling place with Charlie Knott, Gerry Hill and Jim Bailey when on soft, uncovered wickets the finger spinners generally took precedence. Dean left Hampshire in 1949 and went into Devon as professional for Newton Abbot where he was highly successful.

In 1939 Hampshire did not have a designated 2nd XI and there was no competition for the reserve sides so Neville played for Hampshire's Club and Ground while he obtained the appropriate residential qualification. Being on the groundstaff was

> Vastly different from what there is today. We played only two 2nd XI matches each year, one against Wiltshire and one against Sussex. They were played over two days and that was our only two-day cricket.

The gap between first- and second-team cricket was huge. Neville remembered in June 1939 pace bowler Dick Court 'got a call to go to Yorkshire to play for the first team having just played against Lymington's mid-week side'. Hampshire were put out for 174 on the Saturday, after which Yorkshire amassed 493-1 before declaring. Hutton made 280* and Court bowled 20 overs for 120 runs. Yorkshire won by an innings and Charlie Knott replaced Court for Hampshire's next match.

Having completed his qualifying year, the war then interrupted his career. Rogers did not remember being particularly disappointed because this affair was rather too large for such emotions. He suggested that

> You didn't think about cricket. There was a war on and that took precedence over everything. Only Gerry Hill was married and we knew we would all be called-up so we went with our mates.

During the six years of the war, Neville played just one organised game of cricket, when he went home on leave to visit his family and played against London Counties. As the war came towards its end there was a little cricket in 1945 but Neville was still overseas. Somehow Hampshire traced him to Salonica, Greece and a 12-month contract arrived so, after 'demob', he reported to the County Ground on 1 April 1946 'not knowing whether I could still play or not'. Despite this, he did not worry too much as 'we had a couple of trial matches on the middle and you went out and did your bit.'

Not everyone was encouraging. During one trial George Brown umpired and recognised Neville through his father. 'He came across to me and said "they tell me you're Brusher's boy", I said "that's right" and George said "I've had a look at you today son and I should go and get another job"'. Neville laughed considerably and recalled that

> Two or three seasons later George came down and sat on the players' balcony. I went over and said hello out of politeness and he just looked at me and said 'I suppose you must be able to play a bit'. I thought that was praise indeed but he was known as a bit of an eccentric.

Hampshire's last match in 1939 had been against Worcestershire. Coincidentally, with symbolic significance, when Desmond Eagar posted the side for the first match beginning on 11 May 1946, the opponents again were Worcestershire. This match was to be played at Southampton and Neville was chosen. Generally the war was not discussed much but as they toured the country 'someone would turn up and you'd have a beer with them.' Throughout his life Neville continued to meet with a few of his army mates on a Friday 'for a beer and a chat'.

It had not been easy for Hampshire to assemble a side. Under the registration conditions that had kept Rogers out of county cricket in 1939, Eagar for one would not have been allowed to play. A special rule was introduced to ease such complications and Eagar believed that, without it, the low standard of county cricket in 1946 would have been even worse.

One of Hampshire's early games was the tourist match against India at Southampton. It was an opportunity for the newcomer Rogers to form a friendship with the jovial Jim Bailey who had made his debut in 1927. He walked out to bat

And there at the other end was Bailey. I swear he wasn't much further away from me for the rest of his life. Anyway they had three or four wrist spinners and Jim loved leg spinners. This chap's bowling and he plays him back, just having a look. At the end of the over he came down and said 'I've had a look, he's alright, no trouble.' At the end of the next over from that end he was frowning and looking a bit worried so I walked down at the end of the next over and he says 'this bloody bloke's changed his action' and I said 'but it's a different bowler Jim.'

Neville remembers that there was 'usually humour around when Jim was playing' but generally 'the whole side got along well together and a lot of friendships survived the years.'

For the most part though there were also the demands of a professional career. Of Rogers' three particular wartime companions, Dick Court played no more first-class cricket although he spent three seasons on secretarial duties alongside Eagar, Jack Godfrey played a handful of matches before leaving after the 1947 season and only Gerry Hill maintained his professional career alongside Neville. In 1946 everyone had a one-year contract, which was 'what we wanted, something to go back to. Then, if it was not working out you could sort yourself out elsewhere. That was fine.'

Clearly there was justice to this provision of opportunity to men whose best years had been sacrificed in this greater cause but it did have some negative implications for county sides. For example, Jack Godfrey got his contract but after a couple of years left cricket with just 15 first-class wickets at 50 apiece. By contrast Hampshire-born seamer Vic Cannings had to go away to Warwickshire and wait until 1950 to play for his native county because Hampshire could not afford him.

Cannings grew up in north Hampshire and played for Farnham before, in his teens, he joined the Palestine Police Force. In 1938 he played for a Police XI that beat an Imperial Forces XI including the future Australian captain Lindsay Hassett. Cannings's match figures of 6-53 were decisive as the Police won by 15 runs. During the war Cannings remained in Palestine and met up with a number of first-class cricketers including Norman Yardley, Dudley Nourse, Bert Sutcliffe and Jim Laker. In 1946, already 27, he returned to England and wrote to Hampshire who gave him a trial where he remembered bowling at Neville Rogers. But Hampshire had spent their salary allocation on Godfrey, Herman (already 38), Heath (33) and others. They were constrained by the 'Control of Engagements Order' and the inheritance of an ageing squad. Within a few years many of Hampshire's professionals including McCorkell, Arnold, Bailey, Hill, Holt, Dean, Heath and Herman would have to be replaced although, in 1947, Rogers gave hope with 1,542 runs (at 35.04). Sadly they had to reject Cannings but asked him to return the following year.

Meanwhile, Major Jack Marshall, a colleague in the Palestine Police had returned to England to teach in Warwickshire. He recommended Cannings to that county and after a trial he signed in the winter of 1946–7. He had a very successful first season (500 runs and 61 wickets) but could not hold his place in a side that was enjoying success as they moved towards the title in 1951.

Desmond Eagar observed that in 1947, a season of predominantly hard wickets, the bowling 'was not sufficiently hostile to get opposing sides out cheaply enough'.

A comparison between the leading bowlers in each of the first two seasons emphasises that point and draws attention to the fact that bowling sides would tend to prosper on uncovered wickets in wet summers. In addition, Charlie Knott, an amateur, played in only 12 of the 28 matches in 1947:

1946			**1947**		
Knott	111	18.12	Ransom	54	27.22
Hill	49	19.32	G. Heath	74	29.48
Herman	110	20.58	Herman	37	31.83
Bailey	35	23.08	Hill	44	33.00
Dean	20	25.50	Knott	29	33.89
G. Heath	36	31.80	Bailey	51	33.92

Incidentally, in the following season Jim Bailey, 21 years after his debut, enjoyed a wonderful 'Indian' summer, taking 121 wickets (at 18.13) as well as scoring 1,399 runs – the fourth and last Hampshire player after Llewellyn, Kennedy (three times) and Newman (five) to complete the 'double'.

Eagar also regretted the absence of a 'solid and dependable No. 3' although he celebrated the fielding, which 'was nearly always good and at times outstanding'. He believed that 'we can make a show in 1948' but feared that in 1949 or 'certainly from 1950 the outlook is bleak', adding that 'we are looking all over the country for talent.' At home, things were particularly disappointing. Of 200 local cricketers offered trials in the first two seasons 'only one has been considered suitable for a position on the ground staff.'

Meanwhile 'Lofty' Herman did not play for Hampshire in 1949 and he and George Heath retired at the end of that season as a young man called Derek Shackleton took 100 wickets for the first time. Otherwise it was the finger spinners Knott and Bailey who carried their attack, although the quicker Dick Carty showed promise with 34 wickets at 25.82.

During the course of 1949, Cannings played just nine matches for Warwickshire, averaging one wicket per match, but he enjoyed the visit of Hampshire in late August when he returned typically tight match figures of 24-9-44-2. During the game he chatted to Johnny Arnold and Neville Rogers about his future, whereupon they approached Desmond Eagar and Warwickshire agreed to release him. He came to Hampshire for the start of the 1950 season and formed a fine opening partnership with 'Shack' that lasted through the 1950s. His Hampshire career record of 834 wickets at 21.69 is remarkable, not least because he did not play for them until he had passed thirty. Henry Horton has a similar claim with 21,536 runs at 33.49, having made his debut at that age.

Shackleton and Cannings opened the bowling together for the first time at Lord's in 1950 and, while Shackleton dismissed Syd Brown and Bill Edrich, Cannings accounted for Robertson and the Compton brothers. Dennis went for just four during a remarkable period when he became known as Vic's 'rabbit'. Dennis acknowledged this when, in 1959, he played in Vic's benefit match,

> And Leslie, who was a smashing chap, asked me 'how the bloomin' heck did you get him? He wouldn't even play in mine!' I told our blokes, especially young Timms, 'don't you catch him out – they've all come to see him.' He got about 40 and got out.

5 *Vic Cannings bowling at Portsmouth v Northants.*

Hampshire still had very little money but the early years after the war were quite promising for county cricket. In 1946, Hampshire's membership rose from its pre-war figure of around two-and-a-half thousand to 3,694 and over ninety thousand people paid at the gate – about twenty per cent up on the 1930s. Of course, the season of 1947 was even better with excellent weather and the wonderful exploits of Compton and Edrich at Middlesex. They hit the two highest aggregates in an English season as the London side won the title. Hampshire fell away to next-to-bottom but, in this fine summer, their attendances rose again to over one hundred and ten thousand while the membership passed 5,000 for the first time. Another record was the annual turnover of £20,000, mainly due to the large staff. As a result the profit was just £564 but at least it was a profit.

Apart from the weather, the simple explanation for cricket's popularity was a certain post-war nostalgia for things as they had been although this has to be set against the political fact that the people of Britain had thanked Winston Churchill for his wartime leadership before replacing him with the Labour Party's welfare state alternative. The 1940s in Britain were not merely a time of simple nostalgia, but cricket was briefly very popular, as was association football. At that time Portsmouth were the leading side in the South and in the two seasons between 1948 and 1950 they were Football League Champions. Their gates at Fratton Park averaged around forty thousand and a couple exceeded 50,000 in a ground which today holds only twenty thousand.

Hampshire set up 14 area sub-committees across the county as Eagar revealed that 'to run a County side for one year costs nearly £20,000', provided principally through membership and gate receipts. Membership dropped from 2,285 in 1939 to 550 at the end of the war but then rose to 3,694 in 1946 and a record 5,154 in 1947. Cinema audiences too were at a record high but by the 1950s all these

6 *The Hampshire 1947 team.*

figures began to fall. For example, even in the Ashes summer of 1953 Hampshire's attendances were down to 100,000 and their membership fell by about ten per cent. They managed a profit of around £2,000 thanks partly to the regular whist drive fund-raising.

Of course, we have noted that Hampshire were one of the weaker sides. Despite their struggles, in 1947 the senior batsmen McCorkell and Arnold and the promising Rogers all passed 1,500 runs at averages above thirty-five. Rogers received his county cap, which promised a benefit in 10 years but, with Charlie Knott injured, the bowling was weak.

In 1947, Rogers was promoted to open the innings and he stayed there for the next eight years, during which time his regular partners were Johnny Arnold, Neil McCorkell and Jimmy Gray, another life-long friend. In total he had no less than 13 opening partners during his career, which indicated that Hampshire were struggling to replace their senior batsmen Arnold (38 in 1946) and McCorkell (34). Among the 13 were the amateur schoolmaster the Reverend J.R. Bridger, Henry Horton, Gerry Hill and Gilbert Dawson.

Rogers was a very good county batsman but the relative weakness of Hampshire's batting meant that he would receive clear instructions before each innings, either 'stay there' or 'don't get out'. John Arlott noted that Neville was described as a 'dull batsman' simply because he had performed to Hampshire's need. Neville understood that view but added simply 'it depends what you were going to do – play for your side and do what you were told or chase after it.' However, he added with a chuckle, 'I may have been dull – they'd probably want their money back these days.'

His promotion to opener in 1947 was a surprise.

> They tossed at quarter past eleven, the captain came into the changing
> room and said 'I've won the toss, we're batting,' pointed a finger at me
> and said 'you're in first.' I'd had no new-ball practice, no practice against
> the opening bowlers, I just went in blind.

Despite the shock he 'was only too happy to do it' not least because he 'had
always opened' back in Oxford. In his first match as an opener against Sussex he
was lbw to Jack Nye for ninety-nine. 'I didn't say anything about it because the
umpire was Frank Chester. People think it might be disappointing but it didn't
denote any lack of drive, I was happy.'

He was dismissed in the nineties on four more occasions and in one match
against Kent acknowledged his responsibility: 'I thought I could hit Ray Dovey
over his head, went down the wicket and got caught.' On such occasions, the
senior players would suggest quite firmly that such play was not appropriate,
although fellow senior players were generally exempt from criticism.

Rogers' first century came on 1 July 1947 against Cambridge University at
Portsmouth and he added two more before the end of the season, including
another in the naval city where he was often successful. He became a good friend
of Leo Harrison, now back from the RAF, and one of a number of possible
wicketkeepers. David Blake, who played occasionally until 1958, was another
vying to succeed Neil McCorkell as were Ralph Prouton, who was sent to the
MCC groundstaff, and Jack Andrews, brother of Somerset's Bill.

> When I arrived here in 1939 Leo was the batter they were all talking
> about. The question was not if he will play but when will he? We buddied
> up together because in 1946 he was still in the R.A.F. and, apart from the
> amateurs we were often the only uncapped players. We found ourselves
> isolated a bit and became pals.

The pecking order even applied to dressing-room places so that if you were
selected for the first team 'you moved your kit to the pros room' from the junior
dressing room and then at the end of the match the senior players told you to 'get
your kit out, nipper.' By Neville's senior years, youngsters like Barnard, Sainsbury
and Heath were treated more gently.

Immediately after the war in their search for young players, Hampshire despatched
Jim Bailey to the North one winter 'to try to find some young cricketers. I think
he spent some time socialising but settled in and got half-a-dozen names.'

They included Gilbert and Harold Dawson, who both spent a few years on
the staff. The latter came from Todmorden, where Hampshire later discovered a
promising young batsman called Derek Shackleton. According to David Matthews,
who collaborated with 'Shack' on his biography, it was the Hampshire coach Sam
Staples who found Derek on a similar northern trip but if Bailey could not claim
the discovery of Hampshire's greatest bowler he did play his part in identifying
their first Champion captain.

Colin Ingleby-Mackenzie was born in September 1933, 'took up cricket' three
years later and by eight he was at prep school with a headmaster, Alan Barber,
who had played for Oxford University and captained Yorkshire in 1930. It would
not be Ingleby-Mackenzie's last significant contact with Yorkshire cricket. His
final season at the school was in the first post-war cricketing summer when he

scored two centuries and averaged over one hundred. During the Easter holidays preceding the season he reported to Northlands Road for what became annual coaching classes for schoolboys. While there, Jim Bailey, who had first played in 1927, bowled to him and was impressed by the young left-hander. He spoke to Harry Altham, a former amateur batsman, by then the club's President and a friend of Ingleby-Mackenzie's father. Altham and the new captain Desmond Eagar were impressed by the 12-year-old and invited him to stay in touch with the county.

He then moved on to Eton, where he developed a lifelong passion for gambling but also improved his cricket under the coach, Jack O'Connor, who had been an all-rounder for Essex and England. Ingleby-Mackenzie had to wait two years to win a place in the 1st XI and after a poor start scored a century against the MCC that secured his place. He also scored a half-century at Winchester where he again encountered Harry Altham. Towards the end of his career at Eton he scored two half-centuries for the Public Schools against the Combined Services.

During his final summer holidays in 1951 he was invited back to Hampshire and played a few matches for their 2nd XI during their brief period in the Minor Counties Championship. In two consecutive matches against Wiltshire he scored 71 and 77, playing alongside John Bridger, Ralph Prouton, Don Cartridge, Guy Jewell and Ray Pitman. During that season the 2nd XI also included Peter Sainsbury, Mike Barnard, Mervyn Burden, Malcolm Heath and the coach Arthur Holt. Barnard, like Ingleby-Mackenzie, was spotted at the Easter nets, this time in Portsmouth where he was coached by Neil McCorkell.

On the basis of Ingleby-Mackenzie's performances he was invited to make his Championship debut just before his 18th birthday against Sussex at Bournemouth. It was not an auspicious start as he missed a first-ball full toss before Alan Oakman bowled him second ball for nought. Hampshire collapsed to 31-4 before Rogers led a recovery and no further wickets fell as rain ruined the match. By next season he was on national service in the Royal Navy but had time to play in a few county matches and averaged almost thirty with a highest score of 91 against India, although he managed another 'duck' against Oakman.

By then Derek Shackleton was securing at least 100 wickets every season and had played for England – Hampshire's first Test player since John Arnold 20 years earlier. When Sam Staples had travelled north to sign him he did so with the advantage of having seen him in action for the Army. Shackleton eventually signed with Hampshire after national service in July 1947 and played for the Club and Ground side. When he first arrived, Neville Rogers remembers that he 'used to bowl little leg spinners, donkey drops in the nets, then one day he started to bowl with the seam for some reason and began to move it about'.

The reason was that, at the start of the 1948 season, the Chairman, W.K. Pearce, was so concerned about the lack of promising young pace bowlers that he gave orders for everyone to try bowling fast in the nets. Shackleton had bowled in that style earlier in his club career and made an immediate impression. It is interesting to note that county clubs run by committees would give such instructions, which were enacted by the captain and coach – a not untypical example of the ways that amateurs ran English cricket but, as we know from the records, on this occasion at least, remarkably successful.

At this time Neville Rogers was a regular first team player but, a little short of runs, he joined the Club and Ground during a break in county cricket for a match against Wiltshire at Bournemouth. The captain, a local amateur Basil Bowyer, arrived without a regular opening bowler. Someone suggested that 'Shack' could do the job and Neville, who was there for 'a bit of practice' was pleased to witness 'the first time he bowled with the new ball and got eight wickets'.

Neville remembers that 'Shack' was 'so light on his feet' that even after many overs you would not see where he ran in to bowl. He was also 'very good about people dropping catches off him, no moaning, no groaning, no swearing or anything. He was a great bloke to play with.' Bryan Timms believes that if Shackleton had had 'to think about it, it would have been a problem' and his other regular wicketkeeper Leo Harrison remembers his great attribute as his accuracy: 'I've picked up the ball before now and seen

7 *Derek Shackleton.*

six green marks on the seam and none on the shiny part.' In Neville's view the emergence of Derek Shackleton during the 1948 season helped to balance the side. At the start of that season 'Lofty' Herman (40) and George Heath (35) were still opening the bowling, sometimes assisted by Vic Ransom, an amateur from

8 *The Hampshire 1948 team at Aldershot with Field Marshal Montgomery of Alamein.*

9 *Jimmy Gray.*

Surrey where he ran a butcher's business. Amateur pace bowlers were unusual and Desmond Eagar described Ransom as a man of 'tremendous enthusiasm and bulk (but) undoubtedly accident prone'. Neville believes that his presence indicated the extent of Hampshire's difficulties: 'For us to need an amateur seamer from another county was a bit much. Then 'Shack' started to bowl.'

Eagar gradually built a new side, adding bowlers Vic Cannings and Dick Carty and encouraging younger batsmen like Leo Harrison, Southampton-born Jimmy Gray (who also bowled medium pace) and Alan Rayment who had played for Middlesex's 2nd XI. In 1948, Hampshire played two non-competitive first-class matches in a week at Aldershot against Cambridge University and the Combined Services. The week was notable for the visit of Field Marshal Montgomery but in the long term it was more significant for the first-class debuts of Derek Shackleton and Jimmy Gray.

Shackleton became simply the greatest bowler in the club's history while Gray scored almost twenty-three thousand runs, the fourth highest in the county's history and the highest aggregate by a Hampshire-born player. He also took 451 wickets and formed a strong opening partnership with Roy Marshall from 1955.

Hampshire have been involved in four tied matches in their history and three came in the decade after the war when Desmond Eagar claimed a unique record of captaining in all three. The tightest of the three was the Whitsun meeting with Kent at Southampton in 1950. Around lunchtime on the final day Hampshire were 131-9, needing their last two batsmen Cannings and Knott to score another 22 runs to win.

To place the task in context, during 1950 Charlie Knott's batting average was 6.23 and Vic Cannings's 10.75. Their career averages were 7.11 and 9.88 respectively – in both cases, a combined total of five short of their target and they were two of only four players (with Malcolm Heath and Bob Cottam) who played over 150 first-class matches for the county without reaching fifty. Furthermore, over the whole season Hampshire's tenth-wicket pairs accumulated 397 runs in 43 innings at an average of 9.23 and that figure was boosted by a stand of 48 by Carty and Dare in a defeat against Northamptonshire. Hampshire's best cause for optimism was that a week before Cannings and Knott had added 22 against Leicestershire at Portsmouth but that was a seamer's wicket and now Doug Wright was bowling his leg breaks. Eagar remembered that,

> With no great hope except from the batsmen, we watched the resumption. A single here, a pad there and slowly the score crept up. Four leg byes to Charlie Knott were greeted by three hundred people as if Compton had hit Lindwall for his fourth six in a Test Match. Another single, then a classic dab at the square leg umpire for two by Cannings hysterically applauded.

The atmosphere 'was electric' as Hampshire now needed seven runs to win with Wright bowling mainly leg breaks 'and the fielders still attacking'. Four runs came but then Dovey bowled a maiden to Cannings so Charlie Knott faced Wright.

> He bowled and Charlie lashed and connected with an upper edge. The ball flew over gully with no third man. 'Run three' we shouted … it must be three, certainly two. The fielder picked it up and threw at the same time. Cannings would not risk it and the score was tied. What a finish! Again Doug Wright, long run, the same ball, the same shot. Charlie stopped his shot but too late and was caught quickly and easily one-handed by Fagg after a combined stand of twenty-one, a wonderful ending to a match of excitement and interest from the first ball to the last.

Despite the development of players like Rogers, Shackleton and Gray and the acquisition of Cannings, Rayment and Cliff Walker from Yorkshire, during the first nine seasons after the war Hampshire won just 64 matches and lost 100.

10 *Vic Cannings and Charlie Knott, the batting heroes of the 1950 tied match v Kent.*

Despite the lack of success, Rogers recalled that 'if you weren't doing well it reflected in the gate – that was your incentive.' He remembered huge queues for food and drink during the intervals and, against the West Indies in 1950, the authorities reducing the boundary size 'two or three times' to accommodate the crowd – 'Harrison reckons that's the only reason I got a hundred in our innings.' Not only did he score a century but it came before lunch on the third day. With typical modesty and good humour he revealed that the morning session had been extended by 30 minutes but he had got off the mark with a six for the only time in his career. Gerry Gomez was bowling 'little in-swingers' from the pavilion end and 'I picked one up which went over the top of long-leg.' It is perhaps a measure of his general caution that he added 'I vowed never to do that again!'

This was Neville's only chance of facing Sonny Ramadhin, who took four Hampshire wickets including Neville's but not before 'I had sorted something out. I thought I won't try to drive unless I'm absolutely sure which way it's turning. I don't really remember now but it worked apparently.' During that summer Ramadhin and his 'pal' Alf Valentine destroyed the cream of England's batting at Lord's although Hutton and Washbrook enjoyed successful series. However, while Compton was injured and England gave opportunities to Parkhouse, Simpson, Edrich, Dewes, Doggart and F.R. Brown (none of whom averaged 35), Neville never got the chance to prove himself.

He was also called to the Test trial at Bradford but despite the withdrawal of a number of batsmen got no further than 12th Man while Jim Laker took eight wickets for two runs. 'Jim was a particular buddy of mine and after the match we went round to Jim's uncle's in Bradford and had a few beers.' Neville's view of Laker's extraordinary figures was that in a county match it could not have happened.

> Because you had eleven individuals playing for themselves, whereas in a county match the first two or three would have seen the ball turning and gone after it. They might have got out but they would have got twenty or thirty runs. Jim would have agreed with that.

Jim and Neville had become particular friends during a match in Portsmouth in 1947. When the two sides inspected a 'typical Portsmouth green wicket' on the first morning, Alf Gover predicted an early finish with Surrey catching 'the 1.30 train tomorrow'. Someone suggested to Jim that he 'wouldn't get a bowl' but Hampshire won the match only after claiming the 'extra' half-hour on the final day. Neville made 178, which was the second-highest innings of his career and Jim Laker took eight wickets in the match. *Wisden* reported that 'the pitch took spin from the start.' Jim and Neville had a good chuckle over the situation, became firm friends and often coached together in South Africa.

The match between Hampshire and the West Indies in 1950 had a considerable impact on Hampshire cricket although no one could have known it at the time. On the glorious Saturday, Everton Weekes scored a magnificent double hundred but one of the West Indies reserves, a young man called Roy Marshall, also impressed with a hundred before bowling usefully. Desmond Eagar noted that Marshall could not break into the West Indies side on a regular basis. A couple of years earlier

Eagar had approached another West Indian, Alan Rae, but he was now in the Test side. Eagar's approach to Marshall was more productive. He turned his back on Test cricket and arrived in Southampton in April 1953 to spend two years qualifying by residence to play for Hampshire. He could not play for his country because this would break his qualification but, unlike the more recent cases of Hick, Lamb, the Smiths and Pietersen, he was not likely to qualify for England either. In the event his impact was such that there was a possibility of Test cricket in the early 1960s but it never materialised – hence his autobiography being entitled *Test Outcast*. It was good fortune for Hampshire and their supporters.

In 1950 Derek Shackleton made his Test debut against the West Indies but was dropped after one match in which his batting (42 and 1) was more productive than his bowling (1-128) as the West Indies won by 10 wickets. England made eight changes but still lost the next Test by an innings and with it the series. They would not lose another home series until 1961. Shackleton played in the final Test of the following summer against South Africa and the first of the tour to India that winter. After that he disappeared from Test cricket until 1963 when he played in the last four Tests against the West Indies. He took seven wickets at Lord's (including three in four balls) in one of the great finishes of all time. When Shackleton was run out in the final over, England needed six to win and Cowdrey with a broken arm was England's last batsman. David Allen played out the last ball to secure a draw. Shackleton's Test career ended at The Oval in 1963 shortly after his 39th birthday – two years older than Shaun Udal in 2006.

Neville Rogers never played for England but in 1951 he was 12th Man against South Africa, although the playing side had been nominated before he was chosen. In their next match South Africa came to Southampton where Neville scored 118. He eventually appeared in a Test trial in 1953 prior to the selection of Hutton's party to tour the West Indies but he injured his thumb in a car door before the game, which caused him to miss a number of matches. Nonetheless he played in the trial, of which he said 'I didn't do anything, played on to Alec Bedser in the first innings and made fifty-odd in the second but I don't think there was any danger of me being selected.' In fact he and Don Kenyon enjoyed an undefeated opening partnership of 118 in the final innings after being set 222 to win, but neither went to the West Indies where Hutton opened with Watson or Bailey and won the series.

In 1953 Rogers carried his bat for the first time against Leicestershire at Loughborough, making 32* in a total of 68 when 'the ball was turning square'. Such figures were really only likely in the days of uncovered wickets and, in particular, in the 1950s when in English county cricket ball often held sway over bat. Having carried his bat once in 1953 he equalled the English record by repeating the feat four times in the following season, including an innings of 56* for the MCC against Jim Laker and the other champion county bowlers.

Strangely for the man Arlott called the 'master craftsman of defensive batting', he never got to 200.

> It never bothered me in the slightest. I got to 186 against Gloucestershire
> at Portsmouth (1951) and threw it away. Some people I suppose go out to
> set records. I like to think I played my cricket in relation to the way the

> game was going. In 1946 I came in lowdown and was batting with our
> number 11 Jack Godfrey against Somerset at Portsmouth. I was caught in
> the deep for nought and Frank Lee their opening bat asked me 'why did
> you do that?' I told him I was trying to get some runs but he said 'that
> was stupid, there are times when you play for yourself and it will get you
> up the order.' It took another pro from the other side to tell me that.

Rogers remembered that other opponents were helpful and that this attitude
was 'quite common'.

Arlott considered him a particularly good player of spin bowling, yet he was
an opening bat. 'That's because I was hanging around waiting for the spinners to
get on,' he joked, adding more thoughtfully, 'I don't think you ever knew how to
play. If you had a look at a few videos now you'd think "did I do that?"' Apart
from opening on the first morning of a match he also played his whole career
on uncovered wickets which was simply 'the way it was'. This had not worried
him, 'I didn't mind it at all. It's difficult to explain that you spent your first half-
hour testing the wicket out as to whether it was going to lift or keep low.' This
is quite different from the modern game when 'they just take the covers off and
get on with it.' He was sure that uncovered wickets

> helped batting techniques certainly against spin bowling but against quicks
> as well. What you see less of now is the ball lifting from a length as it would
> on a hard wicket where rain had just softened the top. In those days you
> had to take so many on the body with the bat out of the way.

In 1954 Hampshire finished 14th – another poor season. Charlie Knott played in
only three games and acknowledged that he could not sustain his business interests
and his cricket career. On one particular Saturday morning he was at work early
and due to report to the county ground to play Middlesex but at around 10.30
he had to ring Desmond Eagar to say he would not make it. Pompey footballer
Mike Barnard had played once in 1952, scoring 4 and 0, and once again in 1953
when he made a 'pair' against Warwickshire in his native Portsmouth. Now he
had just finished his national service and on this Saturday morning he was able
to take advantage of Knott's late withdrawal and batting at number 10 he top-
scored with thirty-nine. He followed that with 24 not out and then came back to
his home city to score his maiden century against the first-ever Pakistan tourists.
Although he would enjoy the great day in Hampshire's history in September
1961, Barnard still remembers this match as very special perhaps because 'I had
brothers watching and my dad popped in.' In that match Roy Marshall played
his second game for Hampshire and recorded the only 'pair' of his career.

Barnard was one of the young local cricketers being developed by the county,
as were the young spinners Burden and Sainsbury. Hampshire had need of them
because in addition to Knott, Gerry Hill came to the end of his long career
and so Desmond Eagar's spin attack of 1946 (Knott, Hill, Bailey and Dean) had
disappeared. So too had one possible replacement, Reg Dare, and the pace bowler
Dick Carty. More positively, Shackleton and Cannings formed a fine opening
attack and from 1955 Marshall was available to strengthen the batting and bowl
offspin. Jimmy Gray also established himself as an opening batsman and seamer
and Leo Harrison had finally claimed the wicketkeeping position.

11 *Gerry Hill.*

It was encouraging that Harrison and Gray were both local players but Eagar had done far more to support the development of Hampshire's own cricketers. In his first years as captain he had available Arthur Holt, a Southampton batsman who had shown promise before the war. Like so many others, the six-year gap came at a crucial point for Holt and post-war, by now in his mid-thirties, he enjoyed only occasional success. He played for a few years but in March 1949 Hampshire's coach Sam Staples retired through ill health and Arthur Holt succeeded him. He became the professional complement to the architects of Hampshire's later success.

Apart from Hampshire 2nd XI's brief involvement in the Minor Counties Championship in the early 1950s they generally played little competitive cricket until the 2nd XI Championship was formed in 1959. Holt did not work very much with the capped professionals, who considered it their job to help each other and work on their own techniques. His major role was to tour the county with the Club and Ground side as ambassadors for the county club, playing one-day matches against local sides. Holt would invite local amateurs and established club cricketers to play and he would supplement his side with promising youngsters.

When Neville Rogers became involved in Hampshire's cricket committee in the late 1990s he compared the contemporary intensive coaching set-up with his time when most of the players 'were self-taught'. He continued

> You used to get coaching but not all that much and you came on the staff a lot younger, usually at fifteen or sixteen when you watched and learned. As a consequence some players were unorthodox. Neil McCorkell was a very good example. He held the bat with one hand at the top and one at the bottom of the handle but he scored his hundreds.

McCorkell had learned his cricket at school and church in his home city of Portsmouth. He played for Hampshire from 1932–51, keeping wicket and scoring 17 centuries and more than fifteen thousand runs in 14 playing seasons. He is surprisingly the last Portsmouth-born, state-school-educated cricketer to win a Hampshire cap – over seventy years ago.

Arthur Holt had been a Southampton footballer. In the early 1950s the 'Saints' signed full-back Henry Horton, who had played a few matches for Worcestershire before giving up cricket. Holt persuaded him to play some games with the Club and Ground and while Horton was somewhat reluctant he enjoyed some success. As a consequence he played a few first-class games in 1953 and 1954 and signed professional terms with Hampshire.

The development of Gray and the signing of Horton and Marshall brought a new stability to Hampshire's top order, with Rogers now batting at number five. But Holt had another significant impact with the development of young and usually local cricketers. In 1949 he inherited the delightful Mervyn Burden and helped him to switch from medium pace into an effective off spinner. In the same year the committee approved the establishment of a colts side and in the following years that produced young men like Mike Barnard (Portsmouth), Malcolm Heath (Bournemouth), Ray Pitman (Bartley), Ray Flood (Southampton) and most especially Peter Sainsbury (Southampton). Although they all disappeared at some point to do their national service they were still able to play cricket and perhaps returned as more mature young men. At the same time the Hampshire Schools Cricket Association were providing opportunities for representative cricket and Bernard Harrison (Peter Symonds, Winchester) was particularly promising. In retrospect we can identify this as the most productive period for the development of Hampshire-born cricketers in the county's history. These were young men who learned to love cricket in their teenage years as the post-war boom in cricket and other sports occurred. In part they were helped because older players had returned from the war to coach and lead by example. With relatively few competing attractions those who were good enough could find a way into the professional game, while the old supply of amateurs dried up as outside demands of industry and business increased.

By 1955, Sainsbury, Barnard, Burden and Heath, all born locally between 1930 and 1934, were poised to make an impact on the first team. It is not necessarily a simple thing to replace one group of players with another, even when the former have been unsuccessful as a team and it is to the great credit of Eagar and Holt that this was achieved in 1955. Mike Barnard feels that it was to their advantage that these youngsters were all local men but also that they had an important advantage over some of their predecessors in that they were 'too young for anything to be ingrained in us about being a struggling side'. In the first Championship match of 1955 against Glamorgan on FA Cup final day, the Hampshire batting order was Gray, Marshall, Barnard, Eagar, Rogers, Rayment, Harrison, Sainsbury, Shackleton, Heath and Burden. Six of the side were local men, Rogers and Shackleton had been developed by Hampshire and only the captain, Marshall and Rayment were 'imports'.

Barnard was not successful at number three so for the third match at Lord's the top order of Gray, Marshall and Horton was seen for the first time while Cannings replaced Heath. Shackleton who usually performed well at Lord's, took 6-40 as Middlesex were dismissed for exactly 100 but only Marshall (26) and Sainsbury (11) reached double figures. The new batting order failed twice as Hampshire were dismissed for 61 and 86 and lost the match. Horton's first run at number three brought him scores of five, nought, two, two, and six, before Rogers moved up to replace him. Horton was given another chance a few weeks later against Oxford University and improved slightly with a run of low double-figure innings before he top-scored with 89 at Swansea on 27 June. Exactly one month later he made his maiden first-class century v Leicestershire at Bournemouth, followed by two more that year. Hampshire's top three was now established for some years to come.

In 1954 Hampshire had used 25 players in all first-class cricket and the batting line-up was rarely settled for long. The most regular players in a semblance of batting order were Rogers, Gray, Horton, Rayment, Ingleby-Mackenzie, Eagar, Harrison, Dare, Shackleton, Cannings and Burden.

In the following season, Hampshire used just 14 players including Ingleby-Mackenzie who appeared just once as wicketkeeper when Leo Harrison was selected for the Players at Lord's. Otherwise Malcolm Heath played in eight matches and another 12 men made up the regular side. They were Marshall, Gray, Horton, Eagar, Rogers, Rayment, Barnard, Sainsbury, Harrison, Shackleton, Cannings and Burden. Such stability was enormously important and John Arlott in the *Playfair Annual* argued that their 'out-cricket' was 'as fine as any in the country'. The bowling was superb. Only two players made centuries against Hampshire in the whole season, seven bowlers took between 33 and 157 wickets and they averaged between 13.41 and 21.75. As a consequence there were few occasions on which their opponents passed 200. So it was that, after years as one of the weaker sides, Hampshire in 1955 won 17, lost only six and finished third for the first time in their history.

Sadly 1955 marked the end of Rogers' career, although it finished in the best possible way as he captained the side after Desmond Eagar was injured in early August. By this time the newcomer Roy Marshall was opening regularly with Jimmy Gray, so Rogers was usually batting at number five, which he did not particularly enjoy. Captaincy was a different matter. In mid-August they beat Lancashire and had an exciting draw at Trent Bridge (Rogers 85) before they travelled to Weston-super-Mare on Wednesday 17 August. Hampshire were

12   *The Hampshire 1955 team – third place in the table.*

bowled out in 70 overs for just 154 but then Shackleton took 8-4 in 11 overs and Hampshire led by more than 100. They were 16-2 when Rayment joined Horton and decided to play his preferred attacking game on this unreliable pitch. He made a sparkling century and when Shackleton took 6-25 the game was over in two days and by a margin of 264 runs. Somerset's match aggregate was 135 runs, of which wicketkeeper Stephenson scored sixty-seven. Hampshire's 14th victory secured the best season in their history.

After Weston, Hampshire lost heavily to the touring South Africans in front of large crowds at Southampton. They had spent the summer chasing Surrey in the middle of their seven straight Championships but the London county clinched the title during Hampshire's tourist match. The two sides then met at Bournemouth where Horton's century, and five wickets each for Heath and Sainsbury, gave Hampshire a notable victory. The season ended with Rogers' captaincy unbeaten in the Championship. His last match (like his first) was against Worcestershire, this time at Bournemouth. Rogers scored 50 and 29 and Hampshire won despite poor weather.

Rogers 'absolutely loved' captaining Hampshire. He had been in charge for one match in 1954, although the circumstances will seem odd to the contemporary reader. Desmond Eagar was injured at Clacton in August by which time his usual amateur deputy Charlie Knott had effectively retired. The schoolteacher

13   *Roy Marshall and Jimmy Gray opening the batting.*

Rev. J.R. Bridger then led Hampshire for five matches, none of which were won, but he was not available for the last game of the season against Somerset at Bournemouth. At the end of the previous match Rogers recalled being asked

> 'is it the same team tomorrow?' and I said 'all turn up, I don't know anything.' On the next day I went to Bournemouth and told all the players to get changed. At 11.15 Desmond Eagar came into the dressing

14 *Leo Harrison.*

room with Ben Brocklehurst the Somerset captain and said 'there's your side Neville, you're captain.' We won the toss and I elected to bat. I remember Harrison pointing a finger on my chest saying 'now you go out there and get a bloody hundred,' which I did.

Harrison was not merely encouraging his pal, he was making a point about Hampshire's desire to keep appointing amateur captains, even as a stand-in. The players all believed that Rogers could do the job but Hampshire were old-fashioned in this respect. Some counties were different. Warwickshire turned to professional captains from 1948 and enjoyed some success. Sussex flirted with a professional, appointing James Langridge from 1950–2 but then reverted to amateurs. Bill Edrich turned amateur to captain Middlesex from 1951 while Gloucestershire appointed the professionals Jack Crapp and George Emmett from 1953. Kent chose Doug Wright one year later, as did Lancashire with Cyril Washbrook, and Denis Brookes captained at Northampton. Leicestershire had moved backwards and forwards from amateur to professional for some years and Reg Perks had a year at Worcestershire in 1955. The idea was growing but not at Hampshire.

In his first match as captain in 1954, Rogers pleased Leo Harrison by scoring 123, sharing century partnerships for the first two wickets with Jimmy Gray and another amateur, David Blake (100). Hampshire scored 370-8 declared, forced Somerset to follow on, bowled them out again and won by 10 wickets. Neville Rogers was the first professional to captain Hampshire since the war and was unbeaten in the Championship over these two seasons. It is strange to note that Desmond Eagar paid tribute to Bridger's captaincy in *Hampshire County Cricket: The Official History* but made no reference to Neville Rogers' success as skipper. It is difficult to know why this would be unless it does signify his unease with the idea of a professional captain, although elsewhere he suggested that Rogers might have succeeded him as captain.

John Arlott described the tension between professional cricketers and their amateur captain in his account of a match at Portsmouth between Hampshire and Norshire. 'Ain't Half a Bloody Game' was a phrase of Leo Harrison's and this was Arlott's only published work of fiction, but Norshire play against a 'real' Hampshire side that, captained by Eagar and lacking Rogers, was probably in 1956 or 1957.

The tale centres on Yorkshire-born opening batsman George Kennett who, after a solid career, is coming to the end of his contract. Arlott describes how Kennett battles with declining form while his captain looks forward to replacing him with a more enterprising player. The captain K.E.T. Tallis had insisted that

> It's not just a matter of a thousand runs or fifteen hundred runs; it's the way
> the runs are made. We've got to entertain the crowds or they won't come
> – and the committee have made it pretty clear to me that they expect me
> to get something done about it.

When Norshire are set a difficult target in the last innings the captain demands that his players hit out, adding 'If we go down … let's go down with our flags flying and all our guns firing.' The professionals, embarrassed by these 'corny' clichés, are silent. Inevitably, Kennett ignores the instruction but plays an heroic innings to win the match. The captain, impressed in the end, offers a further contract but by now Kennett has received the typical offer of a position as a groundsman and coach at a company, enabling him to play on in Minor Counties cricket.

If it seems strange to be quoting (unremarkable) fiction in a history of county cricket, it is because here Arlott is able to represent the two cultures of the amateur, middle-class committees and captains and their professional employees, whereas much of his 'real' information would have been treated confidentially at the time. A real and rather sad example of the differences came with the end of Neville Rogers' career.

He was capped in 1946. In those days professionals were entitled to hope for a benefit after 10 years with a cap but it was not an automatic right. In 1930, Phil Mead was the first Hampshire player to be awarded a second benefit and his year's efforts accrued £681. In 1934 George Brown, who earned £1,000 six years earlier, had a testimonial earning a further £292. In 1936, Stuart Boyes's first benefit realised £764.

After the war, Hampshire found a solution to reward various ageing professionals when over three seasons, 1948–50, five men, Arnold, Bailey, Herman, Hill and McCorkell received £1,470 each. Then in 1952 and 1954 George Heath and Arthur Holt were given testimonials. Like George Kennett in Arlott's story, Rogers' contract was up and while he was still playing well he had lost his opening spot to Roy Marshall. His old friend Jim Bailey had arranged a job for him with a regional firm, which offered him security, so he asked Hampshire for a three-year contract and a benefit. They turned him down, offering only one year. In the winter, the club eventually revised their offer, but Neville, a man of his word, had committed himself to the company and it was too late. So he retired before the 1956 season when he was 38, although he was awarded a testimonial, which realised about £1,600.

The changing nature of benefits and testimonials indicates how the lives of professional cricketers have been transformed. In 1898, Harry Baldwin, who had played in their second-class days before 1895, was Hampshire's first beneficiary. At that point, the benefit consisted of subscriptions from members and supporters and the receipts from a designated match. Baldwin was awarded the major game against Yorkshire but the first day was rained off and on the second Yorkshire (157) beat Hampshire (42 and 36) by an innings in one day. Fortunately the subscriptions did provide him with £237 10s. Two years later his bowling partner Tom Soar had a similarly disappointing game, which actually made a loss at the gate.

In the 1950s, Hampshire's testimonials were awarded to players after they had retired, whereas benefits were for current players. In 1957 Leo Harrison received just over £3,000 from his benefit. He came from a building family in Mudeford and used the money to build his new home, where he continued to live throughout his life. Since then, most seasons have seen a Hampshire beneficiary. In 1965 Peter Sainsbury received a record £6,250, not bettered until Barry Richards 12 years later (£21,255). After a number of other benefits under £30,000 Malcolm Marshall received £61,006 in 1987 and then from 1990 figures generally exceeded £100,000. Chris Smith took £181,679 and in 1996 Robin Smith £202,000.

Interestingly, Robin Smith's figure included a match income of only £5,047 and in recent years the figure never reaches 10 per cent of the whole. Indeed, benefits are much less dependent upon the gratitude and contributions of regular supporters. They are now highly organised with specialist committees who run expensive dinners, auctions and other high profile events – often now held outside the county. In addition, Hampshire awarded benefits to John Stephenson (2001) and Alan Mullally (2005) although neither had been at the club for 10 years. Nonetheless, some experienced players still do not receive benefits. For example, neither Giles White (1994-2002) nor Will Kendall (1996-2004) left Hampshire with any testimonial or benefit although both were capped.

However, White and Kendall were not professional cricketers in the sense that we think of George Kennett of Norshire or the generations of Harrison and Sainsbury at Hampshire. Both came to Hampshire as university graduates and they were followed in the next few years by other graduates including Jason Laney, John Francis, James Adams, James Tomlinson and Chris Benham. Fifty years earlier young cricketers had returned from the war or later national service. Now, quite a number have the benefit of a degree, some from one of the university centres of excellence although as yet none of those young men have earned a benefit from a full career in Hampshire's side.

2

1956–1961

It felt marvellous – it was nice to be in the side that did it for the first time.

Leo Harrison

HAMPSHIRE'S SUCCESS IN finishing third behind Surrey and Yorkshire in 1955 was as unexpected as it was welcome. At the end of the previous season they had finished in the bottom half of the table as they had done in every one of the previous 16 seasons.

In 1956, Hampshire slipped to sixth, nonetheless equalling their highest position between 1919 and 1954, England and Jim Laker retained the Ashes, Surrey, often without Laker, retained the Championship and Ingleby-Mackenzie, in 11 matches, topped the Hampshire batting averages, including an exciting 130* against Worcestershire at Cowes. In the *Playfair Annual* John Arlott praised the enthusiasm of Eagar's captaincy and suggested that while the side were as friendly as any in the country they were 'probably the hardest against which to score'. But despite this successful period in Hampshire's history, the post-war boom in attendances and interest was waning and English cricket was facing a number of serious problems.

During those years Desmond Eagar maintained a scrapbook, including a series of articles by E.W. Swanton published in the *Daily Telegraph* in September 1956. Eagar had marked sections of these in which Swanton argued that

> There is little question of a lowering of public interest in cricket: quite the contrary … Yet so far as county cricket is concerned this enthusiasm is not translated into active personal support.

But even at the end of a triumphant Ashes summer Swanton observed that, 'scarcely a spark of originality or humour enlivens the play' and he regretted 'the great shift towards the leg-side which was beginning before the new lbw provisions were made law in 1937'. He reminded his readers that 'spectators are, and have always been, attracted by batting.'

By then Hampshire had done their bit by enabling those spectators to enjoy the scintillating batting of Roy Marshall but it would be misleading to suppose that this made them an exciting side. In the field their hostile out-cricket and reliance on the medium-pace seamers Shackleton, Cannings and Gray was effective but hardly enthralling – especially as they too relied upon packed leg-side fields. Sometimes this even applied to Cannings, a natural away-swing bowler who might nonetheless aim on and outside leg stump, restricting the batsman's freedom. In his career from 1950–9 Cannings conceded runs at exactly the same rate as

Andy Roberts for Hampshire. Yet Roberts took a wicket every 7.3 overs at an average of 16.7 whereas Cannings needed two more overs and conceded five more runs. In simple terms, at county level, Cannings was a fine *defensive* bowler who created pressure to take wickets. His opening partner Derek Shackleton was even tighter, Malcolm Heath was effective and even Jimmy Gray, who took 12 overs to capture each wicket, was one of Hampshire's least expensive bowlers. A broader comparison of Hampshire's quicker bowlers reveals how difficult run-scoring was against their attack of the 1950s and is equally revealing about strike rates and about the wickets, which were uncovered and on a wide variety of grounds in most counties. Despite the relatively low scores recorded against Hampshire in the 1950s the wickets were not taken particularly quickly – another sign of slow batting.

In May 1957, Reg Simpson the Nottinghamshire and England opening batsman provided another press cutting from the *Nottingham Evening Post* for Eagar's collection, in which he wrote

> I was particularly interested to see how Hampshire would respond to the pleas of the MCC for brighter cricket as they have always been a side to use negative field placings with bowlers who attack the leg stump in preference to any other method of attack ... I was intrigued to find out whether they had decided upon a fresh approach ... Any such hopes were dispelled when I arrived at the ground and saw Shackleton bowling before lunch on the first day. His field placings told me straight away that nothing had changed. His leg side field included a mid-on, two mid wickets – yes two – another man just behind square and a deep fine leg. Not exactly an attacking field ... . Later in the game Sainsbury actually started without anyone close to the wicket'.

In the match, Hampshire batted first and were dismissed for 279 in the 127th over. Horton scored 106 and leg spinner Dooland took 7-94 in 52.2 overs. In the play described by Simpson, Nottinghamshire took a narrow lead in 137 overs so neither team managed much above two runs an over. Shackleton took 1-55 in 31 overs and Sainsbury 3-79 in 49 overs. On the final day Eagar recorded in the handbook that 'rain mercifully ended proceedings' with Hampshire only halfway through their second innings. In total the two sides scored 837 runs and lost 24 wickets in 346 overs. The over rate puts current performances to shame but otherwise this was dull fare with a scoring rate of less than 2.5 per over, even though Roy Marshall contributed 43 and eighty-seven.

By 1957 Hampshire were a thoroughly professional and competitive side and they were by no means the only team to be accused of dull cricket. Indeed, despite Trent Bridge, their annual report on 1957 recorded them as one of the faster scoring county sides at 45.38 per 100 balls – about 2.75 per over and their best rate since the war. Such a rate in 2005 would see a full day's play yielding less than 300 runs. Their bowlers conceded 10,509 runs in 4,387 overs at 2.4 runs per over and the remarkable Shackleton bowled more than one thousand of those overs at less than two runs per over and with 154 wickets.

One of the problems at Trent Bridge was that the wicket was too placid to obtain a result while the batsmen took their time. However, in those days of uncovered wickets and in the wetter summers, entertainment was not simply a matter of fast run scoring. Low scoring, tight matches could be engrossing.

For example, while Reg Simpson was unimpressed by the Hampshire side at Trent Bridge they had arrived there from a scintillating match against Middlesex at Portsmouth. This was their second home game of the Championship season. The first, in midweek against Essex at Southampton, had a three-day paying attendance of only 766 but Portsmouth was much better, with 2,263 paying on the Saturday and 4,340 overall.

That first day crowd will have regretted Marshall's early dismissal while cheering the partnership between local hero Mike Barnard and Henry Horton, who added 76 for the fifth wicket in an all-out total of just 133 (in 63 overs). Despite the presence of Robertson, Edrich and Compton, Middlesex also found batting difficult and, with Shackleton taking 5-31, Hampshire led by twenty-five. Marshall made the game's first half-century and Horton a second 40 as Hampshire set Middlesex a target of 244 to win. Shackleton soon had Bob Gale caught by Harrison but at the close

15 *Mike Barnard and Henry Horton at Portsmouth, 1957.*

of Monday's play they had nine wickets left to score another 159.

Robertson scored 49, Edrich 50, Compton 52 and Delisle 50 – 201 of the 244 target. Add 12 extras and the other seven Middlesex players had little to do to secure a win. Nonetheless, in the local newspaper, 'Nomad' reported that they 'slumped from 85 for one to 125 for four and at lunch it was anybody's game'.

In his final report 'Nomad' revealed that

> In the 62 years that county cricket has been played there, the United Services ground at Portsmouth has been the scene of many dramatic finishes but none has been closer or more exciting than yesterday's when Hampshire, with 600 spectators holding their breath, beat Middlesex by three runs.

Shackleton's match figures were 44.3-17-72-11. The whole game produced just 699 runs in 309 overs (an average of 2.25 runs per over) but it would be hard to argue that this difficult wicket and quality bowling had resulted in dull cricket. Perhaps a key difference between Portsmouth and Trent Bridge was the wicket, not the cricketers, because Nottingham had not encouraged the bowlers. Nonetheless the 1950s, the final decade without limited-overs cricket, was also the last decade in which ball frequently dominated bat in English cricket. But limited-overs cricket was not simply a reorganisation of the game, it was also crucially a matter of economics.

It was a mixed year for Hampshire at Portsmouth. On Wednesday 19 June they were due to play Sussex there but it rained all day and, in his capacity as secretary, Eagar noted that

> The loss of the day's cricket was a serious blow to Hampshire's finances … The fact that the Test Match with its television draw, will be on during the other two days, will probably mean only a small return for county funds from the game.

Eagar kept another cutting (*Southern Evening Echo*, 22 October 1957) announcing that a Hampshire County Cricket Supporters Club had been formed 'to help rid the club of this awful financial bogey'. The Chairman, Sir Reginald Biddle, announced that the idea had been derived from other counties – notably Warwickshire – and the report told how since the last war the expenses of a county cricket club had increased out of all proportion to its revenue. Biddle commented, 'You ask people to organise a function, then to give a prize, and then to buy tickets for the prizes they have donated! That sort of vicious circle cannot go on for ever'. In fact it does still happen 50 years later although the amount raised is less significant and usually contributes to relatively peripheral activities of the club.

The rain-affected game with Sussex petered out with Barnard and Rayment taking rare wickets. Later that season Hampshire returned to Portsmouth for their festival and entertained the Champions Surrey. A total of 11,194 spectators attended on the two days in 'perfect conditions', and it was 'one of the biggest post-war crowds at the United Services Officers' Ground'. Sadly Surrey were so strong that no third day was necessary. This was Hampshire's second two-day defeat against the Champions. In late June at Guildford they were put out for 66 (Loader 7-36), Surrey declared on 247-4 and won by an innings. It may be unique that in the two matches against Surrey in 1957 Shackleton failed to take a wicket.

The early finish caused some embarrassment. Guildford was celebrating the 800th anniversary of its charter and HM the Queen was to meet the two sides. In the event a friendly was played so that the presentation took place. A local newspaper reported that 'When Mr Peter May the England Test captain was presented to the Queen she remarked jokingly "This is the second time you have done this to me".' She referred to the Lord's Test match on the previous weekend when England had beaten the West Indies on Saturday before Monday's Royal visit.

One of the difficulties for English cricket in the 1950s was that the one competition was dominated by Surrey. They shared the title with Lancashire in 1950, Warwickshire won it in 1951 (Surrey were sixth) and then Surrey won it every year from 1952–8. Yorkshire were second in 1951, 1952, 1954 and 1955 and third in 1950 and 1957 before replacing Surrey as Champions in 1959. In that context, the other 15 counties began most seasons with no prospect of winning the title and probably little hope of even competing.

By contast in the 1950s, six different sides won football's First Division (Portsmouth, Spurs, Manchester United, Arsenal, Wolves, Chelsea) while five different sides won the FA Cup – and only Arsenal won both. With at least ten 'soccer' clubs enjoying success it was possible to attract spectators with the prospect of glory whereas in cricket only the tourists' matches provided regular glamour.

During the last month of his career, Eagar was interviewed by E.M. Wellings in his column *Talking Cricket*. They discussed cricket as a public spectacle, and Eagar suggested that the game had 'Become tighter and tighter. It's more interesting to play than ever but whether the public likes it better I don't know. I still don't know what spectators really want'.   He added that the first innings bonus points for faster scoring 'have made no difference at all. While we've been playing I've never given them a thought.'

One solution to the falling gates and demand for brighter cricket was that English cricket began gradually and intermittently to turn away from the practice of leaving pitches uncovered to the elements. Although this was always a particular feature of English cricket it reduced playing time significantly and gave considerable assistance to the best bowlers. In addition the best English county players like Rogers or Gray will always argue that the demands of playing on such varied and sometimes demanding surfaces was a vital factor in the development of technique.

16   *1957 – Jimmy Gray drives Sobers, Hampshire v West Indies.*

Uncovered wickets did not go immediately and were reintroduced from time to time, while in a season like 1959 when the sun shone most of the year the weather had only a slight impact. A further broad difficulty was that from 1957–60 England successively hammered the West Indies, New Zealand, India and South Africa, winning 15 and drawing the other five Tests. These series were not exciting and the five-year gap between Ashes Tests was too long.

So the cricket authorities continued to worry about brighter cricket while leaving it to individual counties to solve. In Hampshire their solution was the appointment of Eagar's replacement as captain, A.C.D. Ingleby-Mackenzie.

Eagar later revealed that after the marvellous victory at Bradford in 1955, he wrote to the Chairman of selectors proposing that this should be his final season as captain because he 'felt thoroughly stale and tired'. He was especially sorry that Neville Rogers was retiring but hoped that perhaps his new employers

> Could find it possible and see fit to release him for, say, two more summers. I could then retire happily with the knowledge that a great cricketer, respected all over the country and not least by the Hampshire players, was leading the team that I have loved so well.

This is interesting because it suggests that Hampshire were contemplating the appointment of a professional captain in the mid-1950s, although it would not occur for another decade. Eagar had always believed that a captain must be worth his place in the side and felt that while he had 'just about' managed that in previous years 'this happy year of 1955 was to prove the unhappy fact that I was not now good enough.' Sadly Rogers could not be released to become Hampshire's first professional captain and 'we had to think again'.

Gerry Hill and Charlie Knott had also retired so Eagar was 'persuaded to carry on' while 'soundings were made' as to the future availability of Colin Ingleby-Mackenzie. His boss Bryan Valentine had captained Kent after the war and

> In 1956 Colin was released to play but due to injury only had 19 innings in which he scored 620 attractive runs and headed our averages. More importantly it gave him experience. The die was cast.

Eagar agreed to captain Hampshire through 1956 and 1957 and then hand over the captaincy. In 1956 the rain affected cricket and while Laker demolished the Australians, Hampshire's younger spinners were notably less successful, although they still finished sixth. Although the seam bowlers were overused, Hampshire still bowled almost twenty overs per hour and Shackleton 'now seemed to be able to bowl everything except a googly and always on a good length'.

In 1957 Eagar's final side dropped a further seven places as 'the catching let us down' but the batting was 'powerful'. Appropriately, Eagar's final first-class match was against his former county Gloucestershire at Bournemouth. Eagar won the toss and invited them to bat, which they did in scoring just 121. Hampshire took a lead of 67 and Shackleton bowled Martin Young with the score on nineteen. Then, for no apparent reason, Gloucestershire managed just 20 more runs while being bowled out to lose by an innings. John Arlott reported that at the fall of the last wicket

> The Hampshire players turned and ran for the pavilion gate. There they were joined by the Gloucestershire side and, between their two ranks, Desmond Eagar, captain of a winning Hampshire team, walked out of first class cricket.

Eagar was the last of the county captains of 1946 to retire and he recalled that he sat in the dressing-room 'with my hands over my eyes and with an awful lump in my throat'. He expressed gratitude for 'memories of character, loyalty and determination' and a team that 'always kept trying'. As Colin Ingleby-Mackenzie prepared to succeed him, Eagar prophesied a period of 'gaiety and excitement' and wished him 'safe catching, for that way lies the road to the top of the Championship table'. Within four years that greatest goal would be achieved.

One Hampshire cricketer played throughout the period of the two post-war captains, Leo Harrison, the last of their pre-war players. He observed of Ingleby-Mackenzie that 'there's a difference between discipline and leadership and he was a good leader, without having to shout.' He remembered that as a newcomer to the side in 1951 Ingleby-Mackenzie was 'very respectful' and throughout his life he was still 'charming'.

> He never forgets me, always rings me at Christmas and invites me to his box at Lord's every year. He is a very, very nice man. He may have gone to Eton but he's one of the boys.

Similarly, Jimmy Gray remembered that despite his background he was 'delightful' and always a 'good mixer' while Dennis Baldry suggested that he was 'such a great leader, marvellous, if he'd said jump through that wall we'd all have jumped'. As a batsman, Gray remembers him as having a 'very good eye and good timing' but 'very little method'.

Harrison described his two main captains as 'chalk and cheese' with Desmond the 'disciplinarian' but both 'good captains'. He added that Desmond was more defensive 'because we never had the batting to attack teams' and 'he bowled 'Shack' and Cannings into the ground to keep runs down.' Leo felt sure that Ingleby-Mackenzie would have captained that earlier side differently from Eagar and also acknowledged that the professionals of that time had been 'brought up to expect an amateur captain so we didn't generally resent it'.

Superficially, Ingleby-Mackenzie was an almost perfect example of the amateur captain. He had a flamboyant personality with a matching approach to cricket – a player in the mould of Tennyson. He was the son of an Admiral who had done national service in the Royal Navy where he played for the Combined Services. He was educated at Eton but chose a profession over Oxbridge – and a profession in sports sales and then insurance. This 'work' seemed from his autobiography to occupy him for at least two weeks every year. As well as playing county cricket he often went on private overseas tours with Dukes, Lords and fellow amateurs. He had a fine social circle and enjoyed horses, champagne and parties with the top people.

In his autobiography, he describes in some detail an entertaining social tour of the West Indies captaining 'Jim' Swanton's side. They departed on 10 March 1961 following an airport cocktail and dinner party, returning on 20 April. Hampshire's season was to begin on 3 May and, on the day after his return, Ingleby-Mackenzie recounts how he put on his 'city clothes' and visited the office 'In a game attempt to convince my bosses that I had worked hard in the West Indies. They were, as always, more charitable than gullible' (p.146).

But if this sounds a rather demanding return, he reassures us that by the afternoon he was able to place a succession of successful bets on the televised racing from Sandown Park and the next day he went to the racecourse, where sadly he 'lost everything' on the last race. Then he went down to Southampton to compete in the Hampshire Cricket Club Golf Tournament before, on 26 April, he and Ted Dexter visited Newmarket. He had a poor day and the two men then retired to Hove to play on opposite sides in a two-day friendly. He was visited there by his boss and another colleague but it seems that this was purely social.

His was a life which seemed a remnant from 50 years before and while a few other cricketers like 'Lord' Edward Dexter may have enjoyed a similar lifestyle they were a rare breed, even among the amateurs. But there are three remarkable points about this lifestyle and its part in his cricket. Firstly he was very serious about the game despite his enterprising approach; secondly he seemed utterly unassuming about his lifestyle and finally he was happy to share it with his professional colleagues – particularly his two senior professionals Roy Marshall and Leo Harrison.

Ingleby-Mackenzie spent part of his national service stationed in Portsmouth and he played regularly for the Navy and Combined Services with occasional opportunities to play for Hampshire. In 1954 he played almost a full season although his 821 runs were obtained at a modest 17.84 per innings.

After his single match in 1955 he opened the following season keeping wicket for the MCC against Hampshire at Lord's, then played regularly for the county and topped the batting averages. This was probably important for, if this young amateur was to become Hampshire's next captain, the professionals would wish to feel that he was an effective cricketer – not always true of Hampshire's previous amateur captains. In 1957 he passed 1,000 runs for the first time and also gained regular experience as captain, substituting for Eagar. He admitted subsequently that the different approaches of the two captains made 1957 an uneven season but it prepared him to take over fully for the first time in 1958 when he became the second-youngest Hampshire captain in the club's history (R.H. Moore having been 22 in 1936).

He began this first year (after a week of fine parties and heavy losses at Newmarket) with a match in damp Bradford where the first two days were abandoned. Having encouraged his new side to 'entertain or perish' he did his best to meet both criteria in the first match. He won the toss and in the context made quite the wrong decision by batting, although one wonders whether he had any advice from senior players. Hampshire without Gray struggled to 105-7 (Trueman 4-25) whereupon the young captain declared leaving Yorkshire less than an hour to 'win', with eight points now available for a one-day match. With Yorkshire 36-2 Trueman was promoted and scored 58 of 70 to secure the victory.

17   *Ingleby-Mackenzie's first side, 1958.*

Incredibly Shackleton's figures were 7-0-64-0 but Trueman was frequently one of the few batsmen who could collar Shackleton. The Yorkshire crowd cheered Hampshire's sporting approach and their generous captain although they were less enthusiastic about this approach three years later.

He kept wicket as the side then lost their next two matches at Trent Bridge and Old Trafford and must have been relieved to hand over to David Blake at Portsmouth. After three matches they were 15th and had lost 15 hours in weather 'as cold and cheerless as any of the senior players could remember'. Portsmouth provided some relief as the side won their first match by nine wickets, scoring at six runs per over. Their traditional Whitsun match v Kent at Southampton saw them successfully chase 307 to win by five wickets thanks to centuries by Marshall and the young captain. Marshall had opened with Pitman, Bernard Harrison, Blake and Sainsbury before Gray returned in early June and with Leo Harrison fit again the side was more settled and they won regularly.

These victories included Cowes in early June and, in the next match at Yeovil, they found themselves, as in 1955, at the right end of the table. At Yeovil in mid-June, Somerset experimented with midweek days that began at 1.30p.m. and finished at 8.15p.m., anticipating the widespread introduction of evening cricket decades later. Sadly the public did not respond at a time when falling gates were of concern to county treasurers throughout the country. Somerset had been a poor side for some years but in 1958 they emulated the Hampshire side of three years earlier, finishing third. Interestingly they achieved this largely by importing overseas cricketers like Wight, McCool and Alley, and none of their senior players were Somerset-born.

In mid-June Hampshire won at Oxford, after which the captain took Leo Harrison to Ascot. After lunch and the racing came a cocktail party, so that they arrived in Southampton as the milk was being delivered. At Bournemouth a few hours later Ingleby-Mackenzie was lucky to win the toss against Somerset and he slept through the day until with about an hour left he came in at 255-4. Fully refreshed, he and Horton then added 161 in 66 minutes and both completed centuries. On Thursday the rain affected the wicket and as it dried, Burden's offspin took 5-25 but too much time was lost. Following on, McCool and Maurice Tremlett batted towards a draw, despite six more wickets for Burden.

Hampshire were now pressing for the title and Brian Chapman in the *Daily Mirror* wrote of 'England's youngest and most original county cricket captain (who) has led the side to the top of the table in just seven weeks of vivid cricket'. Shackleton returned his best bowling figures (to date) of 9-59 at Bristol and then they beat Glamorgan (72 & 46) by an innings with a score of 120-6 declared. This too was the kind of match that is no longer possible – Hampshire winning with a top-score of 37* by Ray Pitman.

At the end of June at Guildford they dismissed the mighty Surrey side for 106 (Shackleton 7-34) but the wet weather, which generally assisted their attack through the season, again interfered and the match was drawn. Had they beaten Surrey the title might have been theirs. However, they did keep winning. In late July at Bournemouth they dismissed Nottinghamshire for 100 and then Marshall (138) and Gray (154) added 186 for the first wicket in 129 minutes. Their total of 416-9 declared was a huge score in 1958 and they won by an innings.

After 17 matches Hampshire were still top of the table. A crowd of 10,000 at Canterbury watched them on the August Bank Holiday Saturday and E.W. Swanton reported that 'Hampshire are playing attractive cricket and they are simply drawing the crowds'. They won this match narrowly on Tuesday 5 August and it was here that in a TV interview the captain uttered his famous formula for success: 'wine, women and song'.

Sadly, the formula failed suddenly and dramatically. They came to a very wet Portsmouth week where both matches were drawn but then travelled to Burton-on-Trent where, after a rain-ravaged first day, their spirits must have risen as Shackleton and Heath dismissed Derbyshire for 74 in 32.4 overs. Only two men made double figures but sadly this was two more than Hampshire, who were put out for just 23 by Jackson and Rhodes. In Derbyshire's second innings Shackleton and Heath again bowled unchanged on a wicket that was dangerous. In the days before helmets Derek Morgan had his forehead split but came back to score forty-six. He was the only man to pass 20 in the match and Derbyshire, 107 all out, set Hampshire 159 to win. They did not get within 100 runs of the target. Mike Barnard top scored for Hampshire in each innings but surely his scores of five and 16 must be the lowest pair of 'top scores' in first-class history.

The *Hampshire Handbook* recorded, 'that no one was seriously hurt will remain one of the mysteries of cricket'. 1958 was Malcolm Heath's finest season and his match figures here of 34-8-87-13 were remarkable for a man on the losing side, yet decades later the match was still Ingleby-Mackenzie's worst memory in cricket. In retrospect he regretted asking Derbyshire to bat on the 'most dangerous wicket' he had ever played on.

In recent years the wicket would have been declared unsuitable and Derbyshire would have lost points, although then as now this would have offered scant consolation to Hampshire. They recovered by winning the next match at Clacton but that was the only one of their last eight matches that they won. Derbyshire beat them again in the last match at Bournemouth and Jackson brought his season's tally against Hampshire to 20 wickets for 91 runs. By then Surrey were champions again.

In 1955 Hampshire had celebrated third place as though they had won the title. In 1958 this more experienced side and their supporters were proud but also disappointed to be runners-up and Vic Cannings believed that 'we should have won it'. More positively, Heath, still only 24, had enjoyed his best season and a new fast bowler David White had played a few games. He had once been on the Warwickshire staff but was discovered by Arthur Holt playing national service cricket. He took only 29 wickets in 1958 but would have a huge impact in years to come. Marshall, Gray, Horton and the captain all passed 1,000 runs and Sainsbury was a fine all-rounder, but there was a weakness in the middle order and the spinners rarely won matches in that wet year.

At the end of the season, Hampshire's averages showed that 16 professionals and three amateurs had appeared for the county. The published accounts gave the professionals and groundstaff a shared wage bill of just under £10,000 with an additional £1,292 'match money' for the players. The office staff and administrative wages came to nearly £3,000. Travel, hotels and meals cost nearly £3,000 and miscellaneous items *including* amateurs' expenses were £646.

Both members' subscriptions and gate money brought in around £9,000 each. Income from television and Test matches amounted to around £4,000 to which could be added around £1,000 from various fund-raising activities – principally whist drives.

These are not the total figures from the accounts but they give some indication of the earnings of professional cricketers and the costs of running county clubs – especially those without Test match grounds. An ongoing Diamond Jubilee appeal had by then generated around £7,000, much of which was invested to generate further income. On the whole, Hampshire and most county clubs were solvent but in a precarious state. Cricketers, like most footballers, could not expect to earn more than many of their peers in outside employment although some would earn a benefit. In those accounts, Derek Shackleton's benefit was shown at £3,756 – a tax free sum equivalent to about four years of his basic salary. Meanwhile the players continued to prepare and perform on a Victorian ground at Northlands Road or on delightful but often somewhat spartan outgrounds. Hampshire paid £150 in rent to Bournemouth and £225 to Portsmouth.

There was a popular if ultimately unreliable view that county cricket might not – perhaps could not – survive a period of growing prosperity and alternative family entertainment. Many people who did not watch cricket very often kept up to date through the media. In 1959 that would be principally newspapers, especially for opinions, while the radio and television would present the facts and figures of specific matches. Elsewhere there were the specialist monthly publications like *The Cricketer* or the newly planned *Playfair Cricket Monthly*. There were also the annuals, from the counties themselves, from *Playfair* and most obviously *Wisden*.

The gloomy views may have reflected a frequent pessimism in the cricket pages and specialist publications themselves. The glow of the late 1940s had been replaced by pragmatic county cricket, an England side often too strong to provide meaningful Test series and too many alternative distractions in the days of the motor car, television and Macmillan's 'never had it so good' world. There were also a number of specific problems facing English cricket as the 1960s loomed.

During the 1950s, England became the strongest side in international cricket. Although their decade did not begin with promise, after 1950 England were pre-eminent. They gained revenge over the West Indians at home and away, won series against most other countries (losing only one) and – most importantly – regained the Ashes at The Oval in 1953 and held them in the next two series.

There was a blip in the tour there in 1958–9 when the Australians regained ownership of the little urn with a 4-1 series win, but the ageing English side had the comfort of knowing that their opponents had hardly won with honour. From the English perspective, their opponents fielded a succession of fast bowlers with suspect actions who exploited the back-foot no-ball law to bowl from about 18 paces. This was clearly 'not cricket'.

The natural order was restored in the blazing English summer of 1959 when England won all five Test matches against a very weak Indian side. They then toured the West Indies and won that series 1-0 – their first series win in the Caribbean. Brian Statham with 17 wickets at 13.11 and Fred Trueman (24 at 16.7) had crushed the Indians, well supported by the Lancastrian leg-spinner Tommy Greenhough (14 at 18.2). Greenhough had struggled mid-season and, although selected for the West Indian tour, he did not play any Test matches and played only once more for England, in the final Test of the 1960 series against South Africa. By then English leg spinners were becoming deeply unfashionable, although they rarely made any impact in Hampshire until the 21st century.

In Hampshire, the 1959 season began with a new acquisition, Dennis Baldry from Middlesex. Despite Hampshire's success in 1958, John Arlott in his report for the *Playfair Cricket Annual* noted that 'Pitman and Barnard, at numbers four and five, fell short of championship standard.' Although they both played in the regular 11 after Rayment's retirement, neither averaged as high as 17 over the season and Pitman, in 24 matches, managed just one fifty. Hampshire, their ambitions sharpened by recent, unprecedented success were keen to strengthen the batting. So it was that Danny Livingstone and Dennis Baldry reported for pre-season practice at Southampton.

Dennis arrived after a conversation between the Middlesex captain J.J. Warr and Ingleby-Mackenzie, although Leicestershire had also offered him a contract. He said, 'I knew that my position at Middlesex was precarious and I chose Hampshire as a southerner.' Dennis agreed terms with Ingleby-Mackenzie at a meeting at Slazengers during the winter while Desmond Eagar was in Australia with the

MCC. He remembers his captain as 'a tremendous character, a rare breed' and was happy to join his side.

In 1959 Hampshire's batting was still unsettled after the reliable opening trinity of Marshall, Gray and Horton. Livingstone spent his first season qualifying for the county while Pitman, after three unsuccessful appearances, faded out. Mike Barnard averaged 25 but only once passed 50 in 22 innings, while Ray Flood enjoyed his one season of county cricket with 780 runs at 25 each innings. Flood would play one match in 1960 before he too disappeared. In the middle order Sainsbury and the captain were invaluable but the major difference was the contribution of Baldry who had, by some distance, the finest season of his career.

Hampshire's 1959 season began against Glamorgan at Portsmouth on Wednesday 6 May and, after Ingleby-Mackenzie had won the toss, Frank Clarke dismissed the openers and Ray Pitman fell to the Welsh skipper, Wilf Wooller, leaving Hampshire at 55-3. Dennis then joined Henry Horton and the two of them enjoyed a brilliant partnership of 151 before Horton edged Don Shepherd to the wicketkeeper. Hampshire's captain also fell to Shepherd but Baldry and Sainsbury added 93 for the sixth wicket. After Hampshire declared at 350-6, their seamers dismissed Glamorgan twice to win the game by an innings. Dennis Baldry's 151 was the highest innings ever played on debut for Hampshire although, like Abercrombie before him and Richard Hayward, John Crawley, Shane Watson and Andy Bichel since, his century on debut for the county was not his first-class debut.

Hampshire's good start continued with an intriguing game at Bristol where Gloucestershire recovered from 35-7 to 169 thanks mainly to David Allen, who made sixty-two. Nonetheless, with Shackleton taking 9-81 and 3-68 and Marshall scoring 150, Hampshire won again and Dennis then 'went home' to Lord's to play for Hampshire against an MCC side. He came in at 120-2 and enjoyed a century partnership with his captain before completing his second hundred in his first three matches. He says that he 'reached 99 before waking up. I was batting with Leo who was like greased lightning and facing Henry Tilly,' a former Middlesex colleague. 'I played the first ball and called "no", the second was on the spot and I called "no" again, the third ball I called "no" again, ran like hell and Leo was passing me as I left the crease, calling out "well done".' Despite the achievement at Portsmouth, this innings remains most strongly in his memory because it was played on the ground where he had spent his formative decade.

He made 62 and took a couple of wickets in the next match – a defeat against Kent during which he also received his county cap. 'I walked down the steps from the pavilion and had no idea – they all stopped and the captain handed it to me. The contract was the same but it was worth another £100 per year.' The team then travelled to Old Trafford where Lancashire made a good start against Shackleton and Heath before Dennis took 7-76, which remained the best bowling of his career. It was often difficult for Dennis to get on as a bowler because he usually lined up behind 'Shack', Heath, Cannings and Gray but 'I loved it, I always loved bowling,' and on this particular day he got his chance and found the ball 'booming all over the place'.

This was the most extraordinary start and it seemed that perhaps Hampshire had found the batsman who would turn them into a Championship-winning side

18   *Dennis Baldry batting v Kent at Southampton, Whitsun Bank Holiday 1959.*

as well as a useful bowler. After five first-class matches Dennis had scored 360 runs at an average of 45 and had 11 wickets under twenty apiece and he made another century against Somerset in early June. Sadly, this record would not last although in that first season he passed 1,500 runs at around thirty and took 30 wickets at a similar average. In addition he was always an entertaining batsman.

In the following season, Danny Livingstone became available and he, Mike Barnard and Dennis all averaged around twenty over the season, so Hampshire were still looking for a regular number four batsman in a disappointing season in which only their top three managed a century. In 1961 Hampshire selected Danny at number four and Peter Sainsbury at number five throughout the season and they both scored more than 1,500 runs at an average around thirty. Indeed by then, the line-up was so stable that Marshall, Gray, Horton, Livingstone and Sainsbury batted as the first five in all but three mid-season matches when Roy Marshall was injured and Bernard Harrison came in.

Dennis played an important innings at Leeds in 1961, after which he scored half-centuries against Nottinghamshire and Sussex but averaged just under twenty and took only eight wickets. He acknowledged that the constant competition was a factor but admitted, 'I don't think I applied myself as I might have done.' In part this was because he had found himself a good winter job and, 'with a wife, two tiddlers and a mortgage, that was worth a lot. Even our two stars, 'Shack' and 'Marsh' didn't earn that much.'

Dennis continued to play in 1962 although he appeared only intermittently in the first team. During the icy winter of 1962–3, he was offered a permanent position with his firm, which was too good to turn down. In his early thirties he retired from professional cricket.

Meanwhile, the South Africans toured England in 1960 when many of the matches were picketed by protesters, an action that created anger in South Africa at a time when it was rapidly distancing itself from the old Empire and Commonwealth. Generally these protests mirrored the relatively orderly and peaceful protests of CND at this time, although the sightscreens and turf at Trent Bridge were daubed with slogans before the first day's play there. Feelings were particularly high because the first Test match started at Birmingham on Thursday 9 June, less than three months after white South African police had gunned down their own black citizens at Sharpeville near Johannesburg. On that day 69 black people were killed and 178 injured for participating in a peaceful protest against the social, economic and political separation imposed by the laws of apartheid.

The South African tourists were welcomed in the launch of a new monthly magazine, *Playfair Cricket Monthly*. In its first editorial the editors assured their readers that their 'happy memories of fellows' including Learie Constantine, Hanif Mohammed and Clyde Walcott meant that they would 'inevitably regard Apartheid as repugnant'. Nonetheless 'in the same breath we welcome unconditionally … our guests from South Africa … not as politicians but as cricketers'. They emphasised this point by distancing themselves from the Rev. David Sheppard, the former England cricketer, who refused to play against South Africa, suggesting that

> The South Africans must clearly understand that Christianity cannot tolerate Apartheid but at the same time nowhere in the Christian doctrine does there appear a suggestion that the sensible way of dealing with a wrong-doing is a boycott, especially when those to be the subject of the boycott cannot personally be held responsible in any shape or form.

There might be all kinds of retrospective observations about these comments but the key point is to understand that this reflected the mainstream position among the broad cricketing constituency in England then and for some time to come. By-and-large English cricketers, administrators and supporters would have shown no wish to support apartheid but would have been determined to appear 'even-handed' towards the cricketers and anxious to stress that politics should be kept out of sport. In addition, few would have felt any sense that their remarks about a group of black 'fellows' might have been condescending. Very little would change over the next decade but by 1970 the strength of feeling in England had altered sufficiently that the general views of English cricket would be unable to resist the political strength of the British anti-apartheid movement.

Interestingly, about forty years later, the English cricket establishment was more willing to resist playing cricket with a Southern African country with a poor civil rights record but got itself into a diplomatic tangle over matches with Zimbabwe. Their opposition cost them dearly in the World Cup of 2003 and may have reflected a genuine change in the attitude of the cricket world to its role in international politics. Less charitably, it may also reflect the difference between their attitude to the politics of a white colonial country in 1960 and an innate hostility to the anti-imperialist rhetoric of the black Robert Mugabe and his violent henchmen.

Apart from the Rev. David Sheppard, the main opponent of apartheid within the world of cricket was the writer and broadcaster John Arlott. He had witnessed some of the brutality of the regime on a cricketing tour to the country and had also stood as a Liberal parliamentary candidate. In the same magazine, his first regular column took a different, more gentle view, suggesting that 'the tour now faces difficulties more important than the winning or losing of a Test match.' But Arlott too argued against protests and boycotts, although he was more thorough in describing the political constituency of South Africa, criticising the system that elected a 'minority' government. Furthermore, he suggested that it was 'virtually certain' that the majority of South African cricket tourists since the war would have voted against the Nationalist government. He also pointed out that Basil D'Oliviera, a then unknown 'Cape Coloured' cricketer who could not be selected by his country, was about to arrive for his first English season in the Lancashire League. Ten years later, following the D'Oliviera affair, Arlott more polemically announced his refusal to commentate on the South Africans tour of 1970, which was eventually cancelled.

England won the first three Test matches of the 1960 series with ease. It is tempting to suggest that Colin Wesley or Peter Carlstein, who between them scored 168 runs in 14 innings (averaging 12) in the middle order might have been usefully replaced by D'Oliveira – especially as neither bowled. The fourth Test at Manchester was ruined by rain but it is interesting to note that Roy McLean's 109 for the visitors (in a total of 229) was the first century of the series on either side at a time when uncovered wickets still favoured bowlers in England. England's attack generally consisted of three pace bowlers, Trueman, Statham and Alan Moss, supported by Dexter's seamers and one or two slower bowlers, usually the off-spin of Illingworth or Allen. Against this attack and on old-fashioned English wickets, South Africa failed to pass 250 until the first innings of the final Test, when they took 171 overs to amass 419.

England had then won every home series since the 1-1 draw with Pakistan in 1954 but John Arlott's report in the *Playfair Cricket Annual* suggested that the tour 'was the unhappiest ever made by a party of overseas cricketers in England'. He suggested a number of reasons, including selection and results, the first financial loss on an English tour for almost fifty years and the political tensions surrounding the tour. However, in his concluding paragraph he suggested that the strongest memory of the tour for most people would be the calling of no-ball for throwing of the young South African Geoff Griffin.

This occurred at a time when the state of fast bowling in the world was generally causing concerns. England's Australian tour had raised questions about legitimate actions and no-balls and in the following seasons a number of English county bowlers had been called or reported for their actions in what now appears to be a somewhat hysterical response by a few umpires. One of those was Hampshire's 'Butch' White, called by Paul Gibb at Hove in 1960, to the astonishment of all his team-mates.

As he bowled he heard the cry of 'no-ball' from
square leg but he was unaware of what had passed until
he walked off at the interval to be told that umpire
Paul Gibb had called him for throwing. As 'Butch'
walked up the steps he passed Gibb but 'fortunately
Ingleby was behind me and kept me calm'. Gibb
acknowledged he had made a mistake and apologised
but 'it was a bit late'.

1960 was a time of some hysteria about
throwing and, in the Test matches of that year,
South African Geoff Griffin was no-balled out of
cricket. Arlott described a 'purge' of bowlers with
dubious actions at the turn of the century, including
Hampshire's E.R. Bradford. After that, there were
just four instances of bowlers who were no-balled
for throwing between 1908 and 1950. Over the
next 10 seasons he listed 23 more, including nine
in 1960 but for some reason he missed White
– perhaps because like everyone I talked to he
simply could not believe it possible. Roy Marshall

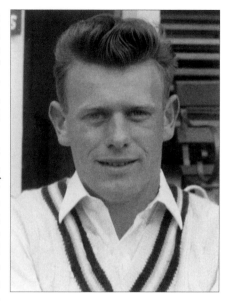

19 *'Butch' White.*

put it succinctly in his autobiography stating 'this was complete rubbish.
'Butch' could never throw with his action.' 'Butch' White was pleased to
hear Marshall's comment and, 38 years later, keen that I should include it.
The incident clearly hurt him.

The MCC arranged to have his action filmed and, while he was never
called again, he feels that this may have affected his career at Test level.
England needed to identify successors to Trueman and Statham and over the
next few years turned to a number of bowlers including Flavell and Coldwell
at Worcestershire, Larter (Northants), Fred Rumsey (Somerset), John Price
(Middlesex) and Ian Thomson (Sussex). In 1963 they selected Derek Shackleton
at the age of 38 but it would be some years before John Snow, David Brown
and Jeff Jones would provide a firm succession.

Following the West Indian tour, questions were raised also about short-pitched
bowling as a legitimate method of 'attack' – the implication being that perhaps
this was not quite cricket. But the South African tour of 1960 brought the
throwing controversy to a head as Griffin was no-balled in the Lord's Test match,
after which his career was effectively over.

At this time then there was a real crisis in English cricket, which was losing
spectators at an alarming rate despite England's considerable success. This was
partly because England's success had been gained in a series of one-sided and
generally dull Test matches – imagine for example a Test series decided 3-0
before any batsman scored a century, as happened in 1960. The South Africans
scored at less than 2.5 runs per over and they were certainly stronger than the
Indian and New Zealand tourists of the previous two summers. And although
England were the dominant side they scored at just 2.3 runs per over while
over rates on fixed days (11.30-6.30) were only around 15 per hour.

John Arlott was one of a number of contemporary commentators who pointed out that cricket's popularity could not be equated simply with attendance at matches, especially as cricket insisted on taking place at such inconvenient times. Some fixtures, like Hampshire's Portsmouth and Bournemouth weeks, took place in early August and many locals and northern holidaymakers would plan leave to coincide with the two three-day Championship matches with a Wednesday and Saturday start. But imagine, for example, a working man watching Hampshire score 252 all out at 2.23 runs per over on a cold May Saturday in 1958 at Old Trafford. In reply Lancashire are 23-3 at the close. Would there be any motivation to take a day's leave to return on the Monday?

The 1959 first-class season ran from 6 May to 1 September, much shorter than today's seasons and the last two holiday months in Hampshire featured 11 home matches, or 33 days of cricket out of sixty-two. It is not surprising that even the most committed supporter would struggle to give up 33 days to watch cricket – 22 of them during the normal working week (and more people still worked on Saturday mornings in 1959). By contrast, anyone wishing to follow their local football team might expect to devote about 17 Saturday afternoons, two midweek matches in September and one game each over Christmas and Easter. Incidentally, that football season of 1959 began on 22 August and finished on 30 April, thereby overlapping the cricket season by just one week. As a consequence Hampshire's Mike Barnard and Bernard Harrison were able to play professional football and cricket.

When cricket had resumed in Hampshire in 1946 both the level of membership (3,694) and paid attendance (91,619) were records for the county and these records were broken easily in the following glorious summer of 1947, with 5,154 members and 113,078 paying spectators. In one sense it is important to remember that comments about sparse crowds at midweek Championship matches should be set against an acknowledgement that members have effectively bought a seat that on a given day they may not be using. It is also interesting to note that the level of membership in 1947 is very similar to that in the early twenty-first century.

1949 was another fine summer but attendances dropped by 11,000 and membership by 142, leaving Hampshire with an annual deficit of £2,000. Two years later in poor weather gates fell by 14,000 but membership was 5,281. Sadly in the following year membership followed suit, dropping dramatically to 4,112 although we must remember that Hampshire were then a poor and not particularly entertaining side.

There is no doubt that members and supporters of most county sides had fairly modest expectations of success in the mid-20th century. Often they would relish seeing one or two star players and look forward to matches with the tourists and major counties. For example, in 1954, which was then the wettest season since the war, Hampshire attracted their lowest paying figure of 73,741 spectators and over twenty per cent (15,598) of them watched the first two days v Yorkshire at Bournemouth in mid-August. The traditional northern visitors, relishing the closure of mills and factories and enjoying Bournemouth's beach and a spot of cricket, would have swelled this crowd.

When Hampshire finished third in their sunny Diamond Jubilee season of 1955 it is not surprising that this was also Hampshire's best-ever financial season with 111,330 paying spectators, almost forty thousand up on the previous year. Hampshire played 16 three-day home matches in 1955 – 14 in the Championship plus one university fixture and the touring South Africans. That is a total of 48 days' cricket although with a record number of victories and only six innings totalling over 300, third days did not necessarily promise a lot of play. But even at 48 days that is an average paying attendance of 2,320 to which should be added members.

Crucially too Hampshire then embarked on a period of some success. They finished sixth in 1956, second in 1958, eighth in 1959 and finally won the Championship in 1961. The membership was virtually five thousand in 1958 and after that record second place increased by almost three hundred in 1959. Although the weather was appalling in 1958, crowds flocked to the Portsmouth Festival in August but both games were rain-affected draws.

Despite this successful period, Desmond Eagar reported in the *Hampshire Handbook* that the financial results in 1960

> were almost disastrous. The club showed a loss of £5,835 which meant that in the three years 1958-1960 Hampshire had shown losses of over £10,000. 'Another year like this and the county club will be pretty well out of play' said our Honorary Treasurer Mr JP Burnett at the Annual Meeting the following March.

In August 1960, *Playfair Cricket Monthly* described how Test cricket had become so slow that the public had become less interested in it 'except' intriguingly 'on television screens'. An example was the first Edgbaston Test where the attendance was 50 per cent lower than three years before. Three reasons were suggested – that bowlers walk back too slowly, that field-setting was laborious and that five days for a match set the pace for play. No specific mention was made of batting tempos but that was implied in the last comment.

There were also changes in the relationships between players and the authorities in English county cricket. The distinction between amateurs and professionals on the field still existed, although fewer amateurs were able to devote sufficient time to the game. Neither were relationships between the two camps always as successful as those at Hampshire.

In this period Hampshire's affairs were driven by Desmond Eagar, who was effectively Chief Executive, and he worked very closely with a small group, including the President Harry Altham and the captain. Nonetheless, while many counties like Hampshire relied on the efforts of a small office staff they were largely managed by committees of well-meaning amateurs, elected by the membership. In a 'shire' county some care would be taken to represent the various areas and in 1958 Hampshire's committee consisted of 28 men, including four officers of Her Majesty's Armed Forces, an alderman and the chief constable of Hampshire. There were two pre-war amateur captains, C.G. Paris and G.R. Taylor, plus J.P. Parker who had played as an amateur for the county under Tennyson. The Chairman was W.J. Arnold, and there were two vice-chairmen – P.C. Ford, whose son and grandson would both follow him and become Chairman and Sir Reginald Biddle, who was co-opted as one of 33 vice-presidents.

During the late 1950s, English cricket was soured by a number of disputes between prominent professional cricketers and their county committees. Towards the end of his career Jim Laker published a book that was critical of some of his colleagues and raised particular issues about the inequalities between amateurs and professionals. Following the publication of the book, both Surrey and the MCC withdrew a number of his privileges.

At Gloucestershire, Tom Graveney led the county to second place in 1959 but when they dropped to eighth in 1960 he was replaced by the amateur old Etonian C.T.M. Pugh. As a batsman Pugh's first-class career average was below twenty so he never warranted a place as a player. In fairness, however, in his two years in charge Gloucestershire performed fairly well but by then Graveney had departed. His move to Worcestershire required a year out of county cricket, qualifying by residence. This aspect of the Graveney affair was highly controversial, and coincided with battles over players' rights in football.

Of greatest interest to Hampshire was the sacking by Yorkshire of their slow left-arm Test bowler Johnny Wardle. He had published a newspaper column without the necessary clearance and his invitation to tour Australia in 1958 was withdrawn. Desmond Eagar went on that tour as assistant manager but intriguingly his scrapbook contains cuttings about the issue including a quote from Eagar that 'the onus of team building rested on the county captain' but 'if Colin would like the committee to offer Wardle terms then I am certain they would agree.' Presumably the captain was sufficiently positive about Sainsbury and Wassell and resisted the opportunity.

Birley (1999) sums up this period as follows:

> Everywhere relationships changed as the old feudal barriers came down …
> Umpires reported players for poor behaviour. Members complained and
> heavy-handed disciplinary committees were brought into play.

Perhaps crucially, he added that 'every incident was grist for the media mill'.

However, none of these issues of slow scoring, throwing, apartheid or players 'rights' would have caused great distress if English counties could balance the books. In this sense the county game is essentially pragmatic but it never has been able to avoid a loss through its own efforts. As a consequence it is highly dependent upon Test match receipts and television and radio fees but in 1960 there were signs that even these were under threat.

In 1960, the four-day attendance at the Lord's Test match when the weather was not very good was 60,000, but that included 15,000 MCC members. Nottingham was awful, with only 12,000 attending overall and Manchester was not much better with thirty-three thousand. Nonetheless, Test match profits including broadcasting revenue were £93,686. This was distributed to the counties in sums of £7,300 to Test ground counties (equalling Somerset's gate receipts), and other counties £3,200.

It was not exclusively a problem of county cricket, for gate income in Lancashire League cricket fell by £2,000 from 1959 to 1960. To a large extent, football pools run by clubs kept them alive. But the Central Lancashire League offered another solution by changing to an over-limit form of the game with bonus points for quick scoring. Other suggestions for improving attendances included Sunday cricket and promotion and relegation.

One question asked more frequently was whether county cricket was too cheap. Desmond Eagar observed that in the first 60 years of the century, cricket ball costs had risen by eight times while membership subscriptions had only doubled. In 1960, the average earnings of a county cricketer were still around £750 p.a., a similar figure to a clerical worker in local government in his mid-30s. Major players might earn more and a Test appearance would produce £100 per match. Compare that figure with Somerset's gate income of £7,100, which would pay for only eight or nine professionals. In 1960 they reduced their staff from 25 to 20 to save money. At Middlesex, gates dropped by 38,000 and they released four players including Bob Caple, who followed Dennis Baldry to Hampshire.

Derbyshire planned to stop benefits because of falling income although they proposed a lump sum to capped players on retirement. Only 47,691 people paid to watch them in 1960 and they cut their staff to sixteen. In May 1961, Nottinghamshire and Yorkshire announced they would follow the example of Lancashire in replacing benefits with pension schemes, guaranteeing players around £1,600 at 40 (which then might buy a modest house).

Gloucestershire had finished as Championship runners-up in 1959 but they withdrew from the 2nd XI Championship £12,000 in debt and their Chairman speculated that 1961 might be their last season. In April 1961 their supporters' club gave £3,000 to add to the £5,000 they had presented in December 1960. This covered the loss of 1960 and we know now that the county survived.

County Championship paid attendances fell from almost 2,300,000 in 1947 to less than one million in the very wet summer of 1958. However, memberships rose in the corresponding period considerably. One extreme example was Sussex, which went up from 638 in 1946 to 7,000 by 1960. In 1959 most counties lost money, although there were some positive signs – especially some increases in gates at clubs like Essex, Kent and Sussex. This may have reflected the change from a very wet summer in 1958 to the glorious weather of 1959. Leicestershire generated £15,000 from their pools scheme and Northamptonshire received the considerable sum of £24,000 from their supporters club. Yorkshire increased membership subscriptions by 50 per cent but they were embarking upon a phase of consistent success on the field.

By comparison, Surrey, after seven consecutive titles, had their worst-ever season in 1960 with gates falling more than 50 per cent by 77,477 to a total of 66,172. The *Playfair Cricket Monthly* suggested that

> With cricket's finances as they stand at present, it is absolutely imperative that next summer's series with the Australians should be a howling success in terms of hard cash.

More expansively, in 1959 Hampshire had joined the new 2nd XI Championship, a competition designed to aid the development of new players but one that had considerable implications for the sizes and therefore costs of county staffs.

Desmond Eagar wrote an article in *Playfair Cricket Monthly* (March 1961) entitled 'The Problem of Cricket Finance'. He pointed out that it had always been difficult at Hampshire, with large overdrafts even between the wars and, anticipating the coming season, also stressed the importance of the Australian visits. Eagar described 1938 as Hampshire's best pre-war season. Although they finished 14th there was an Australian tour and gates and members' subscriptions raised around £8,000. However, expenditure was over £9,000 and a profit of around £2,000 was due 'mainly' to income from the Board of Control, just as today counties rely on their ECB 'handouts'.

By comparison, in 1960's 'disastrous summer' Hampshire's gates produced £7,000 (the lowest numerically since war) but membership subscriptions at £10,500 were a record. Once again, expenditure of £28,780 led to a loss of £11,000, which was reduced to just under £6,000 by the Board of Control and what he called 'other efforts'. He added that, in 1961, 'Supporters' Clubs alone enable first class counties to remain solvent' and suggested that Test match and TV fees should be 'ploughed back' into the game, with clubs existing by balancing their budgets by membership and match income. But he was not sure that that approach was possible.

This all sounds very familiar. While all the sums involved are massively higher, 45 years later, most county clubs still struggle financially and there is still a debate about the best way of using the far larger sums that cricket earns through media coverage.

English cricket decided, as the English often do, to set up a committee of enquiry, although it was not universally welcomed. Eagar asked,

> Is it possible in these days of full employment, television, family cars and the increase in popularity of e.g. sailing and athletics that an answer can be found?

He added, is there too much cricket? Are there too many Tests? Are the Tests too long? By way of something of an answer to his own questions he added,

> I hope that the needs of members will never be forgotten. Membership is our life's blood and over one-third of our total income comes from this source. At the moment we play an average of five matches at each of our three main centres. Could we still retain our members if the number of days for cricket was halved?

He noted the discussions about a knock-out competition, adding 'I see no harm in such a competition being tried as an experiment.' The feeling was that it might be entertaining.

A frequent assertion around such discussions is that cricket is an 'entertainment' and that it should not forget that fact. But there are dangers in allowing this assertion to become a cliché. Professional cricket is an entertainment in the sense that it is marketed to a public who pay to watch it live and on television. The income they generate through these and other activities sustains the game.

But it is not an entertainment like comedy or pop music or Hollywood cinema for one simple reason. Whereas all those other forms of entertainment can be planned around certainties and reasonable expectations there is at the heart of cricket and other professional sports a fundamental uncertainty. And this is derived from the obvious fact that at any given moment one group of players is actively trying to stop the others performing to their best ability. When we watch Warne bowling to Pietersen in an Ashes Test match we have a fair idea of the intentions of the two players but we have no idea what the outcome might be. When we watch a singer or a comedian or a musical or a western our judgements will be related in part to the realisation of our expectations. And if we are at a live concert we will be surprised if someone appears on stage attempting to prevent the star from performing well.

That is what we seek from cricket and other sports yet too often spectators then become bored or annoyed by the consequences. For years, many of the world's finest cricketers frustrated the efforts of English players like Robin Smith, Michael Atherton, Alec Stewart and Darren Gough but not all English 'audiences' found this entertaining. On the other hand, in 2005 we did not worry much that McGrath rarely played or that Hayden or Gillespie were below their best, although we might have objected to understudies and sub-standard performances in a West End show.

So professional cricket has always been the site of a struggle between administrators seeking to make the game more attractive and cricketers who desire to triumph by whatever relatively legitimate means against skilful opponents. In its perfect moments, as in much that occurred in 2005, there is apparently no tension between the two forces but it is not always perfect.

By the end of the 1960 cricket season there was a sense of gloom and anxiety around the English game but also a hope that the Australian tour the following year might bring something better. What no one could know then was that, by the following season, Australia and the West Indies would have competed in one of the greatest of all Test series.

By its conclusion in March 1961 (writing in *Playfair Cricket Monthly*) John Arlott suggested that the series had 'aroused more interest here than any series in history in which England was not concerned'. In the same publication Ron Roberts suggested that it 'seemed to unfold like a fairy tale'. It was successful because it staged the first tied Test match, it was a close series and because the scoring was generally fast, but especially by West Indian batsmen against Australia's pace bowlers. These rates varied from 3.5 per over (Davidson) to 5.9 (Meckiff) while the leg spinner Benaud was the only bowler averaging under three. At the end of the series, in scenes repeated in England in 2005, half-a-million Australians gave their visitors a ticker-tape send off.

Immediately afterwards, Test tickets for 1961 Ashes Tests went on sale in England and the MCC described the level of demand as 'unprecedented'. The *Playfair Cricket Monthly* (May 1961) ran an editorial entitled 'The Dream of a Utopian Summer'. It concluded on the County Championship, 'It is high time a new name appeared at the head of the table. Who is it to be?' The answer would bring delight to Hampshire.

Despite the wet and cold weather, the Whitsun Roses match at Old Trafford attracted an attendance of 40,000, including 23,000 paying customers who contributed over £3,000. This suggested that there was still an audience for cricket if it could be persuaded to come out but the overall picture for county cricket was less clear.

In the County Championship, it did seem that there was evidence of an improved attitude among players although the rain did little to help them – especially early in the season – while May and June were also unusually cold. The 1960s are remembered for many things but one generally forgotten fact is that the English summer weather was the poorest in any decade in the 20th century – a factor that has a huge impact on cricket. It may well be that this was the main reason why the truly English approach to uncovered wickets faded during that decade.

As in 2005, Australia visited as holders of the Ashes. In their early matches they encountered poor weather but defeated Lancashire, Surrey and the MCC before drawing the first Test at Edgbaston, where the receipts of £38,000 were a ground record. They dominated the second Test at Lord's despite a startling collapse chasing just 69, but won eventually by five wickets – England's first defeat in over two years. On Friday and Saturday the attendance reached 32,000 in the days when spectators were permitted to sit on the grass.

The third Test at Leeds finished in just three days and the Australians were defeated for the first time on the tour. On his home ground Trueman took 11 wickets and England won by eight wickets on a controversially unpredictable pitch. Northamptonshire failed by one run to beat the tourists, who went to the fourth Test at Manchester knowing that victory would clinch the Ashes. Australia were dismissed for 190 and England established a lead of 177 on first innings with their captain P.B.H. May scoring ninety-five. Lawry made a century but at 334-9 England were last-day favourites. But Davidson and McKenzie then added the highest last-wicket partnership for Australia in England and instead of chasing around 160 in well over four hours, England needed 256 in 230 minutes.

Nonetheless, Pullar and Subba Row gave support to a glorious innings from Dexter and at 150-1 England were again favourites. Then Benaud, despite an injured shoulder, dismissed Dexter, bowled May for nought and had Close caught. England subsided to 201 all out, losing in the final half-hour and with defeat went the Ashes. Nonetheless, over 130,000 people watched the match. The final Test at The Oval was dominated by Australia but ended in a draw.

The thrilling fourth Test had ended in frustration for England on the afternoon of Tuesday 1 August. At Portsmouth, Hampshire supporters experienced the same feelings as the first match of the 'Pompey' week ended in stalemate. Hampshire were playing Middlesex and those two sides were competing with Yorkshire for the Championship. But while Yorkshire were in the middle of a sequence of five matches without a win, their two closest rivals could not take advantage. Hampshire led by 65 on first innings and set Middlesex 319 to win. In the event Hampshire bowled 69 overs in which Middlesex scored just 118 runs for the loss of six wickets. Shackleton's figures were 28-18-23-3 while Fred Titmus batted for 150 minutes, scoring 34*.

It may seem that the fault lay with a less than adventurous response by the visitors but the *Hampshire Handbook* recorded a 'disappointing match' in which 'Middlesex made no attempt to get the runs and no attempt was made to encourage them to do so'. If this seems a strange comment about the Hampshire side of 1961, it was one of three matches in which Marshall captained after Ingleby-Mackenzie broke his finger. 'Butch' White has described Marshall as, 'tactically astute but as an attacking batsman, the most defensive captain I knew'.

Marshall continued in the week's second match against Sussex, who were put out for 141. Hampshire led on first innings by just 38 and in bleak weather late on the second evening the visitors were 179-4 with Parks and Dexter batting and victory for Hampshire improbable.

White returned for one last over and with the first three balls he dismissed Parks, the night-watchman Thomson and Smith. This was Hampshire's first hat-trick since Tom Dean in 1939 and the next ball was edged by Cooper to a diving Gray who dropped it. Gray tells that a brief apology at the end of the over brought the comment from 'Butch' 'no more than I'd expect!' which says much about the temperament of the fast bowler. To this day 'Butch' will point out that he would have been the first Hampshire bowler ever to capture four wickets in four balls.

Cooper survived the fifth ball but Horton held a catch from the sixth so White had four in the over and Sussex were suddenly 179-8. At least one of their batsmen had to run from the Lord Mayor's hospitality tent to his brief spell in the middle. Sussex added just one leg bye in the morning, Dexter, fresh from the Test, remained not out and Hampshire won easily by six wickets.

This was not the first of White's major exploits at Portsmouth that year. On Saturday 10 June his four wickets helped to dismiss Gloucestershire for 176 and Roy Marshall made an explosive start in reply. On the Monday every match in England was rain-affected but nowhere more than Portsmouth, which lost the whole day. On Tuesday morning, Hampshire's openers continued to 96-0 in 22 overs at which point Ingleby-Mackenzie declared. The captain has suggested that this possibility was a consequence of his 'inbred gambling instinct'. He also claims that the declaration was broached before play whereas Marshall and Gray both say that they were shocked and pretty unhappy at the sacrifice of first innings points.

As both sides were going well at that point of the season, Arthur Milton, Gloucestershire's captain, agreed to pursue a result. Gloucestershire struggled again but at 118-8 in 47 overs they declared. Hampshire were chasing 199 in 137 minutes, during which time Gloucestershire bowled 42 overs – a rate of 18.5 per hour.

Gray went quickly and Marshall followed for thirty-eight. Bryan Timms, deputising for Leo Harrison, recounts that the pair, still angry with the earlier declaration changed and departed to a public house on the outskirts of Southampton. Gray has some evidence to support his contention that Marshall was a better first innings player and that Henry Horton was the man to chase against the clock. On this Tuesday afternoon Henry reached 51 as did the captain but when 'Butch' arrived Hampshire lost three wickets for two runs and at 162-8 Gloucestershire seemed to be winning.

Shackleton and White were batting with only Heath to come. These three had a combined career batting average of 20 but were now required to conjure 37 runs in just 20 minutes to win the 12 points. While Shackleton held one end secure, White hit cleanly, made his highest score of the season (33*) and won the game in great excitement. Heath was not required.

It was on such occasions that Ingleby-Mackenzie attracted media attention and made Hampshire a popular side around the country. The captain was portrayed as a dashing cavalier young amateur whose team evidently partied every night, cared mainly about the racing results and won audacious victories in improbable ways. While Gloucestershire were being beaten, Yorkshire could not create a victory in the rain at Leeds and then lost heavily to the other contenders Middlesex at Bradford. For the northern county this was a period of one victory in six matches while, through June, Hampshire won seven of eight, also losing to Middlesex. The London county were winning seven in a row at this point but won only two from the next 11 and, by the time they completed the double over Yorkshire at Lord's at the end of August, their challenge had faltered.

After a sticky patch during the second half of May this match against Gloucestershire was Hampshire's third successive victory and gave them the confidence to push on to that first Championship.

For 'Butch' a good captain was 'crucial', and he remembers Colin Ingleby-Mackenzie as 'a man's man, everybody was behind him 140 per cent' – except perhaps on that Tuesday morning! Although Colin was an amateur, 'he helped to push it out. We respected him because if he said he would do something for you he did it.' In addition, 'Butch' believed gambles like the game at Portsmouth were astute 'because he knew what he could get out of individuals – I'd bowl all day for him because I respected him – we all did'. 'Butch' is sure that Colin was 'shrewder on the field than most people thought' and was a natural motivator but he was also supported by 'super pros' like 'Jimmy, Roy, Henry and Leo'.

Hampshire's side of 1961 had at its nucleus most of the players who had come close in 1955 and 1958. But in three respects they were strengthened. One was the addition of White, the county's fastest bowler. The second was a useful third spin bowler in Alan Wassell. The third was Danny Livingstone, who brought stability to a sometimes-fragile middle order.

Throughout their history, Hampshire have had many fine bowlers but until the 1950s few of them were genuinely fast. In 1906, John Badcock burst onto the scene taking 212 wickets in three seasons before disappearing, because it was said that he could not be bothered to keep fit. The amateur Giles Baring took 176 wickets through the 1930s but never really recovered from leg injuries sustained in a car accident. In the two seasons immediately before the First World War Arthur Jacques took 168 wickets at 21.52 but he was killed in hostilities. Another amateur, Hesketh Vernon Hesketh-Pritchard, a well-known traveller and writer, took 106 wickets in 1904 but in 14 seasons with Hampshire managed just 233 wickets. In each case these bowlers recorded averages well below 30 but none were regularly available for a sustained period, so Hampshire's regular opening partnerships, Kennedy and Newman, Herman and George Heath, or Shackleton and Cannings had been appreciably below top pace.

The exception came with the debut of Malcolm Heath against Leicestershire towards the end of 1954. He was a tall pace bowler from Bournemouth. Early in the innings Heath bowled a short ball that took off and Neville Rogers, who had been receiving short stuff for some years with no hope of response, declared 'that does me good'.

Heath was appreciably quicker than his regular predecessors but he was still not genuinely fast and he was, according to Arlott and by his own agreement, the 'gentle' fast bowler. Elsewhere at that time, bowlers like Trueman, Tyson, Statham, Fred Ridgway, Terry Spencer, John Warr and Les Jackson attacked county batsmen and Hampshire's aspirations to become a leading side were limited unless they could find a genuinely quick bowler.

At Edgbaston, David William White had been playing fairly regularly in Warwickshire's 2nd XI but found his path to the first team blocked by Warwickshire's seamers, as had Vic Cannings before him. David was playing in the Birmingham League where the club's professional, Dick Pollard, alerted his former county, Lancashire, to the young man's potential. However, David's father wanted him to finish at college, after which national service intervened and a posting at Blandford Forum followed. From here, his commanding officer Colonel Rowley wrote to Desmond Eagar about his promising fast bowler.

Arthur Holt went out to Dorset to have a look at the young man and was sufficiently impressed to invite him back for a trial. At the start of the 1957 season he played in a two-day match at Southampton against the Royal Navy, taking 3-20 in the two innings of an abandoned game and adding 47 in an eighth-wicket partnership with Henry Horton. Charlie Knott still captained the 2nd XI on occasions and recalled David's first appearance for that side at Hove on 29 May. Charlie set a field for a typical fast bowler and the close field settled for the first ball, which beat batsman and wicketkeeper and sped to the boundary! Charlie ordered his players to retreat and 'Butch' had arrived. Although still in the Army, he then took 3-38 in a three-day match against an Army side whose batsmen included John Edrich, Phil Sharpe and Brian Parsons, and he played regularly for the 2nd XI during May and June, taking 17 wickets in eight innings. He made his first-class debut against Cambridge University at Bournemouth.

'Butch' shared the new-ball with Derek Tulk, who had played once before in the previous season against Gloucestershire. Cambridge, with Dexter and Barber, were not significantly weaker and ran up 387 but, while Tulk struggled (0-22 in three overs), 'Butch' confirmed his promise with 3-78. It was also the first of a number of encounters with Dexter. Tulk, without a first-class wicket on his two appearances, went back to club cricket and was still playing for Old Tauntonians when the Southern League was formed in 1969. For 'Butch' the future was brighter although he played no more cricket in Hampshire's colours in 1957.

In 1958 he joined the staff, having completed his national service, and during that season the new captain Colin Ingleby-Mackenzie led Hampshire to second place for the first time in their history. 'Shack', with 163 wickets, and Malcolm Heath with 126 were the leading pace bowlers and Vic Cannings took 44 at 22 apiece but 'Butch' made an important contribution with 29 at less than twenty each.

During the batsmen's season of 1959, Hampshire were unclear about the right man to partner 'Shack', who took the new ball in every county match. Malcolm Heath did the job until 10 June, after which Cannings had it for three games, Heath for two, Cannings for one, Heath for four, Cannings for three, White for two, Cannings for two, White for one more plus the Indians at Bournemouth and then Vic Cannings for a sentimental farewell on the same ground against Derbyshire. Hampshire were in contention for the title until August and perhaps this indecision was one factor that went against them.

After the uncertainties of 1959, Hampshire took the field in their opening match of 1960, against Lancashire at Southampton, and by the close of the first day White (5-71) and Shackleton (3-41) had dismissed Lancashire for 153. Despite a hand injury, which disrupted his early season, in his first five Championship matches of 1960 'Butch' took 35 wickets at 16 each and was firmly established as Shackleton's opening partner for the best part of a decade.

They opened with the new ball for nine consecutive seasons, with 'Shack' exceeding 100 wickets in all of them and 'Butch' averaging 98 wickets per season for the county over that period. Shackleton topped the county's averages in every season except his last full one, when Bob Cottam took his place, but even then the young seamer did not take the new ball. In seven of those nine seasons 'Butch' White was second-highest wicket-taker and only Cottam managed to push him from second spot during the 1960s. It is an historical nicety that – Shackleton's freak figure excepted – 'Butch' took the crown in the first post-Shackleton season and then effectively handed over to a younger generation. Even the extraordinary success of Herman and Mottram in 1973 cannot detract from the fact that Shackleton and White was the most successful opening bowling partnership in Hampshire's history.

'Butch' White remembers that the partnership took a little time to develop during the early years, but when it clicked 'we were great together'. He stresses 'the importance' of partnerships in bowling and while the phenomenon of Derek Shackleton has been frequently and rightly eulogised over the years, the importance of a fit, fierce and young fast bowler at the other end during his later years should not be underestimated.

'Butch' took 124 wickets at 19 each in 1960 and, by August, he had the county cap, which meant greater security. He was mainly a genuinely fast bowler with pronounced inswing but he also learned to bowl the ball that held its line on or outside the off stump. Crucially, after that false start, he stayed fit 'by bowling' and he 'enjoyed playing cricket' in what was, by general agreement, a happy side and, in Butch's view, 'a good side'.

In 1955 and 1958 Hampshire had fallen short of the title partly because their middle-order batsmen did not score sufficient runs and the departure of Rogers and Rayment had not helped. In the 1958 run-in, for example, they never once passed 200 in their last 14 innings. The demands of football perhaps prevented Mike Barnard from reaching a higher standard while Pitman, Flood and Bernard Harrison were never sufficiently consistent. Dennis Baldry began impressively yet in just four seasons with the county his career average dropped to below twenty-five. In 1960 Hampshire gave a few matches to C.A. Fry, grandson of the great C.B. and uniquely a third-generation Hampshire cricketer, but in eight innings he could not reach 40 and with his Oxford University colleague off-spinner Dan Piachaud was the last of the occasional amateurs to play for the county.

Fortunately the problem was solved by the signing of Daintes Abbia 'Danny' Livingstone. He had come to England on national service from his native Antigua and lived in London but Hampshire had given him a trial and he made his first-class debut in one match in 1959. In 1960 he appeared in 18 matches and scored 540 runs at about twenty per innings – a record very similar to Baldry and Barnard. However, in 1961 he was the only man to play in every match, and scored 1,643 runs at 28.32. Baldry often struggled but played a crucial innings in Yorkshire and Barnard's average also improved and he enjoyed a very successful end to the season, which contributed to the title.

Hampshire had also found a local slow left-arm bowler, Alan Wassell, and he complemented the bowling of Sainsbury and Burden, adding to the captain's options. At one time Arlott suggested he might play for England but, despite winning his county cap, he eventually left county cricket at the age of just twenty-six. In Bryan Timms they had a promising wicketkeeper-batsman to understudy Leo Harrison and Ingleby-Mackenzie now had the depth and flexibility to challenge for the title. He may also have realised that a number of the players were reaching senior status so they would need to win it soon.

We have recorded that they came to Portsmouth in August still challenging for the title and the victory over Sussex was very important. The following draw at Canterbury, defeat at Leyton and a trip into Derbyshire may have reminded them of their stumble three years earlier but in 1961 things were different. They beat Derbyshire by 58 runs (Horton 141) and Warwickshire by eight wickets (Barnard 114*) as Shackleton continued to take wickets. Back in Portsmouth they crushed Leicestershire as White had 10 wickets in the match and then won again at Trent Bridge.

Over the last weekend in August a huge crowd came to Southampton to salute the triumphant Australians and the prospective Champions. Hampshire rested Shackleton and White and lost by five wickets but in truth most Hampshire supporters were probably more interested in the match at Lord's, where their two challengers were playing. Yorkshire arrived there under pressure, having just lost to Kent. For Middlesex, Peter Parfitt held Trueman at bay and a full-strength Yorkshire side trailed by 32 on the first innings. After Middlesex declared, Stott and Bolus reached 117-0 but Yorkshire were then dismissed for 214, losing by 85 runs.

Yorkshire went on to Birmingham while Hampshire met Derbyshire at Bournemouth hoping to gain further revenge for that 1958 defeat. With two matches left Hampshire were 22 points ahead but the final game matched them against Yorkshire at Bournemouth. They knew that just seven points more than Yorkshire in the penultimate matches would render that final meeting an irrelevance.

In Birmingham, Warwickshire struggled at 89-5 but a century from Hitchcock took them to 310, including an eighth-wicket partnership of 121. Hampshire also batted and, while they were more consistent, finished with a similar total of 306. Before the close, a direct throw from the Hampshire captain ran out the Derbyshire opener Lee.

Day two was more worrying for Hampshire, as both northern counties batted very well. Johnson (112) and Oates (89) took Derbyshire to 212-2 and, although Wassell took five wickets, Derbyshire had the lead so the four first innings points were lost. For Yorkshire, Ken Taylor made a double century and they declared

20   *Colin Ingleby-Mackenzie leads out his team at Bournemouth (PE).*

in front with only four wickets down. Warwickshire made a stronger start in their second innings and reached the close at 72-0 with their stand-in captain, Yorkshireman Norman Horner, undefeated.

Hampshire batted again after tea knowing they needed fairly quick runs to give themselves time to dismiss Derbyshire and secure the Championship. Gray, Horton and Livingstone went cheaply (40-3) but Marshall was in magnificent form and he and Sainsbury took them to 125-3 at the close.

On the morning of Friday 1 September Marshall adopted a more responsible approach but it did not serve him well and before midday he had gone for 86 out of a score of 141. This brought together the two Hampshire-born batsmen, Sainsbury and Barnard. They compiled a partnership of 99 in just over the hour, not least through quick running, which Jimmy Gray, described as 'the best I've ever seen' and, although four wickets fell cheaply, Derbyshire were asked to score 252 in 192 minutes. In Birmingham, Horner made a century before setting Yorkshire a stiffer task of 270 in 150 minutes. Taylor and Close were run out and Bannister struck twice as Yorkshire slumped to 59-5. Hampshire knew that, if Yorkshire failed, they would be Champions anyway but the best way to be certain was to win the game at Bournemouth.

The first seven sessions of the match at Bournemouth had averaged just four wickets per session with seven batsmen passing 50 including Johnson's century. These were not encouraging statistics on a wicket where Hampshire traditionally picked the extra spinner and, after three overs, Wassell replaced White. However it was Shackleton, not the spinners, who, fittingly, was to dominate this Friday afternoon. He dismissed the first four batsmen for a total of just 24, Wassell struck twice and then 'Shack' had two more as Derbyshire slumped to 52-8. Illingworth and Vic Wilson were leading a recovery at Edgbaston but time was slipping away from Yorkshire as Derbyshire found an unlikely hero in their promising young wicketkeeper Bob Taylor. Taylor (48) and Rhodes added 52 for the ninth wicket and tea was looming as Sainsbury replaced 'Shack' and held a return catch from Rhodes.

Jackson, who had done so much of the damage to Hampshire three years earlier, joined Taylor but, at eight minutes past four, the young man tried to reach his first 50 in the glorious manner and Livingstone held the most famous catch in Hampshire's history. Meanwhile, Yorkshire finished more than one hundred runs short of their target but neither that match nor the meeting of first and second, which was to follow, mattered at all. Hampshire were the County Champions and

21 *Hampshire, September 1961, on the pavilion balcony at Bournemouth 20 minutes after clinching their first title.*

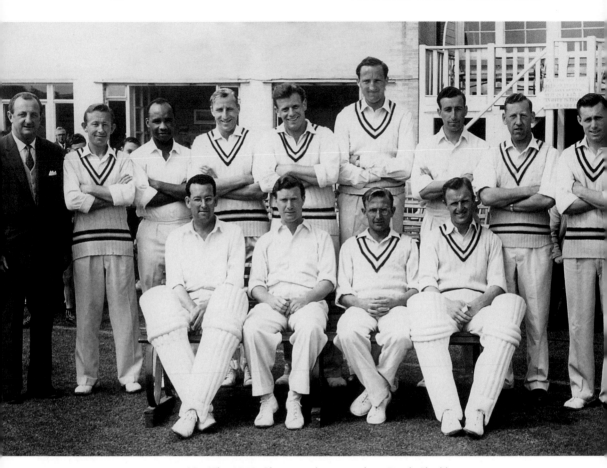

22   *The 1961 Champions line up without Derek Shackleton.*

by 4.30 the team were assembled on the Dean Park balcony for that wonderful photograph. Peter Sainsbury described it as 'the highlight' of a successful career and Jimmy Gray remembered it as a 'terrific feeling'.

Malcolm Heath had a mixed season in 1961, usually competing with Mervyn Burden or Alan Wassell for the final bowling spot. Nonetheless, he took 63 wickets at 27 each and his 4-72 against Yorkshire contributed to Hampshire breaking the Champions' winning sequence. Malcolm took great pleasure in the success, which he attributed mainly to the efforts of 'Shack', the good catching and 'a bit of luck'. In addition he thought 'Colin won about six games with declarations,' Malcolm remembering in particular the Gloucestershire match at Portsmouth where 'dear old "Butch" struck 30 in no time' and the crucial defeat of Surrey at The Oval.

The matter of declarations is now firmly a part of the mythology of that season although the reality is more complex. As the *Playfair Annual* for that season recorded, Yorkshire 'do not care to be second'. They won that last match at Bournemouth although given the celebrations of the Friday night it is surprising that Hampshire managed to compete at all. 'Butch' recalls arriving at Dean Park on

Saturday morning to find his car in the middle of the road but has no idea how it got there. He bowled 11 expensive overs that day and although Marshall made a century, Hampshire were 58 short of their target when Illingworth dismissed 'Butch' for a 'pair' to win the match.

In the *Daily Express,* the Yorkshire captain Vic Wilson suggested that Hampshire's success was against the odds but was gracious enough to compliment their 'splendid and entertaining cricket'. It was perhaps the last kind thing any Yorkshireman was to say about this outcome.

In 1988, Fred Trueman and Don Mosey published some conversations about post-war cricket (*Cricket Statistics Year by Year*) in which Trueman said of Hampshire 'we felt that they did well on other sides' declarations, while no one ever declared against Yorkshire.' Mosey agreed that the assertion was 'probably true', which was odd for a book with statistics in the title since, during the season, Yorkshire had beaten Sussex by just two wickets after Dexter declared at 67-2.

If this was an isolated example of sour grapes it might be tolerable but the story has been repeated in a number of publications. Dickie Bird recorded how the 1961 Champions enjoyed 10 wins from declarations, 'which tells you something of their captain's approach'. Most blatantly (and most grumpily) in a publication entitled *Class of '59*, Ray Illingworth told Chris Westcott that when Yorkshire won the Championship:

23   *Champagne time – September 1961.*

24   *Desmond Eagar congratulates Ingleby-Mackenzie.*

> There were no silly declarations like when Hampshire won in 1961 with
> 16 declaration matches – we had none that year but got within two points
> of them.

In fact the gap was 18 points even with the final irrelevant match, which was
worth 12 points to Yorkshire. It seems that once these stories began they were
repeated sufficiently to become an odd kind of literary 'truth'. Most recently the
same view has been attributed to Brian Close in a biography by Alan Hill. Close
says that Hampshire's opponents 'declared in eleven matches won by Hampshire
while that happened only two or three times to us'.

It is odd that so fine a writer as Hill did not bother to check this claim but
excusing the tale as literary 'truth' is generous, for all these claims are untrue and
reveal a great deal more about Yorkshire resentments than about Hampshire's
achievements as the Champion County. It is interesting that the figures offered
by the various Yorkshire players do not even tally although that does perhaps
confirm many of the tales of that dressing room in those days.

The cricketing truth is very clear because, by and large, Hampshire won that
Championship by dismissing sides twice. In fact both Hampshire and Yorkshire
won 15 matches after taking 20 wickets in the match and they both won one
more match after taking nine in the first innings and 10 in the second. Yorkshire's
other win was the declaration against Sussex while Hampshire won just *three*

games in a run chase against their opponents' closure. One was that famous game at Portsmouth where they lost eight wickets to Gloucestershire's 18 and in only two games might they have been described as somewhat fortunate, at The Oval and against Essex at Cowes. Even in those two cases they had to bat very well in the fourth innings to win matches in which their opponents had every right to expect success and hoped to win. One wonders whether the ongoing fabrications of the Yorkshire professionals are in part a residue of the class tensions of those days, although surely only Yorkshire cricketers could manage to stay annoyed with Ingleby-Mackenzie for such a long period!

Over the season Hampshire won 10 matches in which they declared and dismissed their opponents twice and two more when they declared and won taking 19 Warwickshire and 18 Gloucestershire wickets. On four occasions their declarations led only to a draw but of course a number of these declarations were because the side had scored enough runs in three-day cricket on uncovered wickets. Indeed, from the Yorkshire complaints it appears that they did not approve of declarations and yet in the 121 innings by Yorkshire or their opponents over the season, 29 (over twenty-five per cent) were declared, including no fewer than 20 declarations by the Yorkshire captain. The Hampshire and Yorkshire bowlers took 534 and 535 wickets respectively over the season but Hampshire's opening pair of Shackleton and White were more effective than Trueman and Ryan or Platt, while their batsmen outscored Yorkshire over the same period and *Wisden* pointed the finger at Yorkshire's 'disappointing batting', which 'let down the side'. Strangely, the best average statistics were those of Middlesex, who finished third, although five more points would have taken them above Yorkshire into second place. Worcestershire, in fourth place, had the most potent attack but did not score enough runs. The imminent arrivals of Graveney and D'Oliveira would convert them into title winners.

Hampshire's victory at The Oval was a consequence of the odd rule that, in 1961, teams were not allowed to enforce the follow-on. This may have led to anti-Lord's conspiracy theories in the Dales and on the Moors but it was not obviously a deliberate attempt to deprive Yorkshire of the Championship although it certainly helped Hampshire in this difficult game, and *Wisden* recorded that they were 'flattered' by victory. Surrey declared at 356-4 and dismissed Hampshire for 190 but, obliged to bat again, Surrey declared, setting Hampshire 310 to win. A magnificent 153 by Marshall supported by 85* from Horton won the match by five wickets. They did not deserve victory over the three days but it came because they batted superbly on the last. And the 12 points obtained were not ultimately decisive.

Marshall was as vital on the other occasion, when Essex declared on the Isle of Wight. The West Indian had been injured fielding on the first day and batted at number seven with a runner as Essex took a first innings lead of ninety. They declared at 150-5, setting Hampshire 241 to win in 215 minutes, with Marshall unlikely to bat. Bailey and Preston reduced Hampshire to 35-4 whereupon Ingleby-Mackenzie played his highest and perhaps, in context, greatest innings – 132* in 140 minutes. Marshall joined him at the fall of the sixth wicket to take Hampshire home by four wickets. To summarise, in a match in which the key opening batsman was injured they won, losing 16 wickets against 14 by Essex.

However, while the editor of *Wisden* noted that Hampshire's success 'was extremely popular and rightly so', he added that:

> Apart from Marshall and the captain much of their cricket was of the defensive type which is causing the authorities so much concern.

These concerns would soon lead to some of the most radical changes ever seen in English cricket.

3

1962–1969

SPORT, ESPECIALLY baseball and boxing, has always been a popular subject in Hollywood cinema, while films like *The Arsenal Stadium Mystery, Gregory's Girl, Fever Pitch, When Saturday Comes* and *Bend It Like Beckham* are among those British films which have used 'soccer' as a dramatic backdrop.

Cricket, on the other hand, despite its national status, has only rarely had a significant role in British movies or literature. An exception came in 1953, when the British J Arthur Rank Organisation released *The Final Test*, written by playwright Terence Rattigan and directed by Anthony Asquith. The film opens at Waterloo Station with a wealthy Texan senator alarmed at overhearing comments that 'England's finished. She ain't got a ruddy chance,' and seeing a *Daily Express* headline that ' England May Collapse Today'. Fortunately he discovers that the problem is not an economic or political crisis but simply that England are struggling to avoid defeat in the last Oval Test match of the series against Australia.

The Final Test stars Jack Warner as Sam Palmer, an ageing professional cricketer appearing for England for the last time. His son Reggie, bored by cricket, prefers poetry but his excitement at meeting one of his writing heroes (Robert Morley) is tempered upon learning that the great writer would prefer to be at The Oval.

It is a gentle, conventional drama of families and relationships, evoking many of our stereotypical images of Britain in the 1950s. The film has an authentic feel with contemporary cricketing heroes like Len Hutton, Denis Compton, Jim Laker and Alec Bedser playing themselves alongside Warner, 'real' footage of the Oval Test match of 1953, and commentaries by the BBC's John Arlott.

Where the gentle manners of 1953 were well represented by drawing-room dramas and Test cricket, in 1963 the British film world turned unusually, perhaps uniquely, to Yorkshire's rugby league in Lindsey Anderson's *This Sporting Life*. Murphy records how, shortly before the film was released, Anderson had asserted that it was 'not a film about sport' but 'about a man … of extraordinary power and aggressiveness … a great innate sensitiveness and a need for love'. The man was Frank Machin, played by Richard Harris, and Machin was certainly all those things, but *This Sporting Life* was very definitely also a film specifically about sport and more specifically about *professional* sport, including issues of masculinity, class and environment. Anderson may have tried to 'play down the sociological aspects of his subject' but over forty years later we are provided with a set of representations of the professional, northern English form of rugby, which was necessary for the context and some of the events in the film.

This film too was financed by the Rank Organisation and, compared with *The Final Test*, it represented a significant shift over 10 years from the genteel drawing room and Surrey pub to the working-class streets and terraces of northern England. This change had occurred in much of the drama, literature and cinema in Britain in the late 1950s. In a certain sense it reflected a creative response to the same social situations that had led to difficulties between professional cricketers like Graveney, Laker and Wardle and their county clubs.

There is a marked difference between the worlds of *The Final Test* and *This Sporting Life* but in one respect there is a similarity, for both films recognise the importance of the media in the fortunes of the leading players. In *The Final Test* the film opens with the newspaper headlines that have bewildered the American, we see the lunchtime regulars in Palmer's local listening carefully to John Arlott's radio commentary and we learn that Sam is being criticised by the press for being well past his best. By contrast in *This Sporting Life* we see Frank enjoying his first headline, 'Young Miner for City', after his successful trial. Subsequently, Frank is seen mixing with the local reporter and fans, discussing his photographs in the local newspaper and answering fan mail. He is a part of a new breed of sporting star benefiting from, yet also exploited by, his media image. And while his signing-on fee of £1,000 exceeds his annual income as a coal miner it is not yet sufficient to secure his independence – he is still a 'servant', a term used affectionately of many loyal club men but loathed by 'Butch' White – a near contemporary of Frank. While Sam has done enough in his career to anticipate a secure future as a coach, Frank Machin enjoys a new car and attention in the bar but he is clearly 'owned' by the club's chairman and local businessman Mr Weaver.

Cricketer Sam Palmer, meanwhile, resists retirement and wonders about the point of his life. Of his career he says:

> The trouble with making a game a profession is that you're at the top too
> young. The rest of the way is a gentle slide down – not so gentle sometimes.
> It makes one feel so ruddy useless and old.

Eventually 'old' Sam comes to terms with retirement in gentle and reasonable ways. In many respects his character offers a sense of a particular generation of professional cricketers; men like Neville Rogers or Gerry Hill whose careers were interrupted by the war but who, with little sense of resentment, picked up the pieces of their craft and honed it in those quiet ways of which John Arlott wrote so fondly. Indeed, Sam Palmer is much like Arlott's fictional hero George Kennett, retiring from county cricket at thirty-nine.

But we also see in the film the new breed of the young, brash cricketer, the debutant Frank Weller, who mixes nerves with abrasiveness. In the years following the film, the somewhat earnest application of young amateurs like May and Cowdrey was complemented by the playboy image of the last generation of amateurs like Dexter and Ingleby-Mackenzie, whose Hampshire side of committed professionals inherited something of their captain's image, becoming 'Happy Hampshire'.

25   *Roy Marshall batting v Nottinghamshire at Portsmouth in 1962.*

I reminded 'Butch' of this reputation and he conceded that it 'may' have been true in a superficial sense, but he added 'what time I got to bed at night had nothing to do with anyone else. I think the record proves I was okay.' Ingleby-Mackenzie took the same view, accepting that a player like Derek Shackleton would prefer to go to bed early whereas others would benefit from later nights and a more stimulating social life. White also pointed out how few of the side suffered injuries, which 'says something about our fitness' and, although he did not remember much training once the season started, he spent many winters pounding the roads in army boots. He also spent long hours bowling at unguarded stumps, which helped him to develop his accuracy.

> We had a few beers but we were fit. At the end of play we would drink with the opposition and talk about cricket so that we got to know about other players' strengths and weaknesses.

The Richard Harris character, Frank Machin, is a man who reflects the challenging post-war confidence of the talented working-class youngster who sees in that talent an opportunity to escape the drudgery of menial employment but further seeks to impose his personality on his chosen profession. This man will master his craft, just as the generation of Rogers and Hill (or Hutton and Bedser) did, but he will also see and seize the opportunity to exploit his 'self' and his image. In English cricket, the first obvious example was Fred Trueman, in popular music the most prominent case was John Lennon. For young county cricketers this was perhaps only possible at a local level but it was possible

26   *Arthur Holt with a 2nd XI side at Lord's in 1962.*

to an extent in a world increasingly interested in the culture of celebrity and media characters.

Lennon's ultimately tragic path to fame began in 1963. In the previous summer, Hampshire's success was acknowledged by the Duke of Norfolk as they represented him in the season's opener against Pakistan, while their captain was elected to the MCC's Cricket Committee. Sadly, the reigning champions fell away to 10th place while England beat a weak Pakistan side 4-0 with the match at Nottingham a rain-affected draw. Yorkshire recovered the title that they believed was rightly theirs and English cricket seemed once again dull and predictable. At Hampshire, the top order batted very well and Shackleton took 161 wickets at 19.90 but the support bowlers were less effective. 'Butch' White, who had some rare injury problems, took fewer wickets although he repeated his hat-trick against Sussex, this time at Hove.

His difficulties in the English season of 1962 probably stemmed from the previous winter. With the Championship secure, White was selected for the MCC's tour of India and Pakistan. He made his Test match debut on 21 October in Lahore and dismissed Hanif Mohammed and Imtiaz Ahmed as Pakistan were reduced to 24-4 before a century from Javed Burki led the recovery. 'Butch' finished with 3-65 and England won by five wickets but he then suffered injury problems, which kept him from the next seven Tests before he returned, but was again injured during the final Test. He was not alone in regretting the absence of a professional physiotherapist on the tour, a far cry from contemporary touring parties.

Given his general level of fitness, these problems were a disappointment but 'Butch' believes to this day that 'with a different captain and different manager it might have been different' – the captain was Ted Dexter. Gordon Ross, in the *Playfair Cricket Annual*, observed that 'as a leader' Dexter 'sometimes struggled', adding of White that 'the people in charge' might have tried harder to protect the man 'expected to be the spearhead of their attack'. It was not to be and, although he topped the tour's bowling averages, there were to be no more chances at the highest level. 'Butch' particularly regrets never having a chance in England.

His partner through the 1960s, Derek Shackleton, did win a Test recall in 1963, 11 years after his third cap in India, and at the age of thirty-eight. He partnered Fred Trueman through the last four Tests of that momentous series against Worrell's West Indians and took three wickets in four balls at Lord's – always a happy ground for 'Shack'. His Test appearances and an injury for 'Butch' in June meant that the partnership appeared in just 16 of that season's 28 Championship games,

27   *Derek Shackleton in later years bowling at Bournemouth (PE).*

28   *Mike Barnard.*   **29**   *Mervyn Burden.*

while on other occasions Jimmy Gray or the youngster Bob Cottam performed at one end. In just two matches neither Shackleton nor White appeared – one match was lost and the other abandoned.

The BBC regularly televised Test matches in England in the post-war period and 1963 saw a thrilling Test series between England and the West Indies. The second Test at Lord's was particularly exciting and Barker observed that the match had been 'discussed and reported with as much excitement as the famous Brisbane tied Test'. Part of that excitement was that BBC Television delayed the broadcasting of their six o'clock news programme to show the final minutes of the match.

The *Playfair Cricket Annual* reported that 1963 gave us 'a summer hampered by the weather'. Nonetheless, just as they had done in Australia three years before, the West Indies under Worrell captured the imagination of the public and helped to restore interest in cricket – not least as a modern international media spectacle. After some controversy, the West Indians had been led by their first black captain, Frank Worrell, and included major players like Gary Sobers, Wes Hall, Lance Gibbs and Rohan Kanhai. The West Indies won the series, frequently supported by their fellow countrymen, many of whom had moved to England in the 1950s and early 1960s. Two years later they were the first side, other than England, to win a series against Australia and for most of the next 30 years the West Indies were the strongest side in international cricket.

Hampshire celebrated their centenary in 1963 but managed only 10th place again, although both Marshall and Shackleton were high in the national averages. Ingleby-Mackenzie's magic touch was perhaps waning while Harrison, Heath and Baldry of the Champions had already retired and Gray was to follow shortly. Of the younger players, Timms had replaced Harrison and Cottam showed huge promise but there were no young batsmen pressing for a place. The two most likely had both been recruited from other counties – Keith (Somerset) and Caple (Middlesex). While Timms was a local man, the supply of Hampshire colts from the early 1950s seemed to have dried up.

This is surprising. In the *Hampshire Handbook* reporting the season of 1963 C.J. Cooper traced the development of the Hampshire Schools Cricket Association from its formation in 1946. He reported the active involvement of Harry Altham, Desmond Eagar and Arthur Holt – the three men most responsible for fashioning the Champions of 1961 – as well as an increase in the number of representative matches from three in the inaugural season to 23 in 1963. The senior XI were undefeated and he mentioned fine performances from Newton, Taylor, Watts, Dargue, Lyon, Evans and Wolfe. The latter eventually became a member of the Hampshire committee and was a prominent figure in Southern League cricket but none of them came close to playing county cricket. The junior side is similar, except that a young Gosport schoolboy Trevor Jesty scored one 'brilliant' fifty and another 'fast and powerful century'. He would become the link with the generation of Sainsbury, Burden, Barnard and Heath but he was sadly an isolated case.

Despite Hampshire's somewhat mediocre season and their concerns over an ageing side, 1963 was as significant for English cricket as it was momentous elsewhere in the country. James Bond, the Beatles, Mary Quant and Doctor Who began to transform and enlarge the impact of popular culture and, as the Empire disintegrated and the Conservative government reeled under the chaos of the Profumo affair, its major sporting export, cricket, was transforming itself at a greater rate than any other sport. As cricket lurched into the 1960s the Conservatives attempted to patch their problems by appointing as their leader the man who, as Lord Alexander Frederick Dunglass, had played first-class cricket in the 1920s for Oxford University, Middlesex and the MCC. But in cricket and the country, the old ways were no longer the popular ways.

When Lord Dunglass played first-class cricket he did so, of course, as a gentleman amateur. From the expansion of the County Championship in 1895 the county sides had always been a mixture of amateur gentlemen and professional players. Annual matches were played between the amateurs, known as Gentlemen, and Players at Lord's and elsewhere until 1962. Selection was an honour and the matches often constituted an unofficial international 'trial'. In this sense, cricket inhabited a world somewhere between the almost wholly professional team sports of football or rugby league and the fiercely amateur game of rugby union. The balance of individual sides was often determined economically. When Yorkshire and Surrey dominated the Championship before the First World War they alone would often field nine or 10 professionals under an amateur captain. By contrast, in their early years, Hampshire drew extensively on amateurs from the services. Even during the inter-war years an impoverished club like Somerset could never afford to employ as many as 11 professionals.

By the 1950s there was a general acceptance that professionals would devote more time to the game and would therefore often become better players. In the post-war period, the very best amateurs like P.B.H. May or M.C. Cowdrey would follow the path from public school to Oxford or Cambridge University and then employment in business or the City. The most fortunate found employers who would allow them time to play cricket but they were strictly still amateurs. The strongest view was that amateurs could bring a degree of disinterest and qualities of leadership learned in the public schools, which would make them the best captains. They constituted cricket's officer class. England persisted with amateur captains until the 1950s when Yorkshire's Len Hutton was given the role and, in 1953, won back the Ashes. He may have 'captained' Sam Palmer in *The Final Test* and England against Australia but he never captained his county Yorkshire.

The problem for amateurs in the post-war period was that there were fewer men of the right age and independent income able to devote time to first-class cricket. One man who could was Colin Ingleby-Mackenzie. He completed national service in the mid-1950s and began to work for the sports company Slazengers – mainly in the City – while finding time to play a little cricket. He described (in his autobiography) how he was 'asked to play a full season for Hampshire' in 1957 in preparation for taking over the captaincy in the following year, commenting briefly that 'my boss agreed to this' and referring occasionally to business meetings during matches. His autobiography refers extensively to his successful career as Hampshire's captain but also presents the image of a character who enjoyed horse racing (except when losing money!) and a lively social life, often in the middle of a match.

At the end of the 1958 season he tells us

> I decided to change my job and on the introduction of former Kent captain Brian Valentine, I met my future boss Mr Robert Manson, who offered me a job with Messrs. Holmwoods and Back and Manson, insurance brokers. As I was able to continue free-lancing for *Slazengers* the idea appealed to me, and so I entered the insurance world.

His employers may have changed but his life appeared to remain a combination of county cricket, overseas cricket tours, parties and horse racing. At one point on tour in Bermuda 'work took up little of my time' and at another lunch meeting with various members of his firm 'the talk turned to racing'. At the end of an unsuccessful 1960 season, Ingleby-Mackenzie recalled

> I was glad to finish with cricket and motor down from Scarborough to stay with Lord Belper for the Doncaster St Leger meeting. We had an amusing party including Mr and Mrs Arpad Plesch and more young girls than men. That's always a good idea. I had a monster punt to win the Leger and had no more money worries.

For the upper classes, the swinging sixties clearly began early. In fact, Ingleby-Mackenzie might be considered the natural heir to a previous Hampshire captain, the Hon. (later Lord) Lionel Tennyson, grandson of the poet, who came from an heroic war in the trenches to lead the side from 1919–33. Approaching his 60th birthday, Tennyson concluded his second autobiography by recalling the 'fun' of his clubs White's and Brook's. He described himself as

> A somewhat impoverished Baron of the United Kingdom with the right to sit and vote in the House of Lords, which I have never done since this wretched Labour Government got into power.

By then counties were employing cricketing secretaries who could strictly speaking still play as amateurs without remuneration, and Eagar was one such man. However, Don Kenyon (Worcestershire), one of the first professional captains, told Michael Marshall that by the 1950s 'virtually no one could afford to be an amateur' and some of those so designated were really 'shamateurs'.

Ingleby-Mackenzie, who clearly did have a separate income, took over as Hampshire's captain in 1958 and remained until 1966 when Hampshire at last appointed a professional cricketer, the West Indian Roy Marshall. Nonetheless, Ingleby-Mackenzie always explained his retirement at just 32 partly in terms of his need to work full-time to earn his living.

To some extent, employers of these amateur cricketing celebrities were acting philanthropically although they were also investing in 'names' to attract good business once their careers were over. Often retirement came earlier than for the professionals. J.J. Warr informed the Middlesex committee that 1960 would be his last year as captain because of the demands of business and in the following year Raman Subba Row retired when still England's first-choice opening batsman before his 30th birthday. In the same season, P.B.H. May (Charterhouse and Cambridge University), often considered England's outstanding post-war batsman, virtually retired before his 32nd birthday in 1961 after captaining England against Australia to work full-time in the city. E.R. Dexter (Radley and Cambridge University) made his first-class debut in 1956 and captained Sussex and England in the 1960s but effectively retired at thirty. He told Michael Marshall

> When I came into the game it was still possible for a Cambridge Blue and an England amateur to mix in a social world where there were real prospects of being offered a good career because you were a well-known cricketer.

Dexter added that success at sport ensured that 'no one would ever ask me what kind of degree I got'. Nonetheless, post-war Britain was a less easy environment in which young men could be given paid sabbaticals to play sport, while fewer than ever were of genuinely independent means. The other type of amateur, the schoolmaster on holiday in the second half of the season, was less able to perform sufficiently well to warrant a place in the increasingly competitive first-class game. The last of that breed at Hampshire was Rev. J.R. Bridger, who played only until 1954, although local dentist David Blake continued to play occasionally for them until 1958. In the late 1960s Barry Reed played while also running a farm.

In 1958, the MCC conducted an inquiry into the status of the amateur in first-class cricket. The sub-committee report, which was accepted, expressed

> The wish to preserve in first-class cricket the leadership and general approach to the game traditionally associated with the Amateur player. The committee rejected any solution to the problem on the lines of abolishing the distinction between Amateur and Professional and regarding them all alike as 'cricketers'. (*Wisden*, 1963 p.138)

However, just four years later in the winter of 1962–3, the distinction between amateurs and professionals *was* abolished and from 1963 all players were known

as cricketers. The decision was a surprisingly sudden one, announced while
the MCC (England) were touring Australia, managed by the Duke of Norfolk
and captained by E.R. Dexter. Fred Trueman, a member of the touring party,
described the tour as 'the last fling of the amateur'. Meanwhile, *Wisden's* editor
warned that

> By doing away with the amateur, cricket is in danger of losing the spirit
> of freedom and gaiety, which the best amateur players brought to the
> game. (1963 – p.138)

There is no real evidence that the abolition of amateurs and professionals significantly
altered the 'product' but it did reflect cricket's acknowledgement that the social
world was changing. Previously, amateurs and professionals often used separate
dressing rooms and hotels but by the 1960s cricketers travelled together, and
changes in the old social order made the distinction irrelevant. For example, Bryan
Timms, who had only come into the side in recent years, did not remember the
change occurring and wondered whether that may have been because Ingleby-
Mackenzie was 'a different sort of animal'.

Of itself, however, this change of designation was not bound to have any impact
on the real problem facing cricket, which was falling attendances and a perception
that cricket in the late 1950s and early 1960s had actually become dull. The most
alarming statistic was that the greatest fall in 1960 occurred on Saturdays. With
attendances falling rapidly, English county cricket could not afford a decline in
Test performances. In November 1961 Sir Hubert Ashton, the Chairman of the
Advisory County Cricket Committee, presented an interim report that included
the recommendation that 'a Knock-Out Competition be introduced on the basis
of one-day matches' from the 1963 season. The editor of *Wisden* suggested that

> This will be a diversion and should provide some fun if approached in
> the right spirit, but the game may be killed stone dead if this continuous
> tampering with the laws does not cease. (1962, p.115)

However, the tampering was not difficult to explain. In *The Final Test,* the poet
had told young Reggie that while 'any game can be exciting' to seek a thrill from
cricket is 'as stupid as to go to a Chekhov play in search of melodrama'. Cricket
and Chekhov, he asserts, share a passion for the 'beautifully inconclusive'. That
view would have elicited laughter but also understanding from the audience of
the 1950s but by the following decade fewer followers of the game endorsed
such a view. The age of the television, the family car and greater affluence created
problems for the game.

In 1919 the first-class counties experimented unsuccessfully with two-day
matches. Otherwise, from 1895–1962 the English County Championship was
contested solely through three-day matches between the counties (growing in
number to 17 when Glamorgan were admitted in 1921). As a consequence most
teams other than Yorkshire and Surrey settled for the fact that they were unlikely
to win the single competition each year.

Hampshire won their first Championship title in 1961. They had entered
the revamped County Championship in 1895 and, with allowances for the war

years, were therefore the 57th County Champions and the 10th of the (then) 17 counties to win the title. Until the relaxing of restrictions on overseas players, the County Championship was dominated by Yorkshire, who won the 28th of their titles in 1968. The most successful counties were generally the wealthier clubs with Test Match grounds. By 1961 Surrey had won 11 titles, including one shared with Lancashire (eight). Middlesex had won five and Nottinghamshire and Warwickshire two each. Of the non-Test counties, Kent won four titles before the First World War while Derbyshire (1936) and Glamorgan (1948 at Bournemouth) like Hampshire had each won once.

In the summer of 1962, the Leicestershire secretary Michael Turner organised a limited-overs competition with four Midlands counties. In that year another 100,000 paying spectators disappeared from county cricket and Solan suggested that

> Six-day cricket has no future. That complex and often infuriating character, the average man, has become conditioned to expect some kind of result for his money, and on the one day of the week when he is able to present his toil-worn body at the turnstiles, he is treated to anything but that. It is one of county cricket's most melancholy anomalies that the dullest day's play is almost invariably reserved for Saturdays. The future pattern therefore must have at its centre, a virile and satisfying spectacle on that important day.

Throughout the 20th century all the other major sports in Britain set and maintained a consistent form and structure – 80 or 90 minutes, 11, 13 or 15 players on each side, three or five sets, singles or doubles. But in the 1960s, English first-class cricket suddenly adopted the single-innings match, which had previously been confined to club cricket. Each match would produce a result, and, weather-permitting, be completed in one day, with bowling (and eventually fielding) restrictions that shifted the balance of the game towards batsmen. There is no comparable change in any other major public sport and, although *Wisden* was not alone in thinking it might be a 'diversion', limited-overs cricket has since become the major *popular* form of the game world-wide.

Hampshire's first match in the new competition was against Derbyshire and it was given to Bournemouth, rather than staged at the county ground, on Wednesday 22 May 1963. Shackleton was not fit and since Les Jackson, a similar bowler, took 1-24 in his 15 overs, he was probably missed.

In that first year matches were played over 65 overs and Hampshire packed the side with batsmen, with Ingleby-Mackenzie keeping wicket in place of the otherwise ever-present Bryan Timms and Horton coming in at number nine. White opened the bowling with Gray, Baldry returned from retirement to bowl first change and there were two slow left-armers, Sainsbury and Wassell. Derbyshire scored 250-9 and in reply Marshall went early. Only Baldry failed to reach double figures whereas only Barnard passed twenty-five. He batted superbly but was dismissed from the third ball of the final over, two short of his century and with Hampshire seven short of a victory target. Derbyshire's Derek Morgan scored 59*, took 2-49 and fielded brilliantly and he received the Gold Award. But there was consolation for Barnard, for in that first season a silver medal could be awarded for another outstanding contribution and he is the only Hampshire player ever to receive one.

It had been an enthralling start to the competition, with almost five hundred runs and 19 wickets in 130 overs in the single day. Hampshire followed this with their first Championship victory in Yorkshire since 1955 but by comparison on the Saturday their batsmen took 118.3 overs to amass 260 and Yorkshire replied on the following day with 189 in 88 overs.

A first-round defeat in a 'novelty' competition made little impact on Hampshire's season but, by the time of the cup final in September, the press paid more attention. The first skilled tactician was the Sussex captain E.R. Dexter, known as 'Lord' Ted in recognition of his spirited (Edwardian) approach to the game, although in the field his Sussex side were notably defensive.

So cricket was still rather dull just as the country was about to burst into the colourful swinging sixties. In the British cinema *This Sporting Life* marked the end of the grim world of 'Kitchen Sink' dramas, challenged in particular by the glamour of James Bond. In pop music the provocatively scruffy Mick Jagger ousted the rather nice Cliff Richard. The Tories were on the run and the 'white heat' of Tony Benn's technological revolution was looming. Meanwhile, other sports were moving ahead in the spirit of the times.

Marwick's huge survey of the 1960s pays little attention to sport but where it does, he notes the ways in which George Best and Muhammad Ali 'fused sporting prowess with male beauty'. But if these men provided a glamorous, radical version of the sporting hero there were no equivalents in English cricket. Dexter, for all his wonderful innings, was not a man of the people and could not offer a model of aspiration to ordinary people in the way that Best or Lennon might do. He was, like the popular media satirists of his time, clearly from the public school and Oxbridge class.

English cricket sometimes manages to produce such oddly out-of-time popular heroes. Colin Ingleby-Mackenzie was briefly another while, in the 1970s, David Steele made such an impact as the bank clerk at war with the terrible Australian pace bowlers that he was voted BBC Sports Personality of the Year. In some respects the homesick Steve Harmison or 'wheelie bin' Ashley Giles are modern equivalents. When the side or player has some success this ordinariness can become an attractive element of the public image of the player. But the cricket must be good and the side successful. By contrast, it is patently obvious that figures like Ian Botham, Shane Warne and Kevin Pietersen attract column inches and therefore crowds. In the 1950s Denis Compton had fulfilled this role in a more innocent way but his personality had never really been replaced in a more pragmatic English side in the 1960s. Boycott was a run machine and his obstinacy had a certain negative appeal but by the mid-1960s, when 'Fiery' Fred was in trouble again for his public pronouncements, he was no longer taking the wickets to warrant too much attention.

The cricketer of the 1960s was without question Gary Sobers. *Wisden* in 2000 voted him as the second-greatest cricketer of the 20th century, and as an all-round cricketer he was probably the greatest player of all time. Crucially, through the manner of his play and his approach to the game he became a major media celebrity. When the English authorities recognised the attraction of the 1963 West Indies side they hastily fixed a tour every three years – more frequent even than Australia – but they were still unable to find English equivalents to draw the crowds and county cricket seemed pale by comparison.

At Hampshire in 1963, a week after the first knock-out match, a young pace bowler, Bob Cottam, made his debut, moving ahead of Peter Haslop who had appeared in the 1962 tourist match against Pakistan. Cottam came from Lincolnshire but grew up in the London area and was spotted in club cricket as Arthur Holt flicked through a local scorebook. His figures were promising and, invited for a trial, he impressed in the 2nd XI and was their leading wicket-taker in 1962. After three 2nd XI games in 1963, he made his debut against Kent and took the wicket of Stuart Leary in a drawn game. His next appearance was at Lord's where, at the age of 18 he took 5-74 (9-144 in the match) and, with Shackleton taking 10-76, Hampshire won by 99 runs. 'Butch' White returned for the following match at Portsmouth and the impressive attack of Shackleton, White and Cottam made its first appearance. They each struck as Lancashire fell to 23-3 but Harry Pilling and Peter Marner then staged a recovery and Lancashire, lacking a sense of destiny, compiled 340-7 declared. Nonetheless, Hampshire's trio provided over the next few years the strongest pace line-up in their history.

The new bowling trio enjoyed a remarkable trip to Middlesbrough in May 1965. Yorkshire were English cricket's leading side but Shackleton (6-64) and Cottam (4-45) put them out for 121 although Fred Trueman hit 55 from 22 balls, including 26 in the most expensive over 'Shack' ever bowled. Hampshire took a narrow lead of four runs against Trueman, Nicholson, Hutton and Close. By the close of the first day Yorkshire, batting again, were 7-2 – including Boycott lbw to White – and on the following morning 'Butch' was unplayable. He returned figures of 6-10 in 10 overs as Hampshire dismissed Yorkshire for 23, the lowest total in their history. Unlike Hampshire's 15 in 1922, there was no way back for the champions and Hampshire won by 10 wickets. 'Butch' remembers the 'marvellous' crowd and also that 'the wicket was quick, it swung and neither side batted well.'

One month later Hampshire visited the other side of the Pennines where Bob Cottam recorded the best figures in Hampshire's history, 11.1-4-25-9, as Lancashire slipped from 102-1 to 136 all out. It is often forgotten that Statham and Higgs retaliated, putting Hampshire out for 77, which left Lancashire with a target of just 116 to win. At this point Shackleton (4-15) and White (6-48) took the initiative to lead Hampshire to victory. 'Butch' remembered Cottam as a 'really good bowler, always round about' although, like 'Butch', his only Test appearances were on the Asian sub-continent. One wonders about the prospects for any contemporary 20-year-old taking 9-25 and 73 wickets in a season at 18 each! In 1966 'Butch' almost matched his colleague's performance with 9-44 in Leicestershire's first innings at Portsmouth.

The mid-1960s Hampshire attack of Shackleton, White and Cottam was the finest in its history and the man who experienced most of it at first hand was wicketkeeper Bryan Timms. He recalled their differences, suggesting that '"Shack" was perhaps the most "natural" bowler anyone might imagine although he generally

30 *Roy Marshall who replaced Ingleby-Mackenzie as captain.*

had to bowl himself into form and, given his lack of interest in net practice, this might take a match or two.' In his biography, David Matthews (1998) recorded that Shackleton's two best starts to an English season followed an overseas tour.

While Shackleton relied mainly on the seam 'Butch' was fast 'and swung the ball in steeply'. Bryan believes that 'fast bowling is on the day and "Butch" could be quicker than anyone around on a particular wicket.' He thinks that Fred Trueman 'did it more often' and that this ability was 'mainly a matter of pressure'. Of 'Butch' he added:

> I can remember the Test selectors watching and he'd bowl at medium pace. If you came back in the afternoon when they'd gone he'd be on fire.

Cottam, who also went on to bowl for England, was 'mean'. He bowled an away-swinger and an off-cutter and 'probably learned a bit off "Shack" and he was a thinking cricketer'.

At the end of the 1965 season Colin Ingleby-Mackenzie retired although he returned briefly in the following season's Gillette Cup. He was replaced by Roy Marshall but was never forgotten by his team. 'Butch' White said of him:

> We respected him because if he said he would do something for you he did it. He knew what he could get out of individuals and was shrewder on the field than most people thought. I'd bowl all day for him because I respected him – we all did.

The English sporting summer of 1966 will forever belong to the country's footballers. On the afternoon that the former Essex cricketer Geoff Hurst was winning his place in sporting history, Hampshire's Alan Castell took 6-49 against Derbyshire bowling his new medium pace. Although Hampshire now enjoy the finest leg spinner in history they have never since produced an effective wrist spinner of their own.

For the county cricketers the weather was poor, gates and memberships fell almost everywhere and the authorities came up with one of their least successful ideas for 'brighter' cricket. In some county matches they limited the first innings to just 65 overs per side. Hampshire's first experience of this came on 7 May when Marshall and Reed opened with a partnership of 98 against Somerset but the innings ceased at 197-4. Hampshire enjoyed the best of the match but rain forced a draw, as it did too often in the season. In another match at Cardiff, Hampshire dismissed Glamorgan for 167 but their own innings was closed at 191-5 and they lost the match by 45 runs. The negative impact of the experiment can be seen particularly in the performances of the young off spinning all-rounder Keith Wheatley, who did not bowl once in any of the 12 innings limited to 65 overs and never had the chance to build an innings in those games. In those 12 limited first innings, Sainsbury bowled just eight overs, otherwise Hampshire used only Shackleton, White and Cottam. Roy Marshall viewed the experiment as the 'most harmful' in his career in English cricket. Fortunately it was dropped after one season.

A far more important experiment began when a few Championship matches included Sunday play. Around the country, 14 of the 17 counties saw their midweek attendances fall, with Lancashire's dropping to an alarming 35 per cent of the previous year. Hampshire's fell from around thirty-three thousand to 23,000 and the membership dropped slightly to six thousand eight hundred. They did not play at home on Sundays but those who did enjoyed impressive crowds. Surrey, who finished third, had around forty-five thousand people watching them on weekdays and on just three Sundays over sixteen thousand. Essex, with a season's total of 26,000 on weekdays, enjoyed 6,000 on their one Sunday. Even bottom side Northamptonshire, who were watched by just 14,000 in the week, attracted 9,000 to their three Sunday games. Over the following winter Hampshire polled their members about various experiments in county cricket. The members did not favour a return to unlimited first innings but they did vote against the 65 overs and favoured an extension. They were overwhelmingly in favour of Sunday cricket starting at 1p.m., voting 1,479 in favour and just 316 against. They were also slightly in favour of a limited-overs league competition alongside the Championship, which, given their reputation for conservatism, must have encouraged the authorities. Hampshire's response was to schedule seven days of Sunday play in 1967. By the end of that season, Hampshire were one of 14 counties to have introduced Sunday cricket and 10 of those reported overall increased attendances of paying customers. In Hampshire's case the increase was over twenty per cent and some counties had better figures.

At Hampshire, 1966 was Marshall's first year as captain. He called regularly upon Horton, Livingstone, Sainsbury, Shackleton and White of the Champions while Reed, Wheatley, Timms and Cottam also played in most matches. Harrison,

31   *Roy Marshall pulls to leg against Kent.*

Wassell, Gray and Barnard were reaching the ends of their careers but significantly Turner, Jesty and the Oxford University captain Richard Gilliat appeared for the first time. Hampshire finished 11th and, despite the first innings limitations, they drew 18 of their 28 Championship matches. Marshall sometimes seemed to be a rather cautious captain, not least at Kettering in late July. In the previous match at Edgbaston he had scored 133 and 79 against an attack that included David Brown and Tom Cartwright. On the Wednesday at Kettering, Shackleton took 6-85 as Northamptonshire were dismissed for 280 in 115 overs. Hampshire still had a short time to bat so Marshall sent Timms in as an opening 'nightwatchman' but he was bowled by Durose. A second 'nightwatchman', Wheatley, suffered the same fate and in the following over Kettle dismissed Reed. Horton and Livingstone also went for ducks but still Marshall did not appear although Hampshire closed on 6-5. On the next day he came in at 40-6 and scored 94 as Hampshire passed 200 before the rain returned to ruin the finish.

They enjoyed more success in limited-overs cricket and reached their first cup semi-final, beating Lincolnshire, Kent and Surrey before being comprehensively outplayed at Worcester, for whom Martin Horton made 114 and Coldwell took 4-39. In a Worcestershire total of 253-4 the incredible Shackleton took 1-21 in his 12 overs but White conceded 89 runs while no Hampshire batsman reached forty. Although he had retired from first-class cricket, Colin Ingleby-Mackenzie appeared in these matches in place of Timms, keeping wicket and boosting the batting. He recorded his highest competition score of 59* against Kent but, given his reputation as an enterprising captain, it is interesting that Hampshire's first limited-overs success came after he had retired. In later years he would confess that he took a traditional view in his clear preference for the longer forms of the game. Meanwhile Hampshire would wait a further 25 years to reach the final of this competition.

They began 1967 with the scheduled Sunday play and Richard Gilliat joined them as assistant secretary. The county's treasurer J.P. Burnett told the AGM that Hampshire faced 'a grim year' with a deficit in 1966 likely to be followed by a very small handout from the Board of Control. Roy Marshall suggested that the county needed strengthening on the field and that the solution might lie abroad. His speculation would become reality within 12 months.

Hampshire finished 1967 in 12th place, which was a great disappointment as they were in first place after five matches. At that point the captain praised the 'sound' batting and 'superb' bowling, focusing on Shackleton who was in 'tremendous form'. He also stressed that any willingness to pursue brighter cricket, 'the kind that spectators love to watch', would be tempered by the match situation so that when 'strongly placed', Hampshire would not play 'rash strokes'. They won three of the first five Championship matches as well as both Gillette Cup games. They won again against Essex in late May and at Portsmouth in mid-June but then lost their cup quarter-final at Hove on 14 June, after which their only victory was in Shackleton's benefit match against Yorkshire at Bournemouth in late July. The match was badly affected by rain but the Champions set Hampshire a target that would be unimaginable today and they won with 129-4 in 29 overs.

Across the country, about fifty per cent of matches were drawn, partly because of the poor weather, partly perhaps because Sundays were short days and also because the reward of six points for first innings lead in a drawn game compared favourably with 12 for a victory. Interestingly the two sides with fewest drawn matches, Yorkshire and Gloucestershire, finished top and bottom of the table. Whereas Hampshire had won the title in 1961 with 19 victories in 32 matches (60 per cent), in 1966 Yorkshire won just 12 from 28 (43 per cent). For Yorkshire it was a sixth title in nine seasons following Surrey's seven in a row. Yorkshire would win again in 1968, so there was little variety in the premier competition.

This was all rather predictable in the midst of England's 'swinging sixties'. In 1966 England's Test side lost three of the first four Tests to the West Indies, for whom Sobers was magnificent. In the final Test England fielded a side of professionals led by Brian Close. They dismissed the visitors for 268 but were reduced to 168-8 before Graveney (168), Murray (112), Higgs (63) and Snow (59*) effected an extraordinary recovery and England won. But many of the glamorous figures of the previous decade including Compton, Hutton, Trueman, Laker, Lock, Evans, May and Dexter had pretty much gone and their successors were more pragmatic – perhaps in part a consequence of the new 'professional' culture.

During 1967's summer of 'Flower Power', England won short series against India and Pakistan. Colin Milburn and leg spinner Robin Hobbs were included but without significant success while Boycott, Graveney and Barrington were more dominant. Yorkshire won the Championship and Kent triumphed in the Lord's cup final. England's captain was Brian Close but he fell foul of authorities. They accused him of time-wasting in a county match at Edgbaston and stripped him of the captaincy after winning five of the six Tests. They turned instead to Cowdrey, who led England to victory in the Caribbean.

Over the previous decade the number of television sets in British households increased hugely and there were now three channels, two on the BBC and a commercial channel. While other sports now enjoyed significant coverage, county cricket was missing the marketing opportunities afforded by television, other than the Gillette Cup final on BBC's *Grandstand*. A solution had emerged in 1966 when Rothman's began sponsoring a side of famous overseas cricketers called the International Cavaliers, who played matches on Sundays against county sides. These were often televised and cricket discovered a new public – not just the toil-worn average man but often his wife and children too, both at the ground and in their homes. These new supporters were rarely interested in the distinctions between swing and seam or the fine-tuning of the short-leg field, but they might learn, and they could certainly enjoy stumps flying, boundaries being hit and a clear result by the end of the day. In addition to television coverage, the Cavaliers attracted 115,000 spectators to their 15 Sunday afternoon matches in 1967 so that, for example, the match in Hampshire raised £780 for Shackleton's benefit fund.

The counties already moving into Sunday cricket recognised the appeal of these televised matches and of the new knock-out cup, and their solution was to replace the International Cavaliers matches with televised games between the counties. Since spectators had to be allowed to attend church and enjoy an early

32   *Barry Richards pulls to leg against Middlesex (PE).*

roast dinner, these games began at 2p.m. and therefore were limited to 40 overs
per side. Many traditional supporters believed that this would produce poor-quality
cricket and cricketers but the mass public was certainly enticed.

A league competition between the counties would add a competitive element
that had not been present in the International Cavaliers matches. However, the
great international stars would also disappear and this was perhaps a disappointment.
So, English cricket found another answer – in fact a year before the launch of
the Sunday League. They changed the rules on player registration and, whereas
Roy Marshall had spent two seasons qualifying, the counties were now allowed
to sign an overseas Test player with immediate effect. In the first instance the
press reported the near certainty that Hampshire would recruit the West Indian
batsman Clive Lloyd, but he went to Lancashire.

The Sunday League increased the profiles of many non-Test Match cricketers.
It also gave the viewing public the opportunity to watch great cricketers like
Lloyd, Gary Sobers, Mike Proctor, Majid Khan, Rohan Kanhai, Greg Chappell,
Garth McKenzie and, at Hampshire, Barry Richards.

Leo Harrison remembers his involvement in the arrival of Richards. 'When
I was coach during 1967, Clive Lloyd travelled to Guyana, pursued by secretary
Desmond Eagar with a contract' but, 'on his first morning in Barbados, Desmond
opened his newspaper to the headline "Lloyd signs for Lancs".' Leo roars with
laughter before continuing to describe a simultaneous tip from Geoff Keith, now

coaching in South Africa, suggesting that Barry Richards would be pleased to come to Hampshire. Leo liaised with Cecil Paris and, many telephone calls later, negotiated a deal that brought the great player to Hampshire. Richards confirms that Hampshire were successful by outbidding Sussex and recalled how, on his arrival in England, he spent his first few weeks staying with Joan and Leo and arguing with their student son Martin Harrison about apartheid. The younger Harrison, a university pal of Andy Murtagh, played for Hampshire's 2nd XI but did not make the grade as a cricketer.

When Richards joined Hampshire in 1968 the transformation of the 1961 Champions was nearly complete. Roy Marshall remained as captain, Livingstone and White were still there, Peter Sainsbury played until 1975 and Shackleton retired from Championship cricket at the end of that year. Most of the others had gone.

The 1968 season began with legislation to ensure the bowling of 20 overs in the final hour of the match and a new system of Championship bonus points. The early matches were badly affected by rain and Barry Richards failed to score on his debut at Hove. It was not until the sixth Championship match in Hampshire's season that any side passed 200, and then Hampshire scored 321-4 in their 60-over cup match against Bedfordshire. In the following Championship match at Northampton, Richards moved up to open with Reed, scored 130 and Hampshire passed 300 for the first time at the end of May.

The following match at Southampton was the traditional Whit weekend meeting with Kent. There were good crowds, not least on Sunday. Kent scored 148 in 69 overs and Hampshire 230 in 107 overs – the two first innings being completed late on Sunday evening. Kent, 25-0 overnight, reached lunch on 126-2 and with White injured in the following two hours added less than 100, losing three more wickets. At tea, then, they led by 140. Sadly it was not until after tea that Kent suddenly showed some enterprise but in a meaningless context. The crowd of around 4,000 voiced their disapproval before departing early with Kent closing 260 ahead. It was a 'perfect' example of why county cricket no longer attracted good crowds on a regular basis.

A few weeks later at Bournemouth, Gloucestershire, 206-9 declared in 103 overs, led Hampshire (180-9 declared in 96 overs) by twenty-six. In the Gloucestershire innings Castell had reverted to leg spin, taking 4-38. Gloucestershire began their second innings on the third morning with a lead of 26 and reached 149-9 at the close in 75 overs – a match aggregate of 535 runs scored at 1.95 runs per over. In the *Daily Telegraph*, Rex Alston described the end as a 'merciful death'. In the days of uncovered wickets and wet summers there was some excuse with damp wickets and slow outfields but again this was terribly dull fare and again the players were barracked by the spectators. There was a feeling that despite the innovations of bonus points, overseas players and Sunday play, county cricket might be fading away. Despite these disappointments, Hampshire maintained a position near the top of the table before having to settle for fifth place, failing to win any of their last six matches.

In August, Bob Cottam was chosen to play for the MCC President's XI against Australia and this was followed with selection for the tour of Pakistan. He played in the first two Test matches, taking nine wickets at 20 apiece with best figures of 4-50. All three matches were drawn and two were marred by crowd disturbances. On return to England he did not retain his Test place.

During the changing times of the late 1960s, Hampshire's younger replacements enjoyed mixed fortunes. Some, like Cottam and Barry Reed, were good players; others, including Geoff Keith, Bob Caple and Keith Wheatley, never quite established themselves. The most enigmatic was Alan Castell, last in the line of Oxfordshire men to seek their fortune on the South Coast. He arrived at Southampton in 1959 as a highly promising leg spin bowler although his first major achievement in 1962 was to share with Danny Livingstone in Hampshire's record ninth wicket partnership of 230 v Surrey at Southampton. Livingstone made 200, having been dropped by Sydenham at long leg from Tony Lock's hat-trick ball.

There were periods when Castell's leg spin bowling technique faltered and he also had problems with injuries. In 1966, he began to bowl medium pace and in 110 matches he took 225 wickets for the county before injury finished his career at twenty-eight. He was probably the most successful player in Hampshire's history not to receive a cap and without question quite a number with inferior records have had that honour bestowed upon them – especially amateur cricketers before the Second World War.

There has always been a question about whether Castell's image and manner inhibited his progress. He arrived with a quiff which clearly emulated his early hero Elvis Presley. That affection was reported by Desmond Eagar in the *Hampshire Handbook* and Eagar was apparently more astonished when Castell – with no malice – took his leave of Harry Altham the President with the phrase 'okey dokey mate'. As a school teacher Altham may have been more tolerant.

Through the 1960s, Castell's hairstyles (and occasional beard) often changed to reflect current fashions and he became and remains good pals with the livelier group of Hampshire cricketers including White, Cottam, Richards and Wheatley. None of this implies that they were not serious or able cricketers but the world was changing and the cricketers – young men – changed with it. In the team photographs of the 1960s the hairstyles owe more to James Bond and the Beatles than to the Brylcreemed stylishness of Denis Compton and Derek Shackleton. The faces were more youthful too – perhaps reflecting the better-fed and more affluent post-war period.

Yorkshire won the title again in 1968, despite refusing the opportunity to sign an overseas player, but it was to be the last of their 26 titles in the 20th century. Australia toured in 1968 still holding the Ashes and they won the first Test match at Manchester. Pocock was England's most successful bowler with 6-79 and D'Oliveira top-scored with 87*. He was the only English batsman to pass 50 in either innings and had played in 10 of the previous 11 Tests but both he and Pocock were omitted at Lord's.

The next three Tests were drawn, so Australia retained the Ashes. D'Oliveira was recalled at The Oval and scored 158 as England dominated. On the final day the weather threatened their efforts but the crowd helped to clear the water and on a classic English sticky wicket Underwood took 7-50 and bowled England to victory with five minutes left. The main resistance came from a sixth-wicket partnership of 45, broken with wickets for Illingworth and D'Oliveira.

The story of what happened next is well known. The England selectors omitted D'Oliveira from the party to tour South Africa after two matches against Australia in which he had scored 263 runs at 87.6 and taken 3-48. When Cartwright declared himself unfit, D'Oliveira was reinstated but the South African government exploited the media furore and refused to permit him to tour. English cricket went to great lengths to 'resolve' the issue but in the end the tour was called off and cricketing links with South Africa ceased for decades. The whole sorry affair is explored brilliantly by Oborne.

The issue would reappear when the South Africans were due to tour England again in 1970. The *Hampshire Handbook* for that year, edited by Desmond Eagar, reprinted a memorandum from Lord's that argued for the tour. It stated:

> The firm belief that the severance of sporting contact would achieve nothing in terms of progress towards multi-racial sport. On the contrary, it would have precisely the opposite effect.

It is easy with hindsight to see that, even if this was a wholly honest statement, it was wrong. During their periods of sporting isolation, white South Africa went to great lengths to encourage rebel tours that created complications in England. In 2005 *The Wisden Cricketer* attributed to Nelson Mandela the view that the 1970 Stop the Tour Campaign was a 'decisive moment for the anti-apartheid struggle' (November, p.59).

The memorandum concluded that the Cricket Council knew of and welcomed the 'considerable support' for their views in the counties but it was not universal. John Arlott had been a member of the Hampshire Committee in the 1960s and had long campaigned against apartheid, having witnessed it at first hand. He had also been instrumental in bringing D'Oliveira to Britain. Finding himself in a significant minority, he eventually resigned from that committee. In the press he wrote of the D'Oliveira affair that 'no-one of open mind will believe that he was left out for valid cricketing reasons'. In April 1970 he wrote in the *Guardian* that 'for personal reasons' he would not broadcast for the BBC on the planned tour. He argued that action against a cricket tour was a less productive political gesture than other forms of boycott or picket but he was sure that 'a successful tour would offer comfort and confirmation to a completely evil regime'. Such views were not represented in the *Hampshire Handbook*, presumably because they were not consistent with the dominant view within cricket. Nonetheless, the tour was cancelled and England played instead against a Rest of the World side that included Barry Richards.

Arlott had by that time become the first President of the recently formed Cricketers' Association – a largely moderate body representing players' interests and the nearest equivalent in English cricket to a trades union. It was possible because it came of its time and because all the players were now cricketers with no distinction between amateurs and professionals. It gave them a voice when negotiation was needed.

Hampshire encountered some controversies of their own in the second half of the decade. In August 1965, Worcestershire, the reigning Champions, came to

Bournemouth needing to win their last two matches to hold their title. Rain interfered significantly on the first two days and when Hampshire declared their first innings 146 runs behind on the last day, Worcestershire declared after one ball. Hampshire had sufficient time to score 148 to win but Flavell and Coldwell in just 16 overs and three balls put them out for thirty-one. Worcestershire won the title but the chasing counties were not over impressed.

Two years later, under Roy Marshall, Hampshire scored 421-7 declared at Lord's. The innings lasted 145 overs and Hampshire then bowled 176 overs as Middlesex replied with 371-7. After three full days the match ended with no result. The match was one of the first to feature Sunday play, which added to the general condemnation – Marshall offered two explanations. He suggested that in an attempt to encourage faster scoring some wickets had become too good. He added that the revised bonus points system discouraged teams from chasing victory, a view later supported by Barry Reed. Having fielded through 172 overs at Lord's Hampshire went to Northamptonshire where the home side won the toss and batted. Over those three days (Sunday, Monday, Wednesday) Shackleton bowled 85 overs, Cottam 67, Sainsbury 54 and White fifty-three.

In complete contrast to Lord's, when Hampshire and Middlesex met again at Portsmouth in August 1967 the match finished with a last-ball tie when Bob Herman, who would eventually return to Hampshire, bowled Bob Cottam. In their previous match at Leicester, Hampshire had finished on 267-8, one run short of victory.

Then in 1969, during another rain-soaked match at Bournemouth, the Hampshire side left the ground at tea on the last day with the rain still falling, no likelihood of a result and on the understanding that the match had been abandoned. Only subsequently did they learn that the umpires eventually declared the pitch fit for play and awarded the game to Glamorgan. A subsequent hearing upheld the award of points to the Welsh county but this was eventually overturned, despite which Glamorgan won their second title. They won 11 of their 24 matches, Hampshire finished fifth for the second season running with six wins. Gilliat scored 114 in the Glamorgan match, having made a century in the previous game at Ilford. He then 'failed' at Bristol, scored 100* in a victory over Somerset and then a career-best 223* against Warwickshire at Southampton after which he received his county cap. A fortnight later he captained Hampshire for the first time when Marshall was injured.

In 1967, Hampshire won the 2nd XI title for the first time and Keith Wheatley enjoyed one extraordinary match in an innings victory against Middlesex 2nd XI at Bournemouth, in August. He took 7-53 and 6-61 and top scored with 112. Later that month Hampshire gave a 2nd XI debut to a promising 16-year-old batsman from Reading called Gordon Greenidge. He batted at number seven and after scoring two runs was bowled by Warwickshire's Roger Edmonds. Pace bowler Richard McIlwaine, who joined Hampshire's staff on the same day as Greenidge, recalled that

> When Greenidge first arrived he was a good cricketer but we didn't think
> he would be that good. He amused us one day because he was looking
> pensive and we asked him what was wrong. He said 'well, I don't know

whether to play for England or the West Indies'. We couldn't help laughing. He was about seventeen and not having a good season, running himself out, getting caught on the boundary, sweeping straight balls and getting out lbw That close season he worked in a factory and came back much bigger. Where he used to be caught on the boundary it was landing in the road and we realised he might be right.

In 1969 Greenidge made a few runs in the 2nd XI although he was less successful than Turner, Lewis, Reed and Murtagh. Fortunately Hampshire persevered with him to good effect. He has since told of his loneliness in those early seasons and of the difficulties of being a young black cricketer in the world of English cricket.

Before the 1969 season, Bryan Timms left Hampshire. He had played over 200 matches for his native county but, at the age of 28, he was facing two problems, the first of which was security.

> I didn't think there would ever be money in cricket and my peers were 'Knotty' and Bob Taylor so I was unlikely to break into Test cricket. If you're ambitious it's no good. I couldn't face playing for another ten years and hoping for a benefit. When a marketing job came along I took it.

Bryan also acknowledged that there was some unhappiness in the dressing room about the captain, adding that 'Roy was a great player with a wonderful cricketing brain but he wasn't a man manager. He wasn't good at getting the best out of people.' Nonetheless 'the main reason' Bryan left 'was the job'. Then, in the wake of the D'Oliveira affair, Doug Insole resigned as a Test selector and was replaced by the Warwickshire captain and wicketkeeper A.C. Smith.

> Warwickshire phoned and asked me to cover which I did. I never played for the 2nd XI, I just turned up and played when A.C. was away and I was paid twice the salary. I never played against Hampshire.

Unsurprisingly he remembers Warwickshire as 'a better run club' who eventually invited him to go full-time 'but my people could not release me'. He played 24 matches in the three seasons (1969–71) and then retired completely from professional cricket. Although it had meant leaving his home club he 'never regretted that decision' but looking back on his career he felt:

> Perhaps I had too good a time when I was playing, perhaps I didn't always give it 100 per cent all the time but that's life. You won't get into a Test side playing that way unless you're like Compton but he was exceptional. If Boycott had lived the way I did he wouldn't have played Test cricket but he didn't talk anything but cricket.

In his place, Hampshire signed Bob Stephenson from Derbyshire and also welcomed back Colin Ingleby-Mackenzie to pre-season nets in anticipation that he might appear in the Sunday League. Barry Richards scored over 400 runs in the new competition and they enjoyed the first season as they won 12 of their 16 matches and finished second, just one point behind Lancashire. Their attack of Shackleton, White, Cottam, Sainsbury and Jesty was especially effective and only in the first match did they concede more than 200 runs. In mid-August they beat the eventual champions Lancashire at Old Trafford by 48 runs but, on the following Sunday, in front of a crowd of 8,000 (receipts £878) at Portsmouth, they lost to Essex by 24 runs, falling from 93-1 to 153 all out. Victory would have given them the title but the size of the crowd confirmed the importance of this new competition for the county treasurers. Almost twenty thousand Hampshire supporters watched their eight home Sunday matches – almost as many as watched them in their first-class matches.

Despite this Sunday success, membership had fallen from 6,301 in 1967 to 5,887 two years later. In the Portsmouth sports paper, Desmond Eagar revealed that during the 1957 season Portsmouth had attracted 23,620 spectators whereas 11 years later – the year before the Sunday League began – paying spectators numbered fewer than ten thousand. On the other hand, the cost of running the club had almost doubled over that period, causing concern for the committee, which still comprised 30 men. They included a colonel, three majors, a lieutenant-colonel and a Naval captain but there was also the cricketing experience of G.R. Taylor, Leo Harrison and Arthur Holt. Richard Gilliat was Desmond Eagar's assistant secretary and the Chairman was Geoffrey Ford. In the following year this highly respected man of business posed for photographs outside the John Player caravan at Portsmouth with Miss World and 'two Players No.6 Girls' in fetching miniskirts. On the field, Tom Graveney's Worcestershire were beating Roy Marshall's Hampshire by 41 runs. The swinging sixties were coming to an end while the world of English county cricket continued to change.

4

1970s

It was something you never dreamed of – the Championship title.
Mike Taylor

AFTER THE heady successes of 1955–61, Hampshire had reverted to type during the 1960s, finishing between 10th and 12th in five consecutive years. Towards the end of the decade they improved with fifth place in 1968 and 1969 and also challenged for the first Sunday League title in 1969.

At the start of the early 1970s they slipped again. Shackleton was gone and White was soon to follow. His retirement came as a direct result of damage to knee ligaments. At the end of August 1971, he opened the bowling with Bob Cottam at Canterbury but had to retire after just six overs without a wicket. He did not bat in the first innings but had to join the West Indian off spinner Larry Worrell to defend the final over. Sadly, Derek Underwood snared him for his 10th wicket in the match and 'Butch' went from Hampshire's cricket, with no contract offered. He played a little for Glamorgan after this and then in the newly formed Southern League for New Milton. He still feels some 'anger' at the manner of his going and believes his 'biggest problem' was that people thought him a rebel whereas he had and has a great affection for the game and his memories – '90 per cent of which were great'.

Alan Castell, having struggled with injuries, retired at the same time and Cottam, perhaps feeling that his friends were disappearing, moved on to Northamptonshire. These two men were among the unluckiest of Hampshire's cricketers. Cottam is the only regular, major player at the club in the past 50 years who never won any major cricket competition while Castell is perhaps the best Hampshire cricketer never to win a county cap. In the following year Danny Livingstone's contract was not renewed and John Holder left the county, although Hampshire still had a batting line-up of potential and some strength in Richards, Greenidge, Turner, Jesty, Lewis and the new captain Gilliat.

Having lost Shackleton, White, Cottam, Castell and Holder, Hampshire were struggling for a pace attack. Jesty was a useful swing bowler but not perhaps an opening bowler. In 1968 two promising youngsters Bill Buck (20) and Richard McIlwaine (18) had played in the 2nd XI and they increased their wickets tally in 1969. In that second year, both played in the county side – Buck just once although with neither runs nor wickets.

McIlwaine is one of four post-war Hampshire players to have emerged from Portsmouth Grammar School – the strongest cricketing school in the east of the county, whose most famous old boy is Wally Hammond. McIlwaine followed

33   *Pakistan seek to dismiss Hampshire's new captain Richard Gilliat (PE).*

Mike Barnard into the Hampshire side and later came David Rock and Jon Ayling. The only other Portsmouth schools cricketer since the war to play for the county was Lawrence Prittipaul, who attended Portsmouth's other fee-paying school, St John's College.

McIlwaine's tale is interesting in many respects, because he seemed poised to become a decent professional cricketer at a time when opportunities emerged at Hampshire but did not achieve that goal. His story exemplifies as well as most the huge gap between promise and fulfilment in the world of professional cricket and it is a story that has been repeated frequently in recent years.

McIlwaine impressed initially at school and subsequently in the county's colts side. Their captain was Bill Hughes, later Hampshire's vice-chairman, while Arthur Holt took a careful overview and no doubt reported McIlwaine's promise to Desmond Eagar.

Richard McIlwaine spoke of his bowling ability as 'natural'. Until his early teens he bowled straight with his fingers across the seam, which 'gave me some control'. Then 'somebody told me to hold it down the seam and you might get it to swing'. He tried this with some success but what he never had 'was a natural late away-swinger which is really what's needed'. When he eventually arrived at the county he was told he bowled 'liquorice allsorts', a combination of off-cutters, leg-cutters, away-swingers; 'too many different balls'. Despite this 'they never stopped me and perhaps I could have done with more advice.' He feels that the right advice would have been to develop 'one good, stock ball' and not bowl 'six different balls an over'. He believes that coaching has come a long way in the 30 years since he played county cricket, not least 'because of television'.

His successes at school and for the Hampshire Schools XI were noted by the Winchester master and former Test batsman Hubert Doggart, who recommended him for a trial for the Public Schools XI. He played for them at Lord's and in the following year was also 12th Man for the English Schools Cricket Association. He also appeared in a South of England Schools XI and the *Hampshire Handbook* commended his 'remarkable season', comparing his bowling to Derek Shackleton's. He was 'keen to play cricket professionally' but, strangely, 'Hampshire did nothing' until Worcestershire showed interest whereupon Hampshire 'said "no, we want you to have a trial"'. He reported to Southampton in his last school summer of 1968, and played for the county's 2nd XI, taking three wickets. McIlwaine and Gordon Greenidge were both given contracts for the following season. His local newspaper ran a feature on him under the headline 'Star Bowler in the Making'.

In 1969, Greenidge and McIlwaine were on the staff under the coach Leo Harrison, where they both played for the colts and 2nd XI, in addition to which McIlwaine made his debut in first-class cricket – an unusual range of cricket in one season. McIlwaine, Greenidge, Turner, Jesty and the other juniors would spend hours clearing up after first-team matches and complaints were met with the same comment that 'if Shackleton could do it, so can you'. As a bowler McIlwaine rarely batted in the nets, 'unless the pitch was too worn for the batters'.

He played in the colts with Nick Pocock, Nigel Cowley, Andy Murtagh and Julian Shackleton (who later joined Gloucestershire) while the 2nd XI side included David Turner, Richard Lewis, Trevor Jesty, Keith Wheatley and John Holder. For the colts, Richard took 13 wickets at seven apiece and for the 2nd XI, 22 wickets at twenty-three. The *Handbook* praised his 'variation and control' and, at the end of August, he came into the side to play against Northamptonshire at Bournemouth. His arrival there is an illuminating story in itself.

> I got on very well with Leo but he could be hard. He put me on for two days solid against Gloucestershire 2nd XI and it was sweltering. I bowled 27 overs one day and 28 the next and when I misfielded to my own bowling he went berserk. I nearly gave a mouthful but I thought no, I won't. He was testing me out, wanting to see if I could cope. Shortly after, I was in the first team.

The first match was on Wednesday 27 August 1969. McIlwaine was second change, after White, Cottam and Jesty, and bowled 23 overs without a wicket as Northants recovered from 33-2 to compile 325-5 on the first day. When his turn came, 'Marshall said "next over at that end" then went to stop a ball with his foot and sprained his ankle.' As a result Richard Gilliat took over, which McIlwaine thinks was 'very lucky. I needed encouragement which was unlikely from Marshall'.

Northants' score owed most to an unbeaten 154 from Mustaq, although Peter Willey scored forty-eight. Richard remembers Gilliat advising to keep the ball away from Willey's off stump 'which was absolutely right – I kept it on leg stump but when I strayed it went wallop! Gilliat was a real gent, a nice guy.' But he also remembered him as a 'tough competitor'.

On the second day, only Richards batted well but when McIlwaine went in for the last wicket Hampshire were still 20 short of saving the follow-on. Barry Richards was still there having completed his century and McIlwaine's first ball from Mustaq was 'a googly and I didn't know whether I was coming or going'.

Nonetheless, the pair saved the follow-on and on returning to the dressing room McIlwaine 'got some stick because we had to go out and field again – but it was good-natured'. In the second innings Northants needed quick runs but lost wickets fairly regularly. When Mustaq came in he had scored just two when McIlwaine bowled him a 'slow off-cutter, he tried to hit it over the top and holed out to Gilliat at mid-on'. Not a bad first wicket in county cricket but the target of 283 was almost twice as many as Hampshire managed in a conclusive victory for the Midlands county.

From there Hampshire travelled to London where McIlwaine spent a Saturday afternoon watching Turner (181*) and Gilliat (106) savage Surrey's international attack. Richard remembers Turner's 'great innings' but also that Richards (77) got himself out 'fuming because Turner had taken the strike'. On the Monday it was their turn to enforce the follow-on with Cottam taking 6-55 and McIlwaine weighing in with another Test player, Hampshire-born Graham Roope caught in identical fashion. However, Surrey made a better fist of their second innings and with 0-66 McIlwaine made way for Alan Castell for the last game of the season. He had found the long hours of fielding with no result difficult, and began to wonder whether the life of a professional cricketer was what he wanted.

By the following season Richard had made a significant career move, beginning a three-year teacher training course at Portsmouth College of Education. This inevitably restricted his cricket in the early part of the season, although it is quite common practice nowadays for promising young players to develop in higher education. He was paid to play local club cricket for Waterlooville but the mid-season transition to county cricket was quite abrupt. Nonetheless he played twice more for Hampshire in August 1970 against Sussex at Bournemouth and on his home ground against Glamorgan.

For various reasons Hampshire met Sussex without Richards, Reed, Gilliat, Livingstone, White and Cottam and they struggled to 150 all out, McIlwaine making ten. The young debutant Greenidge was second-highest scorer with 24, 'welcomed by John Snow with a few round the ears'. Sussex took a lead of 108 with McIlwaine recording his best performance of 12-2-40-2. Again there was an illustrious victim as Tony Greig went cheaply: 'I thought I was never a lucky bowler but with Greig I bowled an innocuous ball outside the off stump, he tried to cut it, it hit Stephenson's foot and Sainsbury caught it at slip.' For his second victim he hit the stumps when Richard Langridge on 42 'missed a straight ball. He played all round it and he was furious!' McIlwaine was never confident in the field but he did hold a catch in the deep from Mike Griffith accompanied by shouts from his teammates of 'odds on the ball'.

McIlwaine did not play in the next match at Cheltenham but then returned for Portsmouth. There seemed to be no obvious reason for a promising young bowler to be dropped for one match. His explanation was significant:

> I talked my way out of it. It's amazing really. Richards was fit again and Roy Marshall was in two minds about who to leave out, so I said 'drop me, you don't need me' – I didn't want to play, I was terrified.

I asked whether they pressed him ('no') and whether they should have done ('probably'). By that time he had already 'lost the appetite for the game' and although Cheltenham suited the bowlers he wasn't sure that success there would have made any difference. With Richards missing again he returned for the next match when Greenidge opened for the first time and scored 65 in a Hampshire total of 412-8 declared. The two young men, although very different, had started their careers together but in this same match Greenidge began on the most illustrious of careers as a Test Match opener and 20-year-old Richard McIlwaine played his last first-class match and turned his back on cricket as a career. Majid Khan made 116, Glamorgan scored 361-9 declared and McIlwaine took 0-58 in 13 overs.

> I had bowled reasonably well but all of a sudden I bowled this one over to Majid and the first ball landed halfway down the wicket. I thought I would pitch the next one up but I just seized up and I think it went out of the ground. He took 17 off one over and Marshall just said 'thank you very much' and that was the last over I bowled in county cricket. I think I was tired because I had never bowled such a bad over in my life.

In 1971 he continued to play for the 2nd XI, then coached by Geoff Keith. McIlwaine took nine wickets at 24 each as Hampshire won the Championship with a side that included Turner, Lewis, Murtagh, O'Sullivan, Mottram, Livingstone and White. There were clearly opportunities for young bowlers at Hampshire and Geoff Keith asked 'do you want to play first-class cricket?' The answer was 'no'. He departed instead to a career in teaching and sporting success in his new love, squash. He summed up the reasons for his departure very eloquently and they are worth considering in some detail:

> I think I loved playing cricket at school because I did well at it, so it was easier. When I went on to play for a living it was very different. I really gave it up because I couldn't hack it, I was petrified – especially the fielding. I haven't told many people this but it was the fear of dropping catches or misfielding. I felt I could cope with the bowling and I could throw well enough – stick me at fine leg and provided it came straight to me I could throw it over the stumps.
>
> Physically I wasn't strong enough, brave enough – you have to be brave. I had the stamina to bowl all day but I didn't hit the wicket hard enough compared to someone like John Rice. The other players were that bit taller or that bit stronger. In club cricket I could still get people backing away but in county cricket I was medium pace. Perhaps I had been over-bowled as a teenager. I would bowl 15 or 20 overs on the trot. Now there are directives against that which would have made me mighty frustrated. But I think you can overbowl a young bowler and you drop your pace, get injuries. I think in my last years at school I started to slow down.

If I hadn't given it a go I would still be playing every weekend now. Some of my contemporaries were not treated too well. I was, probably because I had something to fall back on and they knew that. It was a cruel world although I think most dressing rooms were. One young batsman would hit me back over my head in the nets because I was at the bottom of the pile. He was a few steps up and had been got at by other people. It was a bad system with some awkward customers as well as some good blokes. The dressing room wasn't that happy, there was a lot of complaining about the club or the captain (Marshall), a lot of back-biting although the 2nd XI was pretty good. There were some difficult people around.

I think I got out too soon, looking back I could have achieved more. I think I could have been a county cricketer. Perhaps if I could have been a Test player if I had had more ambition but I didn't envy their lifestyle. At the time, I couldn't wait to stop. It wasn't Hampshire's fault that I didn't make it.

To this day Richard McIlwaine has a very real fondness for his 2nd XI coach Leo Harrison but by the end of the 1960s Leo, who had been with Hampshire before the Second World War, was ready to retire. Mike Barnard had been earmarked to succeed him but he and the 2nd XI cricketer Peter Faulkner suffered terrible leg injuries in a cricket tour coach crash in Germany and that was not possible.

34 *Bob Herman – son of 'Lofty' who came back to Hampshire.*

Wilfred Weld, now the club's Patron, helped with the organisation and coaching and appeared in a few matches and he remembers one match in which a student called Tom Mottram bowled very effectively against Hampshire and earned himself a trial at the club. In 1971 he was second-highest wicket taker for the 2nd XI behind David O'Sullivan as Hampshire won the Championship again. Richard Lewis and David Turner also batted well although Jesty, Greenidge and Gilliat were now established in the county side.

Indeed Gilliat was also the new captain, although Marshall would play on for two more years. He did so with some resentment at his successor. He claimed that no explicit reason had ever been given to him for the change of captaincy and declined the invitation to announce his resignation from that role. With Richards and Greenidge opening the batting he, like Neville Rogers when Marshall had arrived, batted down the order. During 1972, under pressure from his other employers, a firm of travel agents, he retired. At the start of his career he earned around £800, by the Championship year of 1961 it had been £1,000 and in his final year he earned just under £2,000 from county cricket. He also enjoyed a benefit and some royalties from his book *Test Outcast*. He continued to play club cricket with Deanery in Southampton until he moved to Somerset, where eventually he became Chairman of Cricket.

Despite the new limited-overs competitions, Hampshire's membership fell again in 1971 from 5,879 to 5,138. In the County Championship, Surrey won the title at Southampton when Intikhab dismissed Gilliat. Peter Sainsbury enjoyed a golden summer with 107 wickets and 959 runs – just 41 short of Hampshire's only 'double' since Jim Bailey in 1948.

35 *The greatest openers: Gordon Greenidge and Barry Richards (PE).*

Hampshire, their pace attack decimated by departures, recruited Hampshire-born all-rounder John Rice from Surrey for 1971 and then a year later 'Lofty's' son Bob Herman from Middlesex. Herman, who had enjoyed only an average career at Lord's, was astonishingly successful for Hampshire in his first three years. In 1972 he topped their bowling averages with 81 wickets at 21.66. Gordon Greenidge made significant progress as an opening batsman but Richard Gilliat's year was so difficult that he dropped himself from the side. It was to be a temporary setback.

On Tuesday 9 May 1972 Herman took 4-20 to help bowl Hampshire to victory in their first match in a new competition, the Benson & Hedges Cup. The English authorities, excited by the success of the Gillette Cup and John Player League introduced this new contest, which amalgamated elements of the league and knock-out formats. As a consequence the county championship was reduced to 20 matches each. By contrast, in 1961 Hampshire had played 32 games to win the title.

The first match finished on Tuesday because the Saturday was rained off and Hampshire were playing in the John Player League on Sunday. The weather then forced the match into two days as Hampshire crushed the Minor Counties but after defeats to Somerset and Glamorgan they did not progress to the knock-out stages. In the Gillette Cup at Bournemouth, Lancashire beat them in the quarter-final despite a magnificent century from Richards.

For the second year Hampshire finished ninth in the Championship and given the loss of so many players they may have seemed content to be a mid-table side. Ray Illingworth retained the Ashes, which his side had won in Australia the previous year, with a victory in the fourth Test at Headingley.

By the end of the 1972 season, Hampshire were able to announce a small profit of about £550, an increase on the £229 of the previous year. These figures contrasted favourably with the loss of £40,000 during the second half of the 1960s although they included a contribution of £27,000 from the central pool. Meanwhile Hampshire's President and former player Ronnie Aird declared that he would support any proposal for promotion and relegation in a two-league Championship. He welcomed the increase of sponsorship in the game and felt that this proposal would make it more attractive. He also pointed out that, unlike most counties, Hampshire's responsibility for two grounds, Southampton and Bournemouth, added to their financial burdens. He added that Dean Park's rent and maintenance cost between £7,000-£10,000 each year.

In 1972 their colts included Peter Barrett soon to join the Hampshire staff but the star was David Rock, who produced a 'breath-taking individual performance' captaining Hampshire colts, the West of England and England Schools. During 1972 Hampshire's first team had won easily at Trent Bridge in the Gillette Cup but may have been impressed by the performance of Mike Taylor, who dismissed Richards and Turner and then top-scored with fifty-eight. When Nottinghamshire did not renew his contract at the end of the season, Hampshire were happy to sign him. Taylor received three offers but thought that with Richards and Greenidge opening the batting Hampshire might have a chance of success.

> Actually Gordon had not made his mark by then but Barry was probably
> at his peak. It certainly attracts you to play with him than against him.

Hampshire fielded only 13 players in the 1973 Championship season. For the
first half Richard Lewis held the batting place that had been Roy Marshall's but
during the final weeks he was replaced by spinner David O'Sullivan. Andy Murtagh
came in occasionally for injured players but 10 men were regulars. They were
Richards, Greenidge, Turner, Gilliat, Sainsbury, Jesty, Taylor, Stephenson, Herman
and Mottram. They won 10 and drew 10 of their 20 matches and became the
second Hampshire side to win the County Championship.

Taylor described that as 'fantastic'.

> It was something you never dreamt of. I just wanted to further my career
> and keep a regular place in the side. One or two lads liked to bet and we
> were given 66-1 for the Championship!

Taylor suggested that the new pace attack had been important.

> Tom Mottram had not done anything previously – he was an amateur
> who would play occasional one-day games. Bob Herman had come from
> Middlesex and had quite a good year in 1972 but he was not the sort
> of bowler to make you think 'God we are playing against Bob Herman
> today'. I am sure he would agree.

In addition Peter Sainsbury was 'still a good cricketer' and Richard Gilliat was
'the best captain I had played under without doubt.' Taylor described him as
'shrewd' and 'encouraging', contrasting the experience with his previous county.
At Hampshire he was asked what he would bowl and sometimes was offered
choice of ends. There was an attitude of togetherness in the dressing room, which
was probably not obvious a few years earlier and this meant that everyone was
'prepared to work hard'. David Turner also remembered Gilliat as a good captain
and 'more venturesome' than his predecessor.

Bob Stephenson, who kept wicket to that attack, remembers that 'nobody
really feared' the bowlers but explained that

> Bob Herman left the bat, Tom Mottram, high bounce and nipped it about
> off the seam – they all fancied him, played shots and got out. To follow,
> Mike Taylor, very consistent, hit the seam and nipped it about, then 'Sains'
> – consistent, Trevor Jesty away swingers – a team of good honest cricketers
> and a bit of variety.

They had one piece of good fortune. When the West Indian tourists visited
Southampton, Hampshire gave a first-class debut to Andy Roberts, not then
eligible for the Championship. A fierce delivery from him put the West Indies
opener Camacho out of the tour and the tourists turned to Ron Headley of
Worcestershire instead of Gordon Greenidge. Headley scored eight, 42, one and
11 before being omitted from the final Test. West Indies won the series 2-0 but
Greenidge was probably the stronger choice. Without him, Hampshire would have
struggled to score their runs at the speed required to dismiss their opponents.

David O'Sullivan had taken only 10 Championship wickets at 35 apiece before
his selection for the Essex match at Portsmouth in early August. In the second

36 *The 1973 Champions (PE).*

innings of a rain-affected game he bowled 27 consecutive overs, taking 6-35. It was the start of an incredible month for him and he finished with 47 wickets at 21.10 – just above Taylor (64 at 21.71) who recalled

> The wicket turned at Southampton. They played a lot more club cricket there in those days and the groundsman didn't mend the ends so by August, in a dry summer, the square was quite bare and the wicket could be a dusty turner.

Bob Stephenson is willing to suggest that O'Sullivan 'won us the Championship that year, there's no doubt about that'. In terms of Southampton, Taylor is not alone in remembering the key match against Northamptonshire which began on Saturday 18 August – not least the very large crowd that had come to watch the top two sides in the table. Richard Gilliat began by losing the toss, which hardly mattered as Herman and Mottram both struck twice, reducing the visitors to 26-4. They never recovered. Bob Cottam, returning to Northlands Road, went for nought and only Bishan Bedi delayed Hampshire with 32*.

Hampshire passed the Northamptonshire score of 108 with one wicket down but Bedi had both openers stumped for 45 and they fell away 167 all out. Mottram, Taylor and O'Sullivan were again in excellent form on the Monday and Hampshire required only 90 to win. Cottam and Bedi had them at 49-3 but Richards was masterful and they won just after 6p.m.

Nottinghamshire subsided in the next match and once again Hampshire clinched the title at Bournemouth with some Thursday afternoon bonus points against Gloucestershire. However, the key had been the Northamptonshire game in which Richards, 45 and 37*, withstood the wiles of Bedi (match figures of 8-105). Taylor says that, at tea on the Saturday, Richards had been critical of the inability of English batsmen to use their feet to a bowler like Bedi but shortly afterwards he was stumped. As a consequence, 'in the second innings he didn't leave the crease!'

As craftsmen, Richards and Bedi were the equal of any cricketers in England in the 1950s but by now the game was responding to the added pressures of media representation, which meant that men like these were not merely fine players but stars. That brings with it different pressures and expectations and of course it is no secret that Richards grew frustrated playing county cricket while being denied the world stage.

As a consequence he was one of the few overseas players available every year to his county side. Not everyone expressed wholehearted enthusiasm for the five-year influx of overseas players and in two end-of-season articles in the *Sunday Times,* Robin Marlar and Norman Harris explored their impact. Marlar identified a boom in cricket complemented by boredom with football but he expressed concern about the state of schools cricket and complained 'of course there are too many overseas cricketers in our game'. That sounds familiar. On the other hand, Harris pointed out that there were still 150 English cricketers eligible for England and he suggested that it was rather the amount and type of cricket in the Championship that prevented English cricketers from reaching a higher standard. He wondered whether in the future English cricketers might become part-time professionals. But of the overseas players he suggested 'for the moment they provide much of the vitality in a near senile championship.' Meanwhile in the *Guardian,* John Arlott insisted that, 'there is no evidence that any young Englishman with the talent of a possible Test player has been put out of the game by one from abroad'.

In *The Times,* John Woodcock wrote of his home county's triumph that Hampshire were the 'most surprising winners' ever in the Championship – even more than Derbyshire in 1936 or Glamorgan in 1948. He added that the arrival of Mike Taylor had been 'as happy for the player as for the club' but that overall it had been a 'team effort'. Richard Gilliat cited limited-overs cricket as having a significant impact on the improvement of their fielding and catching as well as their shot-play and running between the wickets. Although they did not win a limited-overs title they finished third in the John Player League. These successes had a positive impact on the attendances and gate receipts. Comparing his two title-winning sides, Peter Sainsbury felt that the 1961 side had proved themselves capable of success over the years since 1955 whereas in 1973 the success was

37 *The 1973 Champions – the celebrations (PE).*

unexpected. In particular, opposing batsmen would sometimes play speculatively against an attack they expected to dominate but the Hampshire bowlers knew their limitations and bowled to their strengths.

When Hampshire won the title 12 years earlier they did so by playing 32 Championship matches, whereas by 1973 there were just 20 games and at Lord's there were discussions about reducing the Championship to 16 matches – each side playing all others once at home or away. However, the Test selectors under the Chairmanship of Alec Bedser expressed the opposite view of needing more first-class cricket – especially now that international teams had begun to play each other in limited-overs matches. Bedser also feared that an idea to introduce four-day county matches would encourage full covering of wickets. He shared the views of his many of his contemporaries that this would be detrimental to techniques.

As reigning champions, Hampshire began the 1974 Championship season with a defeat at Lord's on Andy Roberts' championship debut. He had been fearsome in the 2nd XI in the previous year while qualifying to play and had won a contract ahead of O'Sullivan because Hampshire could not keep both overseas men. The job of communicating that decision fell to Cricket Chairman Charlie Knott, who always believed that 'purely from a cricketing point of view it had to be Roberts' although he added that O'Sullivan 'took it very well'. In the event, the committee's decision was wholly vindicated as Roberts took 119 wickets at 13.62. However, Gilliat conceded that the decision had unbalanced their attack with only Sainsbury as an established slow bowler although it gave opportunities to young off spinner Nigel Cowley from Dorset.

In the event, the presence of Roberts almost rendered the issue irrelevant. At times his pace was frightening and, in the days before helmets, he dispatched

Colin Cowdrey to Basingstoke's hospital and was often unplayable. Having lost the opening Championship match Hampshire then won four in a row by an innings. A draw at The Oval was followed by two more victories then rain ruined the match at Chesterfield – a harbinger of the gloom to come.

There was more heavy rain at Bristol and Snow at Hove where, without Richards, Hampshire lost easily, as the England star took 11-79 in the match. But then there were two more victories before Worcestershire, in second place, arrived at Portsmouth in a near-replica of the Northamptonshire game of 12 months earlier. As before, Hampshire won it in two days by an innings although on this occasion their opponents fell short of 100 in both innings. And so that surely was that. In August, the *Guardian* ran the headline 'Hampshire's lead is now unassailable,' while the *Daily Mirror* proclaimed 'Hampshire look just Champion!'

But then the rain came as Lancashire (109 and 93-5), survived at Bournemouth. Hampshire went to Cardiff scored 234 and dismissed Glamorgan for 90 – just six past following-on. Roberts had 8-47 but Hampshire – Richards apart – batted carelessly on a drying wicket and Glamorgan needed 282 to win. Roberts bowled 34 tired overs but could not repeat his success, Taylor bowled only 10 overs in the match and Jesty five while Sainsbury's second innings analysis was 63-38-

38 *Andy Roberts.*

39   *David Turner.*

73-1 – and that one wicket an outfield catch. Glamorgan scored 284-5 in 155 overs and won by five wickets. The two sides then met again at Southampton. Hampshire with 393-8 declared made amends but only 15 minutes' play was possible on Bank Holiday Monday and Glamorgan, who were 58-3 overnight, collapsed and followed on 237 behind. Herman then took 6-15 but the visitors survived at 81-8.

The last two matches were at Bournemouth. On Wednesday Somerset scored 264 and, although no one made a century, Hampshire took a lead of 141. Somerset, batting again, collapsed to 22-4 before Close and Parks resisted, but from the last ball on Thursday in bright sunshine Roberts hit Parks on the arm and he could not have batted on the final day with Somerset still in arrears.

It did not matter for the rain came again. Worcestershire had pulled themselves back into contention and over the last three days they took just enough bonus points in Essex to clinch the title. Hampshire's final match with Yorkshire never started. As Mike Taylor has said it must be the only sporting competition where a team can be denied a title because they cannot play. The *Guardian* now ran a different headline: 'Raining Champions', with a photograph of Norman Gifford under an umbrella. At the end of the season Richards was second to Clive Lloyd in the batting averages while Roberts stood alone for bowling. Peter Sainsbury, the only man to have won two Championships with Hampshire, found that no consolation when the rains came in 1974 and he remembers the enforced idleness as 'a dreadful feeling'.

David Turner has suggested that the players were frustrated in part by the poor covering at Bournemouth. Its mossy turf also made it the slowest drying of their venues and no one took consolation when, in the middle of the Yorkshire washout, the two sides managed a restricted Sunday League match at Portsmouth. Bob Stephenson confessed many years later that 'you get philosophical' about such events but if everyone at Hampshire had known it was to be their last title that may have been harder. He confessed, however, that not everyone responded like that and had this to say about dressing rooms.

> You throw 11 people together and there's no chance you will enjoy everyone's company – the secret is to tolerate shortcomings because you will have shortcomings yourself. If you are successful the atmosphere automatically improves – if you're losing all the time it's a different kettle of fish. Any winning side will come out with guff about the great atmosphere but it's human nature.

He added 'we had a team of good honest cricketers', plus Richards, Greenidge and Roberts. At that point Greenidge was still an English-qualified player but that changed in November 1974 when he made his Test debut in Bangalore, scoring 93 and 107. His partner Barry Richards had waited until his second Test match for his maiden century.

Hampshire were continuing to frustrate their supporters in limited-overs cricket. It was difficult to comprehend that a side with Richards, Greenidge, Roberts, Jesty, Sainsbury and Taylor could not reach a final or win the league. They had only once reached a Gillette Cup semi-final in 1966 but lost by the huge margin of 99 runs. They fared better in the new Benson & Hedges Cup. After failing to qualify in the first year, 1972, they topped their south-west group in the next three years. In 1973 they lost a quarter-final to Kent and then in 1974 they seemed poised for a semi-final place.

In the quarter-final, at Taunton they lost their first four wickets at 22, including Barry Richards bowled by a promising teenager called Ian Botham. They recovered to 182 all out thanks to Jesty (79) and Sainsbury (40) who added ninety-five. Botham took 2-33. Somerset lost wickets more regularly at 37-3, 89-5 and then three more at 113. They needed 70 from 15 overs and with only two wickets left. Roberts was bowling fiercely and struck Botham, who had come in at number nine, but he picked himself up and scored runs regularly with Moseley until the latter was dismissed with seven runs required. Botham steered Somerset home with 45* and won the Gold Award. He made his Test debut three years later and never looked back. Jesty added 4-28 to his fine innings but got nothing.

Hampshire began 1975 as bookmakers' favourites to regain the title and for some time they lived up to that rating. They began by winning four of the first five matches, including a huge victory at Hove when they were deprived of bonus points in a strange manner. Richards hit a century before lunch and Turner 150* in the afternoon to allow Gilliat to declare at 401-5. Morley opened but retired hurt and Cheatle too was absent, so Hampshire did not claim maximum points. Sussex followed on 248 behind and Taylor claimed six of the seven wickets needed as Spencer was also unable to bat. So Hampshire won by an innings having taken just 15 wickets!

They beat Nottinghamshire to top the table in early June and then had their revenge over Somerset in a repeat of the Benson & Hedges quarter-final, even though Viv Richards was the only man to pass fifty. The West Indians (and others) in county cricket then disappeared for a month to take part in the first Prudential World Cup. With Gordon Greenidge opening the batting, they won an enthralling final at Lord's against the Australians, helping to establish limited-overs internationals as the primary economic attraction in world cricket.

In Bristol Hampshire won a Championship match in two days and at Cardiff they beat Glamorgan by nine wickets in the Sunday League and were top of that table as well. They looked the most powerful side in the country but things began to go wrong. With Richards injured and batting with a runner, they were beaten in the Championship at Leicester. They went on to Abbeydale Park, the new Sheffield venue, with Murtagh and Barrett opening the batting and lost again. They also lost in the league at Old Trafford and will have welcomed the tourists as a chance to rest before their B&H semi-final.

For Richards, however, the challenge was rather different. Deprived of the chance to prove himself on the world stage he greeted Jeff Thomson and Max Walker (but not Lillee) with two ferocious and accomplished displays of batting. Although Ian Chappell's side won by four wickets, Richards was the star with 96 and 69 (retired hurt). Turner made 87 but broke his finger and Greenidge seventy-four. In the *Guardian* John Arlott wrote of Richards' second innings:

> Whether he wished it so or not his brief but stirring innings was a protest not simply on behalf of the White cricketers of South Africa ... but of those cricketers in South Africa whom their own government will not allow to play national cricket because of the colour of their skin.

It was probably not a point that sprang immediately to the minds of those who watched or heard about it. For Hampshire the sun had shone and they banked around £5,500.

So Hampshire went to Leicester for their latest semi-final. This time Greenidge was magnificent in scoring 111 but he got no significant support as Hampshire kept losing wickets and were 216 all out with eight balls remaining. They had Leicestershire at 115-4 but Chris Balderstone matched Greenidge with an undefeated century, Tolchard gave good support and they won with five wickets and five balls to spare. Roberts took 1-16 in 10 overs.

Two weeks later this unpredictable side smashed a world record 371-4 against Glamorgan in the 60 overs of the Gillette Cup. Richards made 129 but was outscored by Greenidge whose 177 was also a world record innings. Roberts took 3-17 and Hampshire won easily but in the next round Lancashire bowled them out for 98 and halted their progress.

Hampshire recovered with Championship victories over Gloucestershire, Somerset and Lancashire. The latter were also challenging for the title and, in mid-August, this was important but the match at Liverpool finished on Tuesday, followed by a trip south for the following morning in Bournemouth. Mike Taylor recalls a difficult drive in heavy traffic through Ringwood and when his passenger Barry Richards arrived at the ground he was suffering from a bad back. He went for a duck and batted at number 11 in the second innings as Surrey won by two wickets.

He was declared unfit for the following game and Greenidge and Jesty were also missing as Hampshire lost again. Their totals in Bournemouth week were 169, 183, 95 and 159, but with their batsmen restored, they won at Edgbaston and returned to Southampton for two matches that might decide the title. At this point they were second to Yorkshire but with a match in hand the two-point gap made them favourites. Surrey, Lancashire and Leicestershire were in the chasing pack.

A large crowd on the Saturday saw Richards and Greenidge score 88 for the first wicket against Sussex. When Richards left, Greenidge and Turner shared a partnership of 165 of which Turner made sixty-two. On that Saturday, Greenidge hit 259 in 308 minutes, reaching every 50 and century with a six and clearing

40   *The 1975 John Player League Champions celebrate at Darley Dale (PE).*

the boundary on 13 occasions – a Championship record. Hampshire declared at 501-5 in the 100th over leaving themselves a few overs at the Sussex openers. Roberts measured and tested his run, injuring himself in the process and he did not bowl again in the season. In the *Sunday Times* Christopher Wordsworth suggested ominously that this 'affair … looked unhappy in more ways than one'. Elsewhere Leicestershire pulled themselves into third place in the Championship and on the Sunday visited Bournemouth for a televised John Player League match, in which Richards gave an extraordinary performance. He raced away with Greenidge, chasing 195 to win, until Illingworth bowled defensively, firing the ball in towards leg stump with a leg-side field. But as he did Richards simply moved further outside leg and hit him fiercely through the off side. He scored 112 and Hampshire were closing in on their first limited-overs title.

In that year each first Championship innings was limited to 100 overs. On the Monday the somewhat makeshift Hampshire attack of Jesty, Rice, Southern, Taylor, Richards and Sainsbury took wickets regularly but not quickly. The Sussex innings was closed at 259-8 so again they followed on without losing 10 wickets. Jesty and Sainsbury reduced them to 86-3 but old Etonian M.J.J. Faber made his highest ever score of 176, catches were missed and it was left to Greenidge (3-84) and Gilliat (1-51) to bowl them out. Now Leicestershire led by nine points and each side had two matches to play.

After four days' rest, the team played Derbyshire at Darley Dale in the final Sunday League match. It is the only time that two first-class sides have met on this tiny club ground and the television cameras were there as Hampshire had to win to clinch the title. Richards and Greenidge began with 90 and Hampshire set a challenging 223 to win in 40 overs. Mottram, who had lost his regular place to Roberts in 1974, bowled very well, taking 5-21, and Rice with 4-14 maintained his place as their leading Sunday wicket-taker for the season. Hampshire won by 70 runs to clinch the trophy, which was presented to Gilliat on the ground.

On the Wednesday they met Derbyshire again at Southampton and Taylor and Rice put them out for 195. Gilliat made a century as Hampshire declared 175 ahead and the restored Mottram reduced them to 28-3. At this point J.M. Ward joined the obdurate opener Alan Hill. Ward won an Oxford Blue in 1971–3 and had played a few games for Derbyshire but had just learned that he had no new contract on offer. He was selected for this match only because of injuries. He had a first-class batting average of around twenty but on this vital day he stayed with Hill for three hours and eventually reached 104. Even then five wickets went for just 25 runs but Alan Ward and Hendrick held out and the Championship went to Leicestershire.

In the previous year the players had expressed some disappointment with the covering at Bournemouth during the decisive matches. This time, Mike Taylor remembers their surprise at turning up with the 'world's fastest bowler' to find Northlands Road 'flat, true and shaved of grass'. We can only wonder whether Roberts might have bowled had Greenidge not just hit 259. After the sodden disappointments of the previous season it was scant consolation that Hampshire won their final match at Worcester by an innings. Nor did they much care about winning the Fenner Trophy in Scarborough – an unnecessary limited-overs competition that was designed but usually failed to restore pride to Yorkshire.

From the Championship side of 1973 Bob Herman had lost confidence and his career was virtually over, while Mottram, a practising architect, was not always available and not always selected. Sainsbury and Lewis would have just one more year and the replacements, Southern, Cowley and Rice, were good rather than outstanding, while the most promising youngsters Rock and Tremlett were not yet ready. Greenidge and Roberts would be away in 1976 with the touring party and the most successful side in Hampshire's history was to begin its rapid decline. In part this occurred because there were insufficient new players of top class coming through but it was also a consequence of a changing dressing room and a changing order in world cricket. After the positive changes effected by Gilliat in the early 1970s David Turner observed that the next three seasons became a 'very bad time with a lot of bad feeling brewing up' in the dressing room. Nonetheless, the Hampshire side of the mid-1970s should be remembered as their most successful and Gilliat as perhaps the most effective captain in Hampshire's history.

Peter Sainsbury was the one man who played in both sides who had won the title and played under the two fine captains. Of Colin Ingleby-Mackenzie he said that this 'flamboyant' leader had the 'wonderful knack of making you feel important without saying it'. While Gilliat was equally effective he was also 'completely the opposite'. He recalled an occasion when after a long bowl Gilliat asked him to open the batting for the awkward last half-hour. Tired and not fond of opening, Peter protested but he complied with the request, survived and went on to make a big score. Sainsbury had been 'so livid but he proved me wrong and made me more determined'. Gilliat's was a tough side and not quite finished yet.

Hampshire won two trophies in 1976. They retained the Fenner Trophy (beating Yorkshire) and also won the new Tilcon Trophy at Harrogate – yet another limited (to four sides) limited-overs competition. And yet when they reached a 'real' semi-final they fell again. This time it was the Gillette Cup, which Bishan Bedi won for Northamptonshire with a four from John Rice's penultimate ball. They fell to eighth in the Sunday League and 12th in the Championship. Richards was again the dominant batsman and the spinners Sainsbury and Southern bowled well, but the pace attack relied too heavily on the medium pacers Jesty and Rice.

On Saturday 10 June at Bournemouth, Richards (111), Turner (127) and Gilliat (101) made centuries against Glamorgan while Gordon Greenidge hit 101 for West Indies v England at Old Trafford – his second century in the match. England's leading aggregate scorer was extras (44). The West Indies won this third Test by 425 runs (Roberts 9-59 in the match) and took the series 3-0 after England's captain Tony Greig failed in his promise to make them 'grovel'.

England had now failed to win a Test in their last three home series and in recent years their only success had been against India. As a consequence it was no great surprise when Greig enjoyed more success in a series win in India. Then in March 1977 he led England in a single Test match in Melbourne to mark the first ever Test, played exactly, 100 years earlier. Australia won that first match by 45 runs and Charles Bannerman scored the first century. Rod Marsh repeated the feat in this celebration, the first Australian wicketkeeper to score 100 against England. He helped Australia to add 232 for the last five wickets. England had been dismissed for 95 (Lillee 6-26) but in the second innings Derek Randall scored a magnificent 174 as incredibly they fell short by the same margin as their distant predecessors.

The teams were presented to HM Queen Elizabeth and the Duke of Edinburgh and the event seemed like a thoroughly pleasant occasion. But behind the scenes the England captain was engaged in significant negotiations with many of the leading players, persuading them to join an organisation called World Series Cricket in direct competition with the international Test programme. The tale has been told in detail many times but briefly it was initiated by Australian media mogul Kerry Packer after he had been refused television rights to Test cricket. He believed that he could set up a rival competition by purchasing the world's best cricketers and staging matches using coloured clothing, floodlights and other 'innovations'. He recruited Greig to find his players and the cricketing establishment was outraged by this betrayal.

As a consequence the English authorities removed Greig from the England captaincy and gave the job to Brearley for the 1977 Ashes series, although Gilliat may well have been in contention. Brearley was, of course, an inspired choice, Botham made his Test debut and England won the series 3-0. Australia gave debuts to six players but Boycott scored his 100th century and the first 'Jubilee' Test took record receipts of over £220,000.

As the Queen and much of the country celebrated the Jubilee a significant number of young people decorated themselves with safety pins, studs, rings, chains and tattoos, fashioned their hair into vivid colourful 'mohicans' and pronounced their sense of boredom, nihilism and opposition to convention and authority. Many were young, although in Britain they were led by a pair of canny entrepreneurs, Malcolm McLaren and Vivienne Westwood. When their heroes the Sex Pistols released 'God Save the Queen' it went to number one in the charts despite (because?) being banned by the BBC.

In cricket the young punks were led by Packer and Greig, but their dress was more conservative although they expressed themselves, sometimes savagely, on the field. But many of them too were bored, disenchanted, anti-convention and challenging authority. As they schemed and plotted, 1977 became a deeply unhappy English season as rumour and counter-rumour poisoned the county game. Richards, Greenidge and Roberts played for Hampshire, who finished 12th in the Championship and fifth in the Sunday League. In the first Sunday League match, chasing 120 to win, Hampshire were 83-2 and 110-4 but all out 117. There were four ducks and Nottinghamshire won by two runs!

Gordon Greenidge now dominated the batting in both competitions as Richards was less effective. David Rock progressed to the county side and confirmed his promise with Championship centuries against Leicestershire and Nottinghamshire, although he was not yet consistent. Tremlett also appeared but Champions Herman and Murtagh played for the last time.

Hampshire also reached another semi-final in the Benson & Hedges Cup and met Gloucestershire at Southampton. Sadiq and Stovold began with a century partnership for the visitors, who fell away to 180 all out (Mottram 3-21). Greenidge and Richards started well enough but Hampshire fell from 13-0 to 18-4 as Proctor took a hat-trick, roared on by visiting supporters. Turner and Cowley restored hope with a stand of 109 but wickets fell again and Hampshire were seven runs short with three balls left. Procter with 6-13 was Man of the Match and Gloucestershire won the final.

Procter's victims included Richards and Greenidge and all three men were apparently scheduled for the World Series event. For Richards (and Procter), the opportunity to play in an international tournament was obviously hugely attractive but the other players were equally excited by the promise of a lucrative series.

In the *Guardian,* Richard Yallop revealed that Richards had earned around £20,000 during the past 12 months from a season in England and one in Australian state cricket. By comparison, a fully qualified English schoolteacher of a similar age in 1977 might be earning around £3,000. There would be no benefit but they would expect to work until 60 and receive an occupational pension. During 1977, his 10th season with Hampshire, Richards was awarded a benefit and his tax-free sum of £21,255 was about £14,000 more than the previous highest for Peter Sainsbury in 1965, although the next six years all raised similar amounts. The next significant leap came in 1987 when Malcolm Marshall received £61,000. Richards had told Yallop that he was disappointed by press reactions to World Series Cricket because other top sportsmen could earn far more than they were offered.

> Tony Greig is making a protest. If he was paid the same amount that Kerry Packer is offering him, he would play for England. He's the only one honest enough to say that he's in the job for the money.

Of course Richards produced no evidence that *every* other cricketer was in the 'job' for what he could earn, or even that every cricketer saw it as a 'job', but he did identify himself with that view. Tony Baker, who would serve Hampshire for decades on the committee as Hon. Treasurer and eventually Chief Executive, remembers that many ordinary county cricketers at that time did earn 'pretty derisory sums'. In his autobiography, even Richards revealed that he signed a contract to play in the rebel series worth 'as much as I could earn in three years at Hampshire' but his 'main concern' was to protect his benefit.

Richards met with other players including Greig, Knott, Underwood and Snow and he recommended Gordon Greenidge. He argued that a positive consequence of this development was an improvement in the remuneration of county and England cricketers, but in his autobiography he revealed another motivation for his signing – boredom with the county game:

> Though I shall always feel the greatest affection for Hampshire ... I have been disillusioned for some time. Though it has been a voluntary sentence, I have felt like a prisoner within the system.

He criticised the dull routine, the repetitious cricket, the travel and the endless hotels. He acknowledged that some cricketers found it 'idyllic'. He named two other factors that kept him in county cricket: money and the improved spirit in the dressing room from his early seasons and the success of the side. In 1977 he acknowledged that for the first time he did not give the county 'value for money'. He concluded one chapter by admitting that 'When I walk off a county ground for the last time … it will be with an enormous sense of relief'.

The book was published at the start of the 1978 season and by the time most people read that paragraph, Richards had left Hampshire. He had his season in World Series Cricket where the innovations often outnumbered the spectators. At the end of the 1977 season the English authorities were threatening to cancel the county contracts of any 'Packer pirates' and, in a display of on-field sentimentality at the final day of the 1977 season, the Hampshire players sang 'Auld Lang Syne' together to bid farewell to Richards and Greenidge. Roberts was missing injured in a season in which he played in just two-thirds of the matches.

This last match was in Bristol where the home side were hoping to win their first title in modern times as they led the table by five points. On the first day Cowley took 5-94 and Gloucestershire were dismissed for 223, of which Procter scored 115. Emphasising the importance of the overseas players, Greenidge and Richards replied with 108-0. On the second morning Procter (6-68) struck and Hampshire led by just six runs. Gloucestershire 194-4 (Procter 57) were well placed on the second evening and a huge crowd came to Bristol for the final day. John Southern then worked his way through the Gloucestershire batting with 6-81 and Hampshire needed 271 to win in four-and-a-half hours. David Graveney dismissed Richards for 19 (30-1) but Turner and Greenidge were both dropped and they took the score beyond 150. The pace of scoring was relentless and Hampshire reached their target in just 58 overs with more than an hour and six wickets to spare. Kent and Middlesex overtook Gloucestershire and for the first time since 1950 the title was shared.

Trevor Jesty was named as first reserve for the England (MCC) tour of Pakistan and New Zealand but he was never called for. With Roberts not expected to return, Hampshire signed Keith Stevenson from Derbyshire as they had signed Richard Elms from Kent at the start of 1977. They also offered a contract to a 16-year-old pace bowler Martin Doulton from Ringwood, while Paul Terry captained England Schools on their tour to India.

Meanwhile, during the winter, Kerry Packer contested the attempt to stop his players appearing in English first-class cricket and in the High Court won costs of around a quarter of a million pounds. So it was that Hampshire were able to retain the services of Richards, Roberts and Greenidge for the 1978 season. In Australia, Richards scored 207 to pass 1,000 World Series Cricket runs. His partner Greenidge made 140 for the World XI against the hosts, who then collapsed to Roberts and Imran Khan.

While the larger cricket world was changing irrevocably, Hampshire suffered a massive blow in the Autumn of 1977 when Desmond Eagar died suddenly while on holiday. He was only 59, still their secretary and the man who had fashioned the modern Hampshire club and team since the war, although it is doubtful that he much enjoyed the changes then occurring in English cricket. Hampshire's Chairman Geoffrey Ford said of him:

> (He) laid the foundations of the modern Hampshire; he was the money
> raiser, the man who made our present sound financial position possible
> and I am only glad that he lived to see the success on the field for which
> he had sacrificed so much.

This success had begun under his captaincy in 1955 and the three great architects Altham, Eagar and Holt had relished the first title in 1961. But it was really in the 1970s after the registration of overseas players and the establishment of four competitions that counties like Hampshire could compete on equal terms with the major clubs and from that point their success became increasingly dependent upon good management on and off the field. So it was that through the 1970s Eagar, Cecil Paris, Cricket Chairman Charlie Knott and the Committee Chairmen offered support and guidance to Richard Gilliat and his side responded with unprecedented success.

But Hampshire were not alone. For the first time, the county sides began to share success in a way that had been much more common in association football. For example, in the 1920s, although Huddersfield Town won three consecutive titles, seven different sides won the Football League First Division. During the same decade only four sides won cricket's County Championship, with Yorkshire and Lancashire sharing seven of the titles. This was typical until the 1970s, when the impact of changes in the 1960s began to transform domestic cricket and various counties shared titles.

By comparison, until the 1970s English football offered more teams the chance of success than cricket. Since then the situation has reversed and in the 1970s, in addition to the eight counties who won a Championship, five others won a limited-overs trophy. Only four sides won nothing during that decade and each of them were successful around that period:

> Derbyshire NatWest Trophy 1981
> Glamorgan Championship 1969, NatWest finalists 1977
> Nottingham Championship 1981
> Yorkshire Championship 1968
> Gillette Cup 1969
> Sunday League 1983

This change was extraordinary. From the start of the modern Championship in 1890 until Hampshire's title in 1961, only Derbyshire (1936), Glamorgan (1948), Nottinghamshire (1907 & 1929) and Warwickshire (1911 & 1951) had interrupted the 'big five': Kent (four titles), Lancashire (seven), Middlesex (four), Surrey (14) and Yorkshire (24). Surrey and Yorkshire won 38 of 59 titles; indeed in the first half of the 20th century Yorkshire won exactly 50 per cent of the titles – the only competition then available. By 1979, Glamorgan, Hampshire and Warwickshire had triumphed again and were joined by Essex, Leicestershire, and Worcestershire. Only the recent arrivals Durham have failed to win a trophy in modern times. Although this creates the pressure of expectation on players, coaches and committees across the country it does help to spread the interest in cricket and has almost certainly enabled county clubs to remain solvent despite the gloomiest of predictions.

While there are three or four trophies to win (plus promotion) the interest should remain, but football offers a salutary warning. In the first ten years of the

Premiership only a solitary title for Blackburn Rovers (followed by relegation) interrupted the dominance of the big-city clubs Arsenal and Manchester United and they have now been succeeded by Chelsea.

In cricket recently, it seemed that Surrey might dominate the competitions as they did in the 1950s but in 2005 they were relegated, while Nottinghamshire became the fourth different side in four years to win the County Championship. If the era of 'prizes for all' can be sustained, the benefits to the counties are significant. Nottinghamshire, Hampshire, Essex and Somerset won the four main trophies in 2005. In the previous year it was Warwickshire, Glamorgan, Gloucestershire and Leicestershire – eight Champions in two years. Solan's 'average man' of the 1960s – and often his average family as well – now 'expects' more than a result – victories and trophies are the thing. The danger is when this leads to short-term team-building that does not support the development of a strong England side.

Once Kerry Packer won his High Court case in February 1978, the English counties were generally content to re-sign their 'rebels' and discussions began to effect reconciliation between Packer and the establishment. There is an essential pragmatism here, which is often found in English cricket. Conversations with members of Hampshire's committee of that period reveal that there was little if any discussion of the Packer affair and certainly not of it as a moral issue or one harming the spirit of cricket. Cecil Paris, a cricketer and lawyer, was on hand to offer what was considered the wisest of advice and generally the committee got on with their fund-raising, local events and support for the club. Committees consisted of the men elected by the members of the club to get the job done and that was largely a two-part project leading to a degree of solvency and some success on the field. Generally the election and performance of cricket committees was fairly uncontentious outside the two Roses counties, although committees were generally regarded with some suspicion by players.

In one respect the constituency of the Hampshire committee probably did not equip it for these international issues. It held its general committee meetings at 2p.m. because many of its members were retired officers of Her Majesty's armed services, lawyers, barristers and accountants but, unlike football, rarely major businessmen. One exception, Charlie Knott, ran the cricket sub-committee in a highly effective but fairly autocratic way and did not expect much discussion of his decisions in any general committee meeting. Many committee members never spoke about significant matters and while they would mandate their representatives to Lord's, decisions about issues like limiting overseas players or changing competitions would often be made with a view to the best interests of the county rather than England. While matches continued to be played in Bournemouth, Portsmouth and Basingstoke, Hampshire needed an infrastructure of local committee men to organise and run them. There is no reason to suppose that other counties were much different.

Packer, although a tough negotiator, was a businessman and would have been pragmatic. After the first season of World Series Cricket, Gordon Ross (*Wisden* 1979) reported an unofficial estimated loss of around £2 million and crowds were sometimes the size of a Championship Saturday in England. Meanwhile, as in England with Gillette, Benson & Hedges and John Player, the Australian

Board had encouraged sponsorship and increased payments to players. Pictures of Hampshire's home grounds during the Championship win of 1973 or the Sunday League of 1975 show no advertising boundary boards but they are present by the second Sunday League triumph in 1978. Just a few years later the famous Hampshire sweater would come complete with sponsors logo. By the move to the Rose Bowl in 2001, the northern end lacked a name until a sponsor could be found, at which point spectators would hear of a bowling change at the Foreman Homes or P&O Ferries end.

So Packer and the International Cricket Council 'negotiated' from their different positions about the future organisation and broadcasting of international cricket. Pakistan, after a poor tour of England, welcomed the return of their Packer players but Warwickshire told Dennis Amiss that he could not return in 1979. Elsewhere Kent did the opposite and the Warwickshire members were furious. Their concern was for the success of the side and matters of principle could wait. It is largely the culture of English cricket.

The whole affair did not have a huge impact on the game at the time. John Rice was an all-rounder through the 1970s, who bowled when asked to bowl and batted when asked to bat. In 1975 he was the leading bowler in the Sunday League triumph but through the difficulties of 1979 he opened the batting, played in every first-class match and was third behind Greenidge and Jesty in the averages. He recalls that Packer had very little impact on his career: 'I just took cricket day-by-day and hoped I had done enough to win a new contract.' When asked whether it improved the money he smiled and asked 'what money?'

Bobby Parks was, at the time, the promising understudy to Bob Stephenson but he was also a third-generation professional cricketer so had an awareness of the implications of that way of life. He remembered the positive impact of some of the playing innovations and identified fielding circle restrictions as the most important. From the first years of limited-overs cricket, the marketing of it as an exciting form of the game had been threatened by the professional need to win, which often led to defensive bowling to defensive fields. Indeed the otherwise flamboyant Ted Dexter was thoroughly 'professional' in his setting of defensive fields as Sussex won the knock-out cup in its first two years. Bobby Parks remembers that strong batting sides would set large targets and defend them in a way that 'killed the game'. But the fielding restrictions opened it up again and some of the excitement returned.

The Packer 'revolution' took place in Australia but because of the number of overseas professionals playing in England it had a real impact on the county game. In England it mirrored the 1970s as the decade of strife, with organised labour confronting the government and the establishment. Most obviously, the miners effectively brought to an end a Conservative government, which had needed to introduce the three-day working week and restrictions on the use of resources. But the Labour government that replaced it stumbled along under the last months of Harold Wilson and then James Callaghan until the winter of discontent in 1978–9. As the rubbish piled up on the streets 'Sunny' Jim returned from abroad to ask 'Crisis? What crisis?' The crisis was his and within months he had been replaced by Margaret Thatcher.

The Iron Lady was just the person to sort out the economy, the Empire and the decline in moral standards and she would certainly have been the preferred choice of most of the English cricket establishment. One of her closest confidants, Norman Tebbit, would cite traditional Test cricket as a means of testing national loyalty and a decade later her successor John Major would evoke a tradition of England through images of village cricket and warm beer. But in one sense Packer's enterprise and determined business-like approach anticipated many of the key features of the entrepreneurial 'Thatcherite' spirit of the 1980s.

The compromise agreement between the two sides was eventually brokered in May 1979. The Packer legacy includes a whole range of innovations in cricket, particularly floodlights and coloured clothing. There is little doubt too that, in the longer term, it has contributed to better remuneration for cricketers thanks largely to increased sponsorship and marketing. In England the key moment was the ruling in the High Court that preceded the 1978 season and enabled the counties to continue to select players if they wished to do so. Hampshire did and on 22 April Richards (49) and Greenidge (61) opened Hampshire's season in a Benson & Hedges match. Roberts was selected for the Championship match at Lord's on 3 May but that was abandoned in a wet start to the season. In mid-June Hampshire went to Hove where Roberts dismissed Tony Greig for nought and with Greenidge making 211 (Greig 0-55), Hampshire won by an innings.

Three weeks later at the end of another match at Hove against Essex, Sussex announced that Greig would not play for them again and he left English cricket. *Wisden* reported that regardless of the 'rights and wrongs' of the case the Sussex team responded positively by winning the Gillette Cup. In the meantime Hampshire's Packer star Barry Richards had also departed mid-season. After the match at Hove, in which he scored 60, he made 25 and 45 in a defeat at Chelmsford and then three and 29 against Leicestershire at the end of June. He then announced that he would not play any further Championship cricket although he played in a couple of Sunday League matches before disappearing completely.

Things were uncomfortable at Hampshire. Richard Gilliat, in his benefit season, was also captain and secretary. During the disruption of Richards' departure, Andy Roberts approached Cricket Chairman Charlie Knott to ask for a break as he was tired from playing continuous cricket. Despite his status in world cricket he was a junior professional in terms of county experience and the other Hampshire players, perhaps imbued by the some of the sense of 'workers' rights', let it be known that they were unsympathetic. Knott related that acceding to the request might have precipitated trouble internally, but Roberts insisted as a matter of principle and when the request was finally refused he followed Richards in mid-July. Knott remembered Roberts as a 'lovely fellow' but had been disappointed that Richards had departed without speaking to him. Nonetheless he remembered him as a 'quite outstanding batsman'.

In 1974 Roberts's bowling was probably as impressive and effective as any Hampshire player in their entire history. In that one season, he took 119 wickets at 13.62. He toured with the West Indies in 1976 but while his Hampshire career record of 244 wickets at 16.70 is still very impressive it shows the decline after

41   *A sunny Sunday afternoon in Bournemouth where Hampshire won the Sunday League title again in 1978 (PE).*

that first year. He was eventually replaced by Malcolm Marshall and, at the end of his first season, Mike Neasom of the *Portsmouth News* wrote that Marshall's attitude was 'refreshingly enthusiastic and cheerful' adding that this made a 'welcome change from the anti-cyclonic approach' of Roberts.

In their final weeks at Hampshire, Richards and Roberts cannot have helped the mood in the dressing room and neither enjoyed any significant successes. Nonetheless, their departure created difficulties in the Championship. At various points David Rock, Tim Tremlett, John Rice and Bob Stephenson opened the batting. Rock was unable to reproduce the form of his previous season and on his choice he would play no more first-class cricket after this year. Keith Stevenson opened the bowling, often with Jesty or Taylor.

Nonetheless Hampshire finished in a respectable eighth place. The Sunday League was more exciting and to a large extent the key matches revolved around Gordon Greenidge. Andy Roberts had disappeared after a Gillette Cup defeat at Leicester, at which point Hampshire were level second with Somerset in the Sunday League, six points behind Worcestershire but with a game in hand and five matches to play. They hammered Yorkshire at Portsmouth and won again at Cheltenham with Greenidge top-scoring in both matches (116 & 48). They then

travelled to Northants but lost decisively to one of their bogey sides in those early years of the Sunday League.

However, a large crowd cheered a victory at Northlands Road against Kent in the penultimate game as Greenidge scored another fifty. Hampshire's six-man attack of Stevenson, Tremlett, Taylor, Jesty, Rice and Cowley were covering the loss of Roberts very effectively. They arrived at Bournemouth on 3 September knowing that victory against Middlesex would give them a good chance of the title, although victory for Somerset would see the Western county win their first-ever title in any competition. Somerset were not in the best mood because they had lost to Sussex in the Gillette Cup final the previous day.

Hampshire batted first as Gilliat – opening the batting – and Jesty both made useful scores but once again it was Greenidge who led the way with 122. In his first eight matches that season Greenidge scored 298 runs at 37.25 but after Richards departed he scored 339 runs in five innings at 67.8. Greenidge had a difficult start to his career and in later years at Hampshire not everything went smoothly, but he was one of the great batsmen and in a period like this, when Hampshire needed him, he showed considerable character and commitment to the cause.

Hampshire posted 221-4 in their 40 overs and although Radley and Featherstone made a good start, Jesty added five wickets to his 47 runs. Middlesex reached 126-1 but then lost wickets regularly including three run-outs. Hampshire won by 26 runs but the Somerset match was still in play at Taunton and on BBC Two. For 25 minutes a large crowd in the sunlight

42 *Malcolm Marshall bowling (IM).*

in front of the Dean Park pavilion gleaned bits of information about the other match. Somerset needed 11 to win from the last over and four from the last ball but they managed only two and there were great Hampshire celebrations at the end of a sometimes traumatic season.

Jim Laker presented the trophy to Richard Gilliat. On the Wednesday, he captained Hampshire in one final Championship match as they beat Glamorgan but then surprised all the supporters by announcing his retirement. Between 1973–8 he had led the most successful side in Hampshire's history and there are many reasons to suggest that he was their finest captain for, as 1978 showed, this was not an easy side to lead since it contained many strong and sometimes wilful personalities.

So the Hampshire side that began the following season was significantly different. Bob Stephenson, with Taylor the most experienced professional, was appointed captain – Hampshire's second wicketkeeper captain after Charles Robson (1900–2). Both men were given a very difficult task with weak sides although in 1979 there were some promising youngsters in the 2nd XI. Tim Tremlett had already made an impression in the county side and the others included Mark Nicholas, Paul Terry, Bob Parks and Nick Pocock. The Hampshire colts side of 1979, still led by Arthur Holt, included just one future county cricketer, Jon Hardy.

Because Gordon Greenidge had begun his career as an English player he was still specially registered but Hampshire could only sign one overseas man to replace the departing Richards and Roberts. Charlie Knott used his friendship with Peter Short, who effectively ran West Indies cricket, and accepted his recommendation of Malcolm Marshall. Hampshire believed they were signing a pace-bowling all-rounder although there was little evidence of batting prowess in 1979. It is an interesting fact that Greenidge, Richards and Roberts had all joined Hampshire before playing Test cricket and they effectively signed Marshall in the same circumstances. However, Packer intervened again and in the winter before he came to Hampshire and, after just a single first-class match, Marshall was called into the tour of India and Sri Lanka as the West Indies were without many of their major players, who were entertaining the Australian public.

He made his Test debut in the week before Christmas and took one wicket. In the three Tests he took just three wickets at 88.33 each but back at home had more success in the Shell Shield before joining Hampshire. He began at a cold, damp Derby by dismissing Peter Kirsten but Hampshire lost. He had a reasonable season, taking 47 wickets at 22.36 and missed a few matches mid-season when he and Greenidge were in the West Indies squad that won the second Prudential World Cup, beating England in the final by 92 runs.

In 1979 Hampshire were 12th in the Championship, 10th in the Sunday League and made no significant progress in either knock-out competition. The 1970s had been the most successful decade in the county's history but Gilliat's fine side was disintegrating rapidly. A new and fairly successful era would emerge soon but not without complications.

5

1980–1990

BOB STEPHENSON was the first captain appointed by Hampshire from the ranks of their English professionals. He was also one of the last of the professional footballers in county cricket, had played cricket on a match-fee basis for Derbyshire as understudy to Bob Taylor and had been with Hampshire throughout the 1970s. While the amateur/professional divide had been abolished for the 1963 season, in many respects Richard Gilliat was an old-fashioned secretary and 'amateur' captain with a public school and Oxbridge background (and three initials). His predecessor Roy Marshall was certainly a professional cricketer but he was an overseas Test cricketer. Stephenson was a real English 'pro' and the first to be appointed as captain of Hampshire.

His was not an easy task. The loss of Richards, Gilliat, Roberts, Sainsbury, Herman, Lewis and Mottram over the previous four seasons meant a period of rapid rebuilding. The new pace bowler Keith Stevenson who had followed from Derbyshire performed very well, as did Greenidge, but neither Jesty nor Turner was at his best and the promising youngsters were not yet ready for a full season of county cricket. In his autobiography Malcolm Marshall revealed that he and his new captain had a difficult relationship during Marshall's first season, with the suggestion that the attitude on the field was far too defensive.

Some committee members had misgivings about the new appointment but this was still not really a matter for discussion. Meanwhile, Bobby Parks had a full season in the 2nd XI and, just into his twenties, he was pressing Stephenson (37) for his place in the side as wicketkeeper.

In 1980 the West Indies would be touring England, which would further affect the Hampshire squad. Perhaps recognising that this was a period of dramatic change rather than transition, Nick Pocock replaced Bob Stephenson as captain after just one season. In 1979 under Stephenson's captaincy, this stylish batsman had scored his maiden century against Middlesex at Portsmouth and he was a fine fielder but, at 28, he had been promising for too long. In that same season he had played 14 innings in the 2nd XI Championship with an average of under ten.

Stephenson described losing the captaincy as 'a terrible shock' and wondered whether his position was not helped because he was the players' representative from the Professional Cricketers' Association. He believed that Hampshire should have given him one more year with the inexperienced Pocock serving an apprenticeship as his vice-captain. To some outsiders it appeared that Pocock had many of the

43 *Wicketkeeper Bobby Parks.*

attributes of the typical Hampshire captain. He was another product of public
school cricket, he worked with Colin Ingleby-Mackenzie, he was a flamboyant
player and he had three initials.

Stephenson did continue for one year as the county's senior professional and
a member of the cricket sub-committee which he had joined when appointed
captain. The General Committee was still 30-strong and was responsible for all
aspects of the club but in reality it rarely discussed cricketing matters. Rather it
elected and received reports and recommendations from the cricket sub-committee

44   *Nick Pocock, the new captain in 1980.*

under its Chairman Charlie Knott. That sub-committee consisted of 16 people, some including Stephenson co-opted, and it was considered too large. When the General Committee cut the numbers, Stephenson found himself removed although he was the only one with recent experience – especially of limited-overs cricket. In later years he was able to describe his great fortune in coming to Hampshire and his career as 'a great life' but there was always a sense of disappointment at the way he was treated in the end. He played for most of that final season and then retired to take up a teaching and coaching role in a local school. Twenty-five years later he was still there.

In 1980 Pocock's career as captain began unhappily, as the still-young David Rock walked away from county cricket before the season began. Subsequently he played a little Southern League cricket with South Hants Touring Club but fairly soon turned his back on that as well. Pocock inherited Jesty, Turner, Cowley, Rice, Stephenson and Taylor from Gilliat's golden period, as well as slow left-armer John Southern, although Taylor acknowledges that he played for at least a season more than he should have done. Having begun his Hampshire career with the Championship he retired at the end of the season – this time with the wooden spoon. He was appointed assistant secretary and eventually marketing manager and stayed with Hampshire for another 20 years. Bob Stephenson hit a rapid 65 against the Australians in early August but was then replaced by Parks and he too retired.

Among the other younger players, Tremlett and Nicholas appeared quite regularly in the county side and Terry, Parks, Hayward, Massey and Hardy showed promise for the 2nd XI. Although they were not all Hampshire-born, they had all arrived at the club from school and were in this sense genuine Hampshire cricketers. They were perhaps the most promising group of young players since the mid-1950s, with Peter Sainsbury from that era as their coach.

Of the regular bowlers only Keith Stevenson averaged under thirty and the Australian Shaun Graf enjoyed little success, while spinners Cowley and Southern shared 91 wickets between them in 1,000 overs. Another pace bowler, Steve Malone, had joined from Essex but took just 13 wickets in seven matches. During the 1960s Shackleton, White and Cottam provided Hampshire with a regular and very fine pace attack. Since then, Hampshire's opening bowlers had included Holder, Rice, Herman, Mottram, Roberts, Elms, Stevenson and Malone but there had never been a really settled opening pair. During the 1980s Marshall would lead the attack and Tremlett became an excellent first change, but otherwise a succession of pace bowlers was tried and generally discarded.

The one real success of the summer was a young South African batsman who had played a little with Glamorgan 2nd XI. Chris Smith was the only man to pass 1,000 runs and average over thirty. His parents were British, he held a British passport and, while he had played as an overseas signing in 1981, the cricket authorities agreed that by 1983 he could qualify as an English player. It was said that his younger brother was also a promising batsman.

Hampshire won only one match all season in the Championship, in late August at Bournemouth, and they were bottom of the table for the only time since 1905. The victory owed much to Tremlett with two half-centuries as an opening batsman but also to Malcolm Marshall. He returned from the Test series for a few games and in this defeat of Worcestershire returned match figures of 9-92. Sadly in the next match at Trent Bridge Hampshire lost by an innings after collapsing to 29-9 in the second innings. It was a measure of their problems that Steve Malone top scored with twenty.

They lost all their Benson & Hedges Cup matches but defeated Derbyshire in the Gillette Cup thanks to a magnificent century from Jesty. He then had a cartilage operation and Yorkshire won the quarter-final with ease. Only Glamorgan managed fewer than Hampshire's six wins on Sunday afternoons.

1980 was, then, a very hard season. For 1981, the returning West Indians Marshall and Greenidge replaced Graf. Those major players led the averages and ensured an easier year for Pocock. The batting was fallible but Hayward showed promise and with 101* against the Sri Lankans at Bournemouth became the third man to score a century on first-class debut for the county. John Rice played in only half the matches and bowled rarely but he enjoyed a golden end to the season. At Hove, Tremlett opened with Greenidge in a tired state after the birth of his son and future Hampshire bowler Christopher the previous night, and was run out without facing from the first ball. Rice then hit an unbeaten maiden century – perhaps a unique achievement in carrying his bat apart from the first ball? Hampshire lost heavily but went on to Edgbaston where Rice opened and scored 161* and forty.

By the season's end Warwickshire replaced them at the foot of the table while Hampshire rose to seventh place. They also won a Benson & Hedges match although they contrived to lose by three runs to a Minor Counties side including Richard Lewis, now playing for Dorset with Bob Herman. Malone took 8-50 in his NatWest Trophy season but Lancashire won their quarter-final meeting. Hampshire also rose from 11th to sixth in the Sunday League. Hampshire's 2nd XI won their Championship for the third time as Chris and brother Robin Smith played some fine innings, while Southern and off spinner Mike Bailey were their

45   *Trevor Jesty.*

leading bowlers. Meanwhile at Headingley, Botham and Willis enjoyed themselves against the Australians as England retained the Ashes.

On and off the field Hampshire's fortunes improved. The 1982 *Hampshire Handbook* included an architect's impression of the new squash and social centre on the site of the indoor school, which, when built, would be called 'The County Club'. On the field, Hampshire rose again in the Championship to third place, although 75 points behind the Champions Middlesex. They were fourth equal on Sundays but less successful in the knock-out competitions. In the NatWest Trophy their home quarter-final against Surrey began at 10a.m. in misty weather. Jackman took 6-22 and Clarke conceded just 11 runs in his nine overs and Hampshire were 17-3 and 38-4 before Turner dragged the score past 100. Surrey won by eight wickets in mid-afternoon.

Greenidge and Marshall were again in excellent form but there were other remarkable performances, none more than from Trevor Jesty who at last fulfilled all his promise, scoring eight first-class centuries and 1,645 runs at 58.75. He was also second in the bowling averages where the top six all averaged less than twenty-five. Most remarkable was Kevin Emery from Wiltshire, who opened the bowling with Marshall and took 79 wickets. He won the national 'Bowler of the Year Award' and it appeared that Hampshire had a settled attack at last.

In addition Mark Nicholas played regularly, scored three centuries and passed 1,000 runs for the first time. The one sad story was that of John Rice. He has said that in most seasons he would worry whether he had done enough to win another contract. He opened the batting with Greenidge for most of the season but his 777 runs came at less than twenty per innings and he rarely bowled, even on Sundays. In late August he heard that this time the contract would not be forthcoming and having been dismissed cheaply by Gloucestershire he walked off Dean Park, depositing his bat in the nearest rubbish bin. Many supporters thought and hoped he might be offered a coaching role but he went instead to Eton where he remains, although he has worked effortlessly with Barry Reed, coaching Hampshire Under-19s. Recent products of the school have included Alex Loudon and James Bruce.

Richard Hayward, reserve wicketkeeper Chris Curzon and Mike Bailey also left the staff. Chris Smith, still qualifying by residence, scored most runs for the 2nd XI while brother Robin scored 854 runs in 10 completed innings and Paul Terry outscored him. The young batsmen began to look very promising.

In 1983 much of the promise was realised. Mark Nicholas scored 1,418 runs at 37.31 – a very similar return to 1982. But whereas he was third then, by 1983 seven players had higher averages. Greenidge was again top of the group but he and Marshall missed some matches as the World Cup returned to England. While he was away Hampshire could play Robin Smith, who scored three centuries in seven matches. One was against Lancashire at Bournemouth and it gave Hampshire supporters a taste of the future. Hampshire's first four batsmen were Paul Terry, Chris Smith, Mark Nicholas and Robin Smith, and the two brothers both made centuries as Hampshire scored 357-3 declared. Over the season, Chris Smith scored 1,845 runs at 57.65 and he was selected for England against New Zealand at Lord's, the first Hampshire cricketer to play in a Test in England for 20 years.

In the circumstances there was some sympathy for Trevor Jesty, who never won that honour, and in 1983 was also overlooked for England's unsuccessful World Cup side. Their first six were Fowler, Tavaré, Gower, Lamb, Gatting and Botham, while Greenidge and Marshall appeared in the final where they were unexpectedly and quite heavily beaten by India.

Jesty had topped Hampshire's averages as they reached the Benson & Hedges quarter-finals before losing to Kent by just five runs. Chasing 199 to win, Terry and Greenidge took them to 131 before the first wicket fell and they should have progressed. In the NatWest Trophy victories over Hertfordshire, Glamorgan and Gloucestershire took them to Canterbury again, this time in a semi-final, but they lost this more heavily. They were fifth in the Sunday League and had clearly rebuilt successfully over the three years but there was one real disappointment that may well have cost them the Championship over the next few years. Kevin

Emery, after his stunning first season, bowled a spate of no-balls on the first day of Championship cricket and three days later no-balls and wides in the Benson & Hedges Cup. He never recovered his form, taking just five wickets in the season and his career was effectively finished after just one year. Steve Malone worked hard in his place while Tim Tremlett had a fine season, taking 63 first-class wickets at 21.36. Nigel Cowley was the leading slow bowler.

Nick Pocock was never more than an average player but he was an enterprising cricketer who deserves great credit for rebuilding the side over this period. Tim Tremlett remembers his captaincy with great fondness. In retrospect, Charlie Knott doubted whether he was 'really good enough' at the start in 1980 but he became a good captain. 1984 would be his last season in charge. Unlike his predecessor he went willingly, but sadly the change again brought real difficulties.

The season itself was less successful than 1983 as Hampshire slipped to 15th in the Championship, ninth in the Sunday League and nowhere in the knock-out cups. There were two main reasons, the absences of Marshall and Greenidge who were engaged in humiliating England at the time. While England's batsmen

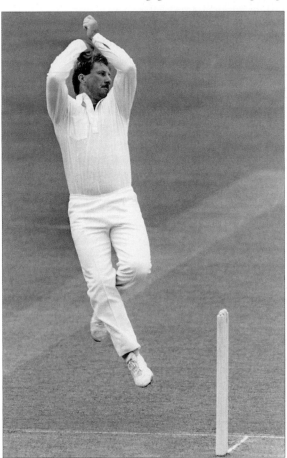

46 *'Dougal' – off spinner Nigel Cowley.*

failed regularly, Jesty scored 1,625 runs at over forty per innings but was still not selected for a failing England side. Chris Smith was less successful and lost his Test place, although Paul Terry began the season in fine form and was picked for England.

In the first Test, debutant Andy Lloyd was struck on the helmet by a ball from Marshall, retired hurt with 10 and never played Test cricket again. The West Indies won by an innings. They won the second Test by nine wickets as Marshall took 6-85 and Greenidge scored 214* and England lost after declaring for the first time in 36 years. Terry replaced Gatting at Leeds but scored just eight and one – Marshall took 7-53 with a badly fractured left thumb and batted one-handed.

Greenidge scored another double century at Old Trafford but England started well with an opening partnership of ninety. Terry, batting at number three, reached seven when his arm was broken by a ball from Winston Davis. He returned at the fall of the ninth wicket to bat one-handed as Tennyson had done for England in 1921 and Marshall at Leeds. This enabled Lamb to reach his century

before Garner bowled Terry. England
followed on, Terry followed Lloyd into
Test oblivion and the match was lost.
The fifth Test completed the 'Blackwash',
with Marshall taking 5-35.

For Hampshire, Terry missed the rest
of the season. Nigel Cowley passed
1,000 runs, as did Nicholas and Turner,
but apart from Tremlett the bowling
was not consistent. There were two
spinners, Cowley, whose fine season
included 56 wickets, and Rajesh Maru,
who had been signed from Middlesex
to replace John Southern. He took 47
wickets and was a good slip fielder.
While missing Greenidge and Marshall,
Hampshire did field two West Indians.
One, the evocatively named Elvis Reifer,
is sometimes rumoured to have been
a case of mistaken identity. In truth
he was not the worst overseas signing.
He was innocently delighted to be
with Hampshire and took 49 first-
class wickets. The second was a Home
Counties club bowler, spotted through
the Charlie Knott network and offered

47   *Slow left arm Rajesh Maru who came from Middlesex.*

a trial with the 2nd XI. Knott always remembered the situation very clearly
and it reveals something of the team-building at a club which was spreading
its nets beyond the county to recruit good cricketers.

The demise of Kevin Emery and the gradual disappearance of Stevenson and
Malone left Hampshire's attack somewhat bare again. They had signed a promising
young bowler, Steven Andrew, London-born and Dorset-based, but he needed
time to develop. In addition to Raj Maru, Hampshire had signed Chris Goldie
from Middlesex as an understudy to Bobby Parks. He still played in London
league cricket at weekends and Charlie Knott asked him about the pace bowlers
in the leagues. He provided a list of five but identified Cardigan Connor as the
best, so Charlie Knott and Peter Sainsbury invited him to play at Bournemouth
against Somerset's 2nd XI.

Knott did not plan to spend too long at the ground but was impressed with
Connor in the warm-up. Malone, Emery and Stevenson struggled initially against
the openers Wyatt and Ollis (who scored 131), but when Connor came on he
took 5-58 in 21 overs. Peter Sainsbury was not completely convinced but Knott
was sure, walked around the boundary and offered Connor a contract. Knott
remembers that he 'jumped up in the air as excited as anything and that was it'.
Within a fortnight he was called into the Championship side and against the
same county took 4-31 and 2-53 in a 10-wicket victory. He finished the season

with 62 wickets and if they were a little expensive he was learning the game and took 7-37 against Kent at Bournemouth.

Hampshire gave a debut to another promising batsman in that match, the opener Tony Middleton. Unfortunately Connor's figures reflected a pitch of variable bounce and movement and Kent had Derek Underwood, who was well suited to such conditions. He took 4-34 and 8-87, Middleton scored 10 and five and he returned to the 2nd XI as Hampshire lost.

By this time Mark Nicholas was leading Hampshire. In mid-July vice-captain Trevor Jesty replaced Nick Pocock for two Championship matches but in early August Pocock announced his retirement from the first team. He revealed that he had been somewhat 'reluctant' to continue in 1984 and was happy to make space for younger players like Hardy or Middleton. Mark Nicholas was appointed acting captain and under him Hampshire drew three and lost four of the remaining seven matches, but the worst outcome was that Jesty was sufficiently upset to leave his home club of 20 seasons.

On the day after Nicholas first led the side, Hampshire won a thrilling Sunday League match against Warwickshire at Portsmouth by just one run, but the headlines in the local newspaper were reserved for Jesty's angry response. At the end of the match he resigned as vice-captain and told the *Portsmouth News*, 'I feel as if I have been kicked in the teeth.' In later years Charlie Knott revealed that he had indicated to Jesty that he was likely to get the post but then changed his mind. The pair had met at Knott's home and after two hours of discussion had parted 'good friends'. He expected Jesty to remain at Hampshire but later the same day Jesty telephoned him to say that he would leave when his contract expired at the end of the season. He moved to Surrey and captained them in some matches before again being overlooked in favour of Ian Greig. His playing career finished at Lancashire but he still lives in Hampshire and is now a first-class umpire.

One man who had advised on the succession was David Turner, and he had opted for 'positive reasons' for Nicholas – in later years Turner believed that recommendation to have been the correct choice and Nicholas's record suggests much the same. Nonetheless, the acrimonious departure of Jesty was a tragedy for he is one of the greatest of Hampshire's local players and as good as any of his generation never to play Test cricket. Another outcome was that for some weeks the Hampshire players were forbidden from talking to the press about any aspect of their cricket. At the end of the season, the county committee confirmed Nicholas as the new captain and in the week before Christmas they agreed to release Jesty to join Surrey. The *Guardian* quoted him as saying:

> If they had told me the real reason I might be prepared to stay on but they have been dishonest with me … It definitely seems like old school tie to me … Perhaps I don't have enough initials in my name … but I have nothing against Mark, it is the Hampshire committee I cannot now play for.

With the emergence of Connor, the promise of Andrew and the imminent return of Marshall, Hampshire released Malone, who joined Glamorgan, Emery and Mel Hussain, who never played for the county side but whose younger brother Nasser would have a significant impact on Essex and England in the following decade.

Even with Jesty gone, Nicholas's first real side was overstocked with batsmen. Robin Smith was now 'English' and he joined brother Chris, Paul Terry and Gordon Greenidge in an international line-up, supplemented by Nicholas, Hardy and Middleton. The new captain began the season scoring 121 for the MCC against Champion county Essex. In his first appearance, Robin Smith scored 85 against Dilley and Underwood and there were further eighties for Terry and Chris Smith in the second innings. It augured well for the Championship season with the West Indian players still to arrive. In Marshall's place, another former Middlesex man, Kevan James, opened the bowling. Charlie Knott remembered that he had not been 'bothered about money one bit – he was just pleased to come'.

He batted and bowled left-handed but strangely threw with his right. In this first season he batted down the order and opened the attack with Connor in the early weeks. Then at Taunton Hampshire subsided to 90-5 overnight and lost Marshall and Cowley at 107-7. Tremlett joined James and the pair rescued Hampshire with their record eighth-wicket partnership of 227. Both men made their maiden centuries – in Tremlett's case his only one on his father's old ground against a Somerset attack that included Garner, Botham and Marks. On the third day, Marshall thumped Garner for six into the river as Hampshire won in the final over. They repeated the feat in the next match against Glamorgan.

Hampshire fared well in the Benson & Hedges competition and against Somerset Parks held five catches and unusually won the Gold Award for his wicketkeeping. They met Leicestershire in the quarter-final but lost by four runs. They had their revenge with a four-wicket victory over the same opponents in the NatWest and went to Taunton for the quarter-final. Terry and Robin Smith hit centuries and 299 looked beyond Somerset at 43-5. Botham threatened to rescue them, unilaterally declared the setting sun too bright and walked off. Marshall dismissed him next morning and Hampshire entertained Essex in the semi-final.

Essex chose to field and Hampshire struggled to 224-8. Only Gooch stood firm but with his score on 53 at 125-5 Robin Smith threw down the stumps with Gooch out of his ground. Hampshire-born Barrie Meyer declared not out and Essex came off for bad light. There was a delay on the second morning but Essex eventually won with the scores level, having lost only seven wickets. A Lord's final was still a dream and, of that 1985 side, two men, Tremlett and Greenidge, would never get there with Hampshire. Essex also won the Sunday League title with Hampshire third.

Meanwhile, Nicholas had gone back to Lord's to score another century for the MCC against Alan Border's Australian tourists. Jon Hardy, who could not break into the side, was proving too good for 2nd XI cricket, scoring two centuries in the match at Eastbourne.

After eight matches Hampshire led the table from Gloucestershire and Middlesex but at Bournemouth they were thwarted by the London county in a match that would have a crucial bearing on the title. They set Middlesex 265 to win in 67 overs and after 38 overs reduced them to 82-8, but Jamie Sykes and Simon Hughes held out and the match was drawn. James cheered the side by taking 6-22 as the Australians were dismissed for 76 and Hampshire had them struggling to avoid defeat on the third day. Sadly the bad weather, which helped the bowlers in this match, also thwarted Hampshire in a number of Championship games when they looked well placed.

Hampshire won the two Bournemouth week matches and were heartened by Andrew's 6-43 against Gloucestershire. In early September they drew at Folkestone and then met Northamptonshire in the penultimate game. They scored 300-8 declared thanks to a Greenidge century and Marshall reduced Northamptonshire to 61-5, but Capel and Harper rescued them. Hampshire declared, setting Northamptonshire 241 to win in 60 overs. They started well but Nicholas took two wickets and Maru worked his way through the batsmen. Nicholas kept him on to encourage the chase – he took five wickets but conceded 5.5 runs per over. Northamptonshire were 214-7, 228-8 and 234-9. Maru bowled the last ball to Harper with the batsman needing to score six and Hampshire needing a wicket. The ball sailed over the boundary, Hampshire lost and the 16 points and the Championship went too.

Middlesex began the final game one point ahead and secured the title with a maximum-points victory. Hampshire's final match at Trent Bridge was drawn and Hampshire were runners-up for the third time in their history – disappointing but also riches compared with five years earlier and a tribute to the team-building of Knott and Sainsbury. In that final match Chris Smith completed 2,000 runs while his brother, Greenidge, Nicholas and Terry all exceeded 1,000 runs. Jon Hardy scored 742 at 35.33 but chose to leave to seek a more regular place with Somerset. Malcolm Marshall's 95 wickets cost 17.68 and Tremlett and Maru both took over seventy wickets. If Andrew, Connor or James had been more incisive with the new ball, Hampshire must have been Champions.

For 1986, Hampshire signed the Dutch pace bowler Paul-Jan (P.J.) Bakker and they gave contracts to two promising local players, all-rounder Jon Ayling and wicketkeeper Adrian Aymes. Both had come through the Hampshire colts, as had David Hacker, Mark O'Connor and Ian Chivers, who all spent time on the staff in the mid-1980s without breaking into the first team. The colts side in 1985 also featured Rupert Cox and Ian Turner. In the following year Julian Wood was the colts' leading batsman and Shaun Udal impressed with his off spin bowling. Jimmy Gray and Mike Taylor were now involved in their coaching.

The performance in 1985 suggested that Hampshire were now a strong side but in 1986 they failed to progress in the Benson & Hedges or NatWest competitions. In the Championship they slipped to sixth place, not least because of a considerable number of injuries.

The players were too inconsistent, although Greenidge passed 2,000 runs for the first time, but there was a strange incident at Lord's that perhaps presaged the end of his county career. In a rain-affected game, Middlesex asked Hampshire to score 224 in 54 overs and with Greenidge undefeated this might seem a reasonable task. In fact Hampshire lost wickets at 40, 51 and 78 and Greenidge (70*) decided to call off the chase. With Nicholas injured, Tremlett, batting at number five, was instructed to urge an attempt but apparently Greenidge was not talking. After 43 overs and at the earliest opportunity, Greenidge walked from the field but there

48 *Kevan James.*

was an unhappy dressing room and allegedly a physical confrontation with his captain. There were occasions in the later stages of his Hampshire career when Greenidge could be uncommunicative but it cannot outweigh the enormous contribution of this great batsman. Tremlett takes the view that the death of his young daughter had a terrible impact on him for a while and may explain some of the difficulties. Happily the season ended well for Hampshire and Greenidge, as in late August he played successive innings of 222, 103, 180* and 128 – a Hampshire record for consecutive centuries.

In the Sunday League, Hampshire began by winning eight of the first nine matches. There was a mid-season blip followed by wins against Yorkshire and Derbyshire and on the penultimate Sunday a trip to The Oval where, as events transpired, victory would bring a third Sunday League title.

They batted first but only Greenidge helped them to stumble to 56-4 when Kevan James scored a good half century. Hampshire's 40-over total of 149-8 looked inadequate but they bowled well and Surrey were 17-2, 45-4 and 117-6. They needed a difficult 29 from 16 balls but Thomas hit successive boundaries. Connor, who had dropped Thomas, bowled the last over with Surrey needing just seven

49   *Mark Nicholas with his squad that won the 1986 John Player Special League.*

runs. He bowled two dot balls before James caught the Surrey batsman, Needham hit a single, then James threw to Connor for a run out. Gray needed six to win from Connor's last ball but he failed, Hampshire won and the title was theirs – their first for eight years and the second Hampshire trophy in Tremlett's career after he took 26 wickets. Robin Smith scored 629 runs and averaged almost seventy. This was the final year of John Player's sponsorship. From 1987 it would become the Refuge Assurance League but, once the tobacconists departed, Hampshire never won it again, switching their preference to Benson & Hedges.

Although cricketers will always say they value the Championship most highly, the limited-overs trophies do provide great excitement for players and spectators and Nicholas's side now set about establishing themselves as pre-eminent at the shorter game. From 1986–92 they won four trophies – more than any other side in that same period, and also reached a number of other semi-finals.

To a large extent their success was built around their batting. Terry, the Smith brothers, Nicholas, Turner and Middleton all contributed and the all-rounders James, Cowley and Ayling could score runs and bowl effectively. Parks and Aymes were the wicketkeepers and Connor became an important bowler. At various points two overseas bowlers, Steven Jefferies and Aqib Javed, played their parts while Shaun Udal emerged as a rival and partner to Raj Maru.

Hampshire eventually reached a Lord's final in 1988 when only Jon Ayling on either side represented the county of his birth. Nonetheless, most of the Hampshire side were products of their colts or 2nd XI. They got to Lord's after a rain-threatened victory in Chelmsford with a century from Paul Terry. Oddly, just

50 *Chris Smith, Hampshire and England. (PE)*

51   *The young Robin Smith batting without a helmet. (IM)*

52   *Lords B&H Cup Final, 1988 – the winning run.*

as they had beaten Derbyshire to win their first Championship in 1961 and first Sunday League in 1975, so they would beat the Midland side in their first final.

The game hinged on Nicholas's inspired insistence that he should field at forward short leg to Jefferies' considerable swing. The South African enjoyed only modest success with Hampshire but this was his great day and brought him a special place in the county's history. He and Connor bowled nervously at first as extras and Barnett took Derbyshire to 27, but they fell away rapidly to 32-4. John Morris sought a recovery but was run out by fine fielding from Cowley and Derbyshire slipped to 117 all out. Holding, Malcolm and Mortensen attacked Hampshire but Robin Smith played a brilliant innings until he fell for 38 to an astonishing catch by Goldsmith. It was perhaps fitting that Nicholas the captain and the very senior pro Turner saw Hampshire home by seven wickets before opening time in the London pubs.

In 1987 Hampshire had finished fifth in the Championship and seventh in the Sunday League. Despite their cup success in 1988 it was a West Indies year and, as Greenidge, Marshall and the others trounced England again, Hampshire slipped to 15th – a familiar story in summers without Marshall. They were ninth in the Sunday League but did reach the NatWest semi-final, losing in the gloom at Worcester as Hick took 4-54.

He was of course the latest Southern African to help England during a mixed decade. Australia were still not strong and Gower and Gatting both won Ashes series, but the West Indies ruled Test cricket. In 1988 the first Test was drawn,

53   *The day after – Sunday celebrations with Saturday's hero Steve Jefferies.*

54   *Mark Nicholas celebrates on the balcony.*

but Marshall served notice with 6-69 and West Indies won the next four Tests. Marshall finished the series with 35 wickets at an incredible average of 12.65 yet was only in third place. Greenidge managed just one century but a new Hampshire batsman appeared in the series. Robin Smith made his debut in the fourth Test at Leeds, scoring 38 and 11 and passed fifty in the final test. Unlike his brother Chris and teammate Paul Terry, this was the start of a lengthy Test career.

Although Terry's Test career was over, he was still a fine county batsman and in 1988 he made his highest innings of 190 against the touring Sri Lankans. Mark Nicholas was keen to declare but his teammates were willing Terry to his first double century and to help him Tim Tremlett turned back the dressing room clock. Sadly Terry got out and Nicholas was not amused. 'Trooper' is a respectable Director of Cricket but he has a playful streak, which perhaps he reserves for his skippers. Early in his career he was amusing the dressing room with an imitation of Gilliat's left-handed 'hoik' over midwicket – unaware of the presence of his captain behind him. Incidentally, Terry with 37 centuries, Horton (32), Turner (27) and Rogers (26) are the only Hampshire batsmen to have passed 25 centuries without ever reaching 200. Rogers and Terry share another strange 'non-achievement' record as the only Hampshire players with more than 250 appearances, except wicketkeepers, who never took a first-class wicket.

In 1989 a stronger Australian side won the six-match Ashes series 4-0, although Robin Smith led the English averages with 553 runs at 61.44 and two centuries. Meanwhile, Marshall returned to Hampshire but, after more than twenty years, Greenidge did not. He had scored almost twenty thousand first-class runs for the county, averaging in the mid-40s and his 315 catches came at more than one per match. He had moreover given wonderful pleasure to generations of supporters and, with Barry Richards, had formed one of the truly great opening partnerships in county cricket. Nonetheless there was a feeling that, in later years, incidents like the one at Lord's had driven a wedge between him and his younger colleagues. Towards the end of 1988 he was seen walking around Dean Park with Charlie Knott trying to negotiate a deal, but it did not come. Having left, he severed all links with the county until the new regime of the 21st century and there was an assumption among many supporters that, as with Roberts, the going had been difficult.

This negotiation was one of Charlie Knott's last major activities as he handed over as Cricket Chairman to Jimmy Gray. Jimmy brought Neville Rogers in to work with him and Neville expressed optimism about the strength of the younger players, including Ayling, Aymes, Cox, Scott, Shine, Ian Turner, Udal and Wood. Under Peter Sainsbury this promised to be another fertile period for Hampshire's colts. In the Championship Hampshire rose again to sixth but in that and the Sunday League they had a disappointing final month. They also quickly lost their hold on the Benson & Hedges Cup. In the end the excitement was reserved for the NatWest Trophy and yet another semi-final. They beat Cheshire and Glamorgan with ease before, at The Oval, Robin Smith (125*) led them from 23-3 in successful pursuit of 229. In the semi-final against Middlesex at Northlands Road, the visitors opened with a stand of 165. Hampshire did well to hold them to 267 and Chris Smith compiled a marvellous century in reply. But a beamer from Angus Fraser broke his thumb and Hampshire finished four runs short.

In 1990, Hampshire were third in the Championship but two wins behind Middlesex and fifth in the Sunday League. They had released Jefferies and Cowley, who joined Glamorgan, Tim Tremlett effectively retired from playing to move into coaching and Steven Andrew joined Essex. Hampshire signed local spin bowler Darren Flint, West Indian Linden Joseph and, most surprisingly, David Gower. His arrival undoubtedly strengthened the side but it did little to encourage young batsmen like Scott, Wood and Cox. However, Tony Middleton passed 1,000 runs for the first time. The batting was strong but only Marshall (19.18) had a bowling average below thirty-five.

The Championship was probably decided in August when Middlesex compiled 430-7 at Bournemouth thanks to a rare Emburey century. Neil Taylor, a Southern League bowler from New Milton, took 3-44 for the London county as Hampshire struggled in reply and the match was drawn. Hampshire won only three of their last eight matches.

So once again supporters thrilled to the NatWest Trophy. Things were tight for the most part as Hampshire beat Leicestershire by one run and Essex by scoring 307-5 against 307-6. This was some revenge for 1985 and the highest score chasing in England. The quarter-final against Yorkshire was much easier. Hampshire scored only 229-9 in 60 overs but won by 111 runs. At one stage Yorkshire were 40-6 until the future Hampshire player Peter Hartley hit a fifty. Marshall took 4-17 and must have hoped at last for his first final.

They met Northamptonshire in the semi-final at Southampton. The visitors batted first and while no one passed 60 they set a target of 285. At 55-3 Hampshire were in trouble but Gower (86), and Marshall (77) added 141. They reached 246-4 but the required rate was high. P.J. Bakker needed to hit the last ball for two but managed only a single. Nicholas and Marshall were visibly upset on the balcony with Marshall reluctant to collect his match award.

Rupert Cox scored his maiden Championship century at Worcestershire but played mainly in the 2nd XI, where another promising young batsman, Sean Morris, topped the averages with 812 runs in 10 innings. Hampshire were moving into the 1990s still poised for immediate success but with the additional comfort of a group of young players with real potential.

6

1991–2000

WINNING THE Benson & Hedges Cup in 1988 did not immediately solve Hampshire's semi-final anxieties for they reached the same stage in the next three years in the NatWest Trophy, losing by increasingly small margins to Worcestershire, Middlesex and Northamptonshire. The last defeat was a particularly bitter blow to Malcolm Marshall, who was missing in 1991 on his final tour of England with the West Indies. During his Hampshire career his presence had a huge impact on the team's performance in the County Championship yet his only Hampshire success at that point was in the 1986 Sunday League.

During the winter of 1990–1, Richard Scott, like Jon Hardy before him, left Hampshire in search of a regular place, joining Gloucestershire. With Marshall absent, Pakistani Aqib Javed was Hampshire's first overseas signing from the Asian continent – there has still never been one from India. He was a promising pace bowler in the Test side behind Wasim Akram and Waqar Younis. At the climax to the season his path would cross Waqar's on a momentous day.

Before that, Hampshire struggled. They won their first Championship match in late July, eventually slipping from third to ninth and they never once took 20 wickets in a match. Worse, they were for the first time bottom of the table in the Sunday League. They did reach the Benson & Hedges quarter-final but lost at Chelmsford, while in the rain at Reading they had to wait until the second day to beat Berkshire in the NatWest Trophy. But then suddenly, in that one competition, they played superbly. They beat the powerful Lancashire side by eight wickets and Nottinghamshire by seven wickets. Robin Smith scored 43*, 79* and 67, brother Chris 66 and 105* and Connor and Udal bowled particularly well. Against Nottinghamshire they even survived the controversial run out of Paul Terry, accidentally impeded. Nicholas strode out to debate the verdict with umpires and opposing captain but the decision stood.

So they went again to a semi-final, this time at Edgbaston. Seven times in this competition, in 1966, 1976, 1983, 1985, 1988, 1989 and 1990, they had fallen at this hurdle but this time they made no mistake. They dismissed Warwickshire for 172 with Connor taking 4-29 and Maru and Udal conceding just 50 runs in their 24 overs. By contrast, Terry 62* and Robin Smith 64* took Hampshire to a nine-wicket victory with 10 overs to spare.

Chris Smith was the one man out, for twenty-three. During the season he scored over one thousand five hundred runs at an average around sixty-five and passed 15,000 career runs for the county. This record included 41 centuries and a career average over forty-five but the semi-final was his last appearance for the county. The immediate offer of a lucrative position in sports management in Australia was sufficient to lure him away a few weeks before the final.

Tony Middleton played in 18 of the 24 matches in 1991 and after Chris Smith departed he remained in the side with relatively little success in the Championship or the Sunday League. He had never played in the NatWest Trophy but was earmarked for the final against Surrey and opened the batting against the same side at The Oval in the three preceding days. In this 'phoney war' Surrey dealt Hampshire two major blows, beating them by 171 runs while Waqar Younis broke Nicholas's hand, denying him his chance at Lord's.

It had been a long journey for Middleton who had come through Hampshire's schools and colts sides with players like Adi Aymes and Richard Scott. He made his debut for Hampshire 2nd XI in 1982, scoring 21 v Surrey, opening with Chris Smith, and 14 v Middlesex, opening with Paul Terry – two players who would block his path to a first-team place over the next decade. The Middlesex attack that day included three future Hampshire bowlers, Maru, James and Cowans.

Middleton's progress was rewarded when Hampshire offered him a contract for the following season: 'I was very excited – Peter Sainsbury asked me would I like to be a professional cricketer? It was a moment I will always remember.'

At the start of the 1983 season he opened for the 2nd XI at Taunton against a Somerset side for whom a mysterious D.C.S. Compton appeared at number 10 but did not bowl, bat, captain or keep wicket! The Hampshire line-up indicates the level of competition for batting places: Terry, Middleton, Smith (R.), Hardy, Scott and Hussain (Nasser's brother), all batsmen and all under 25 years of age. In the first team that year Chris Smith, Greenidge, Nicholas, Jesty, and Terry all passed 1,000 runs while Robin Smith and David Turner both averaged above forty. Nonetheless, Middleton passed 30 regularly and finished the 2nd XI Championship season with 500 runs at around twenty-seven apiece.

He remembers his first season in such illustrious company as 'a bit daunting' but also recalls that he 'loved it'. In the early season the senior players reported back first and the newcomers' involvement was limited to 'fielding in practice matches and bowling in the nets'. There was only one coach – Peter Sainsbury – and Tony was willing to accept that this was the way it was, although 15 years later, he runs a very different system for his young charges at the county ground. He thinks that one or two of his younger colleagues felt overlooked and as the years progressed he became more frustrated and perhaps 'resentful', but the first year was highly enjoyable.

But his patience was eventually rewarded – albeit later than he may have wished. In the county match at The Oval in 1991, not one of Hampshire's batsmen made 50 and Waqar's match figures were 12-92. Middleton was dismissed for six and three but with Nicholas's injury he was definitely playing in the final, where David Gower would captain Hampshire. Shaun Udal and Cardigan Connor, who had missed this Championship defeat, came into the side in place of Nicholas and Shine.

55 *David Gower who captained Hampshire to the 1991 Nat West Trophy. (IM)*

Gower won the toss and went with tradition in these finals, inviting Surrey to bat. Robinson was injured early and retired hurt and Ayling bowled Bicknell at 25, but Alec Stewart and Graham Thorpe added a century partnership before Ayling struck again. David Ward and Thorpe took Surrey beyond 200 when Connor took three late wickets and, despite losing only five men, Hampshire restricted them to 240 in their 60 overs.

Terry and Middleton weathered the Waqar storm and survived until the tea interval. Shortly afterwards, Terry was run out and Middleton and Robin Smith took the score to 160 before Middleton was bowled for an excellent seventy-eight. There was a brief slump as the blazing hot day turned to twilight and in the gloom Ayling hit an incredible flat six backward of point into the Tavern stand. Hampshire needed 10 to win from 13 balls when Smith was run out for

78 following a lucky ricochet. The final over started with a single but next ball Aymes was run out at 238. Maru pushed another single and with two needed from three balls Ayling hit a four to long leg and the trophy was Hampshire's.

Tony Middleton's recollections of that marvellous day are still clear and he says it was the 'most memorable day of my career'.

> Partly because I played well and it was a lovely day with great weather. I was nervous, especially the night before when I was petrified but our Championship defeat over the previous three days did not affect things. Mark's injury made selection easier but I don't know who would have been left out. Mark did not play a massive part because David Gower did it his way – he was more conservative than Mark and more defensive but he was also relaxed and encouraged us to go out and enjoy ourselves.

Of the detail of the game he remembered that Hampshire's bowling was good 'especially before lunch' and he noticed how the support lifted the team: 'I had played at Lord's before but with a full house the noise was massive.'

Although he remembered Robin Smith's 'brilliant' innings he felt that it was bettered when he scored 191 against Australia at Southampton two years later. At the end of the final he felt delighted but also 'absolutely shattered'.

Winning the cup was a marvellous achievement at the end of an often difficult season. Nicholas's side was beginning to age but the 2nd XI showed promise, finishing in fourth place. Their leading players included batsmen Sean Morris, Cox, Wood and the youthful Laney. Slow left-armers Ian Turner and Darren Flint were leading wicket-takers and a promising batsman/wicketkeeper Mark Garaway from the Isle of Wight played a couple of games. At the end of the season the club announced that Richard Hayward would return to coach these young players. Peter Sainsbury finally retired after about forty years at the club and Tim Tremlett moved up to work with the first team.

There was a sad moment in December 1991 when the death was announced of John Arlott. It is a comforting thought that he did so after his county had won the fourth and last of the major trophies. Although now living on Alderney he was Hampshire-born and had actively supported the sides of the 1920s and 1930s, making one appearance for Hampshire as 12th Man at Worcester.

He was not much of a cricketer but after war service in the police force he fell into cricket commentating and then journalism by chance – an amateur who quickly turned professional and reached the highest standards. But even when commenting on England v Australia from Lord's or Melbourne there was always something of rural Hampshire about his delivery and his manner. Through the 1950s and 1960s he befriended many of the major Hampshire players and Neville Rogers and Leo Harrison remained lifelong friends. If you asked Rogers how a man of such modest playing talents became such an astute observer of players he would reply that Arlott knew which questions to ask and was a good listener with a reliable memory. But he also commanded his medium, written and spoken language, in a manner perfect for its purpose. As well as supporting Hampshire, he had been a member of the General Committee and a vice-president.

56   *1992: David Gower wins a B&H match for Hampshire on their way to Lord's.*

So Hampshire began 1992 without Chris Smith, Peter Sainsbury or John Arlott but Marshall was back. In 1991, England delighted their supporters by sharing the series with the West Indies two matches apiece and Robin Smith averaged 83.2 with two centuries and 416 runs. By contrast Graeme Hick scored just 75 runs in seven innings to frustrate his admirers. DeFreitas was England's leading bowler and his 22 wickets were two more than Malcolm Marshall managed. It was also unusual to see a West Indies side lacking Gordon Greenidge, as Haynes and Simmons opened the batting.

It seemed then that Marshall was no longer the phenomenal force of the 1980s and unusually with him in the side Hampshire fell to 14th place in the following year, but the season did not begin like that and perhaps hinged on one match.

Before the end of May, Hampshire won three of the first four Championship matches during which time Smith, Terry and James all made hundreds and Middleton enjoyed an incredible run of scores. In his first five first-class matches he registered 153 v Sussex, 55 v Yorkshire, 121 v Oxford University, 221 & 1* v Surrey and 73 & 138* v Lancashire. He will talk about being able to achieve runs like this as a mental activity in which he focuses on what he is doing right and replicates it from the start of the next innings. In this respect he was at his best a very consistent batsman in the 2nd XI and Championship side. In the game against Lancashire, the enigmatic fast bowler Kevin Shine enjoyed his finest match, taking 5-58 and 8-47 including the hat-trick. Hampshire had set Lancashire 344 to win and they reached 132-0 before Shine's efforts reduced them to 171 all out.

57 *1992: Hampshire beat Somerset at Northlands Road and win a home semi-final for the first time in the 30th limited overs season.*

But Shine would often frustrate and on the next day he was omitted as Hampshire beat Middlesex by six wickets in a Benson & Hedges quarter-final. On 10 June Somerset came for the semi-final and Connor with 4-32 put them out for just 218. Terry, Smith and Gower ensured a comfortable victory and a third Lord's final in five years. Meanwhile Hampshire enjoyed the best of drawn Championship matches against Yorkshire and Warwickshire and both sides came close to victory in a thrilling game at Leicester where Hampshire, chasing 309, finished 294-9.

So they came to the crucial match against reigning champions Essex at Bournemouth over a mid-June weekend with both sides chasing the title. Nicholas (81) led the way, as they posted exactly 300 and the bowlers shared the wickets as Essex collapsed. At 149-8 Essex needed one run to make Hampshire bat again and Hussain was 63*. Then Udal trapped Illott and Middleton took a magnificent diving catch in the deep from Marshall's bowling to dismiss Hussain. Had he missed it, Essex would have avoided the follow on as the batsmen had crossed.

Essex batted again and lost Pritchard to Marshall for one. There was some resistance and Marshall was tiring but at the close of the second day (a Saturday) Essex were 105-4 and still well behind. On the Sunday Hampshire maintained their reasonable start in the league with an easy eight-wicket victory and they returned to the Championship final day in good spirits.

Connor soon dismissed nightwatchman Illott and at 165-7 Essex were only 14 ahead. But Garnham and Pringle made half-centuries, Shahid 48 and eventually Hampshire had to score 160 to win in a *minimum* of 26 overs. Victory would now be difficult and Middleton went first ball but Hampshire pursued the target. They also lost Terry and James, then from 54-3 they simply disintegrated. In the 28th over they were all out for 80, Essex had won a magnificent victory and Hampshire's Championship season – indeed their Championship decade – fell apart. They won only one more match in 1992, a rain-affected forfeiture at Arundel, and, when they lost at Chelmsford in late August, Essex were

Champions again. By contrast, Hampshire finished 15th with Durham bottom in their first-ever season.

Tony Middleton believes that the players did not realise the significance of that Essex match at the time but he was sure that the dressing room was 'awful' and as professionals there would have been a deal of swearing and anger. Ironically, had he not taken his spectacular catch Hampshire would probably have drawn the game. The memory of that match prompted him to describe cricket as 'all highs and lows' adding, 'I am more relaxed now but I miss the highs.' He believes that 'with Macko we should have won a Championship' but it was not to be.

Nonetheless, there was some cheer in the success of the local men as Middleton was the leading run-scorer and Udal the main wicket-taker while Wood and Shine also showed promise. In the NatWest Trophy they lost to Kent despite a Terry century two days before the same sides contested the Benson & Hedges final. This was the highlight of Hampshire's season and a special moment for Marshall, which heavy rain could not dampen, although it did cause the final to spill into the Sunday. On the first day Hampshire scored 253-5 in 55 overs with Smith again run out at Lord's, this time for ninety. Marshall scored 29* and, after a couple of Kent overs, the day finished. On a grey but clear Sunday morning Marshall took 3-33 and each bowler took wickets as Kent struggled with the chase. They were

58 *Robin Smith at Lord's, 1992 – a third winners' medal and second Man of the Match award.*

59   *1992 at Lord's: the B&H Cup Final – The Champions on the balcony.*

eventually dismissed for 212 and while Smith again won the match award, for Hampshire this was Marshall's match. Less prominently, an injury to Aymes also enabled Parks one last day on the big stage in his benefit season.

At the end of 1992 Parks retired and P.J. Bakker also left the staff. Hampshire signed Martin Jean-Jacques from Derbyshire and three young men, Jim Bovill, Jason Laney and Mark Garaway, were given contracts. Ayling had enjoyed his

60   *Cricket Chairman Charlie Knott and Malcolm Marshall (IM).*

third successful cup final, as had Terry, Smith and Connor, but he was seriously troubled by his injured knee. The *Hampshire Handbook* listed 25 non-contracted players who had appeared for the county in 1992, of whom only Will Kendall would progress to the county side although Jon Batty would enjoy a good career with Surrey.

Hampshire had enjoyed a decade of successful rebuilding under Pocock and Nicholas, resulting in four trophies and a number of 'near things'. But although it was not immediately obvious, that period was now coming to an end. Over the next few years Hampshire would bring little joy to their supporters on the field. Elsewhere, however, plans were in place to transform the Hampshire County Cricket Club of the 20th century. And English cricket too would lurch through a series of poor performances, leading to a radical overhaul of the game from junior levels through to the England side.

In many respects the 1990s was a deeply disappointing decade for cricket in Hampshire and England, and on the world stage there were many shabby, discouraging events. However, simultaneously, away from some of the glare of publicity, both the English game and Hampshire County Cricket Club were engaged in a complex, radical overhaul that can be seen in the county and the country as the basis for the excitements of 2005 – and hopefully beyond.

In Hampshire, 1992 ended with another trophy for Mark Nicholas's side despite a sense of disappointment at the overall performances. Marshall's Lord's medal could not disguise the fact that the great bowler was past his peak and from the powerful batting side of the mid-1980s Greenidge and Chris Smith had gone. Wicketkeeper Bobby Parks was replaced very capably by Aymes and another local youngster Shaun Udal showed real promise as an off spinner, but Jon Ayling's

61   *Jon Ayling – three cup medals and great promise, wrecked by injury.*

62   *Former Hampshire cricketers meet to dedicate the 2nd XI pavilion to Arthur Holt.*

potential was threatened and ultimately cut short by his injury. In 1991 it was reasonable to suppose that those three and Middleton (at least) might provide a solid spine of local cricketers in the Hampshire side to rival the team of the 1950s. In the event only Udal and Aymes survived through the decade.

But while Nicholas was now leading an ageing side, there were promising players developing in the 2nd XI. From 1946 until the 1990s Hampshire had generally had one coach at a time: Sam Staples, Arthur Holt, Geoff Keith, Sainsbury and Tremlett. During the 1990s the coaching 'empire' would expand. Jimmy Gray remained as Chairman of Cricket and the General Committee included former players Barry Reed and Keith Wheatley, who worked with Gray, Neville Rogers, 'Butch' White and the coaches on the Cricket Committee. During the 1980s the club's Chairman Donald Rich had also reduced the General Committee to 21, with seven retirements or re-elections each year. In the early 1990s he was replaced as Chairman by Brian Ford – a third-generation leading committee member. During that decade, the committee would reduce in number again. A smaller executive group working with the President Wilfred Weld, the Chief Executive Tony Baker and the Marketing Manager Mike Taylor would be increasingly responsible for much of the important business.

One of the executive members was Bill Hughes, who was principally responsible for the most important initiative at Hampshire during the 1990s, the building of the new ground at West End in the borough of Eastleigh just off the M27 corridor between Portsmouth and Southampton.

Through the 1980s and 1990s Hampshire continued to play cricket at Basingstoke, Portsmouth and Southampton but in 1992 they played their last home match at Bournemouth although they appeared once as the away side in the NatWest Trophy in 1998. The use of these outgrounds served an important function in taking cricket around the county and there were many supporters who would only watch in their home ground. However, Hampshire had relatively little control over Basingstoke or Portsmouth and, at a time when the quality of wickets was coming under increasingly stringent inspection, this was a worry. So too were the logistics of moving around, especially now that all boundary advertisements had to be displayed at every match. Furthermore, Hampshire were less able to control or generate income from catering and bars if they did not own the ground.

None of this might have led to the decision to move had it not been that county cricket had finally outgrown the Victorian ground at Northlands Road. Many plots of land around that area of Southampton were being built upon and, as car use increased hugely, parking spaces declined. In addition to the new County Club, Hampshire had created an Executive Club facility in the new Philip Mead stand but this was more attractive than robust. The main pavilion – joined from two separate buildings in the 1960s – was increasingly fragile and in the wake of new legislation covering safety at sports grounds it had a limited future. The ground limit was now around four thousand and on semi-final days and other big occasions it creaked. Hampshire had to move.

The plans for the new ground were hatched one evening over dinner between Hughes, Weld and Nicholas. Hampshire had announced in the late 1980s that they were looking for a new location and they began to cost the project and to consider what a 21st-century ground might need. Since Hampshire was a traditional county members' club, all plans and proposals were communicated via mailings, newsletters and in particular the annual general meeting. This was always held prior to the season and it reflects the constituency of the membership that it was held in alternate years in the evening to accommodate working people and in the afternoons for the benefit of the retired, elderly and independent. At these meetings, a few members would ask questions about the plans but there was generally more interest in playing prospects.

63   *1992, Bournemouth – Nicholas's Hampshire take the field for the last ever session v Middlesex.*

64   *Cricket at Northlands Road (PE).*

After the years of promise and success under Mark Nicholas, the matter of cricketing achievement became a constant worry at Hampshire. In previous chapters the attention to detail of matches and seasons is a reflection of the unprecedented success enjoyed by Hampshire between 1955–92. During that period Hampshire won eight trophies, including two Championships, and finished second in the Championship on three occasions. Shackleton, White, Cottam, Terry and Chris and Robin Smith all represented England in Test matches and Hampshire supporters were also able to enjoy the brilliance of the two Marshalls, Richards, Greenidge and Roberts. The local cricketers included Gray, Sainsbury, Jesty, Aymes and Udal and, while the county continued to exasperate as often as they delighted, they also maintained their 'Happy Hampshire' tag.

But the Benson & Hedges triumph of 1992 signalled the end of this successful period as Hampshire fell rapidly into a spell of poor cricket and poor results that rather more resembled the 1930s. Like then, they had a variety of captains and cricketers who were unable to translate promise and ability into collective achievement. Unlike the 1930s, they had a core of supporters who had come to expect a degree of success provided by high-quality cricketers. For the rest of the decade that expectation was generally disappointed.

There were four principal reasons. Nicholas's side had aged and was past its best, overseas players of variable quality came and went, too many mediocre players were signed from other counties and Hampshire's supply of good local cricketers virtually disappeared. While it is a simple matter to state these reasons, explaining their root causes – especially the latter – is less straightforward.

One version is that Nicholas, having inherited the basis of a fine side from Nick Pocock, so much revelled in his successes that in his last years he encouraged short-term signings in the hope of further trophies. In the case of Gower, if this was the aim then it was successful but it cannot have encouraged the prospects of young left-handed batsmen like Rupert Cox, Richard Scott or Julian Wood. In addition, other signings were much less successful, not least the much-publicised opening bowling partnership of Winston Benjamin and Norman Cowans. Benjamin was an overseas signing who moved from Leicestershire where he had often been troubled by injury, while Cowans, who had bowled fast for England in the 1980s, came from Middlesex. In the previous season Marshall, Connor, Shine, Thursfield, Jean-Jacques and Bovill had all taken the new ball for Hampshire in first-class cricket but with little success. None of the regular bowlers averaged under thirty and none, not even Marshall, took 30 wickets. The leading wicket-takers were Udal, James and Flint.

In that same Ashes summer, Benjamin had played in only half of Leicestershire's matches and Cowans in just five games for Middlesex, although both players led their respective averages. In the following year Cardigan Connor, who took 72 first-class wickets, usurped their new partnership. Benjamin and Cowans managed 50 between them but again Benjamin appeared in only half the matches. Meanwhile, at Southampton, Kevin Shine, who had moved to Middlesex, opened their bowling and dismissed his former captain.

While Benjamin's contribution was as disappointing as it was predictable there were odd occasions when he showed himself to be a cricketer of outstanding natural ability. What he never revealed was the commitment of fellow countrymen Greenidge and Marshall. Cowans, on the other hand, was simply past his best and, having taken 26 wickets in his one season, he disappeared. Martin Jean-Jacques was perhaps never good enough and suffered injuries. In two seasons his nine wickets cost almost fifty each before he retired.

During the 1990s Hampshire signed many players who had been with other counties. The first was Gower in 1990 and the others who played first-class cricket in that decade included Martin Thursfield (Middlesex), Martin Jean-Jacques (Derbyshire), Matthew Keech (Middlesex), Norman Cowans (Middlesex), Giles White (Somerset), Paul Whitaker (Derbyshire), John Stephenson (Essex), Stuart Milburn (Yorkshire), Peter Hartley (Yorkshire), Alex Morris and Zac Morris (both Yorkshire). Of those, Gower, White, Stephenson, Hartley and Alex Morris were capped by Hampshire but Gower, Stephenson and Hartley were already established county cricketers in the later years of their careers. White was a steady opening bat, who played with some regularity over eight seasons, averaging around thirty. Alex Morris was a very promising all-rounder whose career was blighted by injury. The others generally supported the increasingly prevalent notion that county cricket gave employment to too many players of no more than average talents. They also reflected the increasing tendency of county sides to sign players from other counties, the most successful example of which was Nottinghamshire in 2005, who acquired virtually a whole side to win the County Championship.

Hampshire's 11 signings from other counties in the 1990s compare with three in the 1960s (Caple, Keith and Stephenson), six in the 1970s (Rice, Herman, Taylor, Watson, Elms and Stevenson) and five in the 1980s (Malone, Curzon, Goldie, Maru and James). Over those four decades 12 of the 25 were capped by Hampshire and the difference in numbers indicates an increase in these 'transfers' and Hampshire's needs in terms of their level of success.

In signing such players in the 1990s, Hampshire were implicitly acknowledging their problems in producing their own cricketers, despite the increasingly careful organisation of their junior representative sides. In a changing world it did not follow that every cricketer that came through the Hampshire colts, under-19 and 2nd XI sides was born in the county – indeed this was the case with the generation of Nicholas, Terry, Tremlett and Parks – but it was the case that Hampshire's increasingly elaborate scouting and coaching structure had contributed to the development of talented county and occasionally even Test cricketers. Now, suddenly that system failed them.

The statistics about the players who came through Hampshire's junior sides are alarming. In 1988, Shaun Udal joined Hampshire and went on to become a capped and international player. In 2001 the same applied to Chris Tremlett. In total over that period, Hampshire signed 34 players who were learning their trade. Six of them won a county cap. Of those six, Udal, Laney, Kenway and Tremlett were genuine products of the county's youth development programme but Laney and Kenway never fulfilled their considerable promise and both left county cricket in their twenties. Will Kendall had played for Surrey as a colt and also won his Blue at Oxford University. He reached the position of vice-captain but was really only a regular player from 1999–2002. At the end of 2004 he retired, having scored nearly seven thousand runs at an average of 33.27.

Mascarenhas has become a fine county all-rounder and is still close to international selection in limited-overs cricket. But while he was born in London he grew up in Australia and made a rapid transition from Bournemouth in the Southern League to Hampshire 2nd XI and then the county side. In the first team Hampshire have done much to nurture his talent but it would be stretching a point to argue that they discovered it.

Of the others, the Francis brothers moved to Somerset but both have struggled to establish themselves, although John played in every first-class match for Somerset in 2005, scoring over 900 runs at an average of 37.44. He slipped back in 2006 while his brother Simon was released. At Hampshire, Jimmy Adams finally made the breakthrough in 2006 and Tremlett was hoping to be fit enough to play at the higher level. But 26 of the 34 entered and left first-class cricket without a complete career or the comfort of and recognition of a benefit.

One of the first to go was Rupert Cox. Although born in Guildford he lived most of his life in Hampshire, was educated like Mark Nicholas at Bradfield and progressed through Hampshire's junior age groups to the colts and 2nd XI sides. He was a left-handed batsman and good fielder and he made his 2nd XI debut in 1986, approaching his 19th birthday. He joined the full county staff in 1989 and made his first-class debut the following year at Arundel. A few weeks later at Worcester he made his maiden first-class century and played in a few Sunday League matches, scoring 56 at The Oval in 1992.

However, despite the departures of Greenidge, Turner and Chris Smith he was only one of a number of young players trying to force his way into the side. In 1992 he captained the 2nd XI and topped their batting averages but played in just three first-class matches and one Sunday League match. Given that this was his fourth year as a professional cricketer he was beginning to be frustrated by the lack of opportunities.

One of his Championship appearances was at Cheltenham in late July. In the previous game Hampshire's first six were Middleton, Terry, Gower, Smith, Nicholas and James but now Gower and Smith were playing for England against Pakistan while Terry and James were both injured. So the revised line up was Middleton, Morris, Cox, Nicholas, Marshall and Aymes. Courtney Walsh took 6-33, Smith dismissed Morris for four and Ball had Cox lbw for one. Middleton with 64 helped Hampshire to 167 but they trailed by 172 on first innings. When Hampshire batted again, Middleton and Morris posted 102 before Morris (64) and Cox (13) were both run out. Hampshire looked safe when Nicholas suddenly declared, setting Gloucestershire 103 in just 10 overs. Richard Scott showed Hampshire what they had lost with 42, including five sixes, but Udal took 4-36 and the match was drawn with Gloucestershire 95-7.

Cox was unlucky to be run out but Morris had done enough and he retained his place when Terry and James returned. At the same time, Cox went back to the 2nd XI for a match against Durham 2nd XI at Southampton. He scored 45 and 103 and there was also a century from Julian Wood.

During the match Cox spoke of his disappointment of the run out at Cheltenham, which meant a return to the 2nd XI. He might have been playing at Worcester and, remembering the century of 1990, felt that his career was 'going backwards'. He commented on the 'big difference' between first- and second-team cricket 'especially since the limitation on one overseas player'. Tony Middleton makes the same point, offering the example in the 1980s of Surrey where they employed Geoff Howarth and Tony Gray as their two overseas cricketers but could only ever field one. In the early 1990s, Hampshire had done the same with Marshall and Jefferies or Linden Joseph. This often meant an overseas pace bowler in the 2nd XI providing good experience for the opposition batsmen. By contrast, when Durham chased their total at Southampton the Hampshire attack consisted of P.J. Bakker in his last weeks with the club, Thursfield, Bovill, Flint and a trialist spinner, Chris Sketchley.

Cox also drew attention to the different 'mental approach' in the first team and the danger of believing that opposition players were better. Given the frustration, there was the option of moving to a county with fewer top-class batsmen but he was not sure that he would attract sufficient interest. He added, 'In addition I've lived in Hampshire since the third week of my life and I dearly want to play for Hampshire, especially in such a good set-up.'

Leading the 2nd XI in 1992 was not always straightforward because until the students, such as Bovill and Laney, returned for the vacation they were using a number of trialists. Cox had experience of captaining sides at school and for Hampshire under-19s before moving on to the 2nd XI, but he was still a young man and sometimes found it particularly difficult to captain the older players not being picked for the county side.

Another issue for the uncapped professionals was what to do in the winter. Hampshire do not pay 12-month contracts but they have usually tried to find employment or coaching and in the 21st century many of the younger players spend winters in Perth, connected with Paul Terry. This was

65 *Robin Smith (PE).*

not the case in the 1990s, however, and Cox concluded the conversation by suggesting that:

> The problem for Julian Wood, Sean Morris and me is that we have such a strong batting side … By the time (we) get a regular chance they will probably have found a couple of 21-year-olds.

In fact, Cox played 19 matches for Hampshire but left at the end of the 1994 season. Wood appeared in 27 first-class games but he had departed a year earlier and has since enjoyed a long and successful career in Minor Counties cricket. Morris came closest to establishing himself, playing 37 matches in five seasons, but he suffered a bad hand injury batting against Courtney Walsh and his career finished in 1996. Before then, in 1994, he actually finished the season at the head of the Hampshire averages (686 runs at 49.00) but none of them could sustain their early promise and all three left with career batting averages in the twenties.

By 1996 Hampshire had built a new batting line-up around Robin Smith. The top order included Giles White, Jason Laney, Paul Whitaker, Matthew Keech and John Stephenson, who had been signed to succeed Nicholas as captain. In 1996 Keech scored 793 runs at 44.05 and Laney 1,163 at 38.76 and both seemed poised for long county careers. Benjamin appeared in only two first-class matches and for 1997 Hampshire replaced him with Matthew Hayden – not yet established in the Australian Test side. In addition to Sean Morris, Paul Terry left Hampshire in rather unhappy circumstances midway through the season when told that he would not be offered another contract. Thursfield and Liam Botham also left while Kenway and Savident were signed for 1997.

These regular changes did not affect the playing results much – they remained poor as the following table shows:

YEAR	C Ch	Sun. League	NatWest	B&H	Captain	Overseas
1990	3rd	5th	SF	Group	Nicholas	Marshall
1991	9th	17th	Won	QF	Nicholas	Aqib Javed
1992	15th	3rd	Rd 2	Won	Nicholas	Marshall
1993	13th	15th	QF	QF	Nicholas	Marshall
1994	14th	12th	QF	SF	Nicholas	Benjamin
1995	13th	18th	Rd 1	Group	Nicholas	Streak
1996	14th	15th	QF	Group	Stephenson	Benjamin
1997	14th	15th	Rd 2	Group	Stephenson	Hayden
1998	6th	8th	SF	Group	Smith	McLean
1999	7th	8th R*	Rd 2	Super Cp	Smith	McLean

(*In 1999 the National League was in two divisions and Hampshire were relegated from the First Division. They had qualified for the Benson & Hedges Super Cup, which replaced the old competition, but lost in the first round at Headingley.)

The great years of Nicholas's side from 1985–92 vanished rapidly after the mid-season defeat by Essex in 1992. For the first time with Marshall in the side they were not a force in the Championship.

Nicholas, preparing his succession, persuaded Hampshire to sign John Stephenson from Essex where he had been overlooked for the leadership role. He played from 1995 and became captain in 1996, by which time Malcolm Marshall had returned to Hampshire as coach. Meanwhile, Tim Tremlett was moving more towards his current role as Director of Cricket.

Stephenson was a very different captain from Nicholas. The latter was flamboyant in his batting and his declarations, he displayed his emotions for all to see and when his sense of justice was injured he would engage in legal debates with umpires and opposing captains. His approach to county cricket is evident in his subsequent career as a media star but he was a fine batsman who might have achieved more had he not been captain. On occasions his captaincy created tensions within his dressing room but generally he enjoyed significant successes, although the supreme county prize always eluded his team.

In some ways the great failing of his regime came in its end, when the team that he handed on to Stephenson was considerably weaker than the one he

66 *1996: new captain John Stephenson goes out to bat at Basingstoke.*

had inherited from Pocock a decade before. In broad terms this is true of all the more successful Hampshire captains as Tennyson, Ingleby-Mackenzie and Gilliat also left their successors with problems of team-building. Gilliat was the one captain who inherited problems – especially with the bowling – but overcame them to create significant success in a short time.

In Stephenson's first season as captain his regular players included Laney, White, Smith, Kendall, Keech, Whitaker, James, Aymes, Udal, Connor, Maru, Bovill, Milburn and Benjamin. Too many of these players were promising cricketers who never quite made the grade. Meanwhile, Robin Smith was available throughout the season because his Test career had come to a rather abrupt end. In 1995 he averaged 43.57 against West Indies and in the winter he toured South Africa, where he scored 43, 52, 44, 34, 2, 66 and 13 in the Test matches. These were not huge scores but they were fairly consistent. However, England then had a poor World Cup campaign in Pakistan, losing to the eventual Champions Sri Lanka and Smith's career was finished. He had scored 4,236 Test runs at 43.67 – at the time a higher career average than any other England batsman including Gooch, Thorpe, Atherton or Stewart but, although just 32, he was surplus to requirements.

For Hampshire in 1996 he top-scored in both major competitions and expressed his frustration at being omitted by England. He formed a strong alliance with Adi Aymes, who might have played international cricket, and Shaun Udal, who had been omitted by England after 10 limited-overs internationals in 1994 and 1995. These three, known sometimes as USA, were a powerful group within the dressing room and it may be that Stephenson struggled to impose authority on his side. He was a quiet man and it seemed that his strategy was to lead by example on the field as a batsman and a bowler. Sadly he was often more successful in the latter role. Although he had won a Test cap as an opening batsman he never found runs easy to come by for Hampshire. He was also unlucky in 1996 that he could rarely call upon his overseas professional Winston Benjamin.

Benjamin was replaced in the following year as Hampshire's batting was strengthened significantly with the signing of the Australian Matthew Hayden. He was the highest scorer in the country in the National League and the only man to pass the thousand-run target for Hampshire in the Championship, scoring 1,446 runs at 53.55. White, Keech, Smith, Stephenson and Laney all batted usefully on occasions but the bowling was now terribly weak. At the end of the season Bovill gave up the struggle with a back injury, Milburn retired and Chetan Patel, having played one game as a non-contract player, was not retained. No bowler took 40 wickets and only James averaged under thirty. Stephenson, Renshaw and Udal were the leading bowlers in the two league competitions while two young pace bowlers, Simon Francis and Tom Hansen, made their debuts at Southampton together in the toughest circumstances. They bowled against Worcestershire at the end of the season while Graeme Hick (303*) recorded the highest score ever conceded by Hampshire and in partnership with Tom Moody (180*) set a third-wicket record for their county of 438* – watched coincidentally by the previous holders Tom Graveney and Martin Horton. Neither debutant took a wicket and although Hampshire passed 300 twice they lost by nine wickets.

During the season, the Champions Glamorgan used just 14 players in the Championship while Hampshire selected from twenty-two. In these difficult times for the first team, Hampshire were hoping that their increasingly sophisticated colts structure would produce a new generation of county cricketers. Under the tuition of former players like Barry Reed, John Rice and Richard Lewis, the various age groups featured Lawrie Prittipaul, Ian Brunnschweiler, James Bruce, James Adams, Charlie van der Gucht and Chris Tremlett, who would all play first class cricket for the county.

During the close season Stephenson's unhappy reign came to a close. He was disappointed but typically stoical and remained as a player. Robin Smith was one of the few major England players of his generation not to captain his county

67 *Adrian Aymes.*

68   *Robin Smith's senior players: Laney, Udal, Kendall, Smith, Aymes, Stephenson, White and Mullally (IM).*

side but now Hampshire turned to him. There was a general feeling that he was simply too nice, too relaxed to be an effective captain but there was a slight revival of fortunes in 1998 as Hampshire finished in the top half of both tables and reached only their second semi-final in six years.

Indeed, even the previous occasion had been rather fortunate for in 1994 the Benson & Hedges Cup changed to a straight knock-out, so reaching the semi-final required just two victories. The first was a fairly convincing eight-wicket victory over Yorkshire but they then beat Essex on the afternoon of the second day in a 19-over rain-affected contest. Essex scored 124-3 — modest by today's Twenty20 standards — and Robin Smith hit Hampshire to an easy victory. In the semi-final they had lost at Worcester by three wickets and three overs despite a Smith century and Norman Cowans' best day (4-36).

In 1998, the NatWest Trophy took Hampshire back to Dean Park to visit Dorset. Julian Shackleton bowled with an action so like his father's that it increased the sense of nostalgia and extraordinarily White, Stephenson and Whitaker were all dismissed without scoring. But from 0-3, Smith (144*) and Aymes (73) rescued Hampshire who reached 315-5, winning by 161 runs. Jon Hardy was Dorset's top scorer, followed by another former Hampshire man, Matt Swarbrick.

The next round started similarly as Cardigan Connor took three Essex wickets in the first over and, while Hampshire stumbled, they reached the target of 130 with three wickets left. In the quarter-final they played magnificent cricket at Lord's, setting a target of 296 and beating Middlesex by 144 runs. There were fine innings by Laney, White and Aymes and the bowlers shared the wickets with only Justin Langer resisting.

69 *2002 – a reunion of wicketkeepers at the Rose Bowl: Bryan Timms, Ralph Prouton, Adi Aymes, Colin Ingleby-Mackenzie, Leo Harrison and Bob Stephenson.*

So, unlike four years earlier, Hampshire had earned their semi-final appearance and, for the last time, it was a home tie at Northlands Road. However, their opponents were Lancashire, who frequently beat Hampshire in this period. Crawley and Fairbrother led them to 252 with Connor and Mascarenhas each taking three wickets. The Lancashire bowlers struck as a unit reducing Hampshire to 28-5 and, although Mascarenhas, James and McLean staged a recovery, Hampshire were never close to victory.

During the course of the season McLean, White and Mascarenhas were awarded their county caps by the Cricket Chairman David Robinson, who had succeeded Jimmy Gray in 1997. He was a member of the General Committee and had been a good club and Minor Counties cricketer but, unlike his predecessors Charlie Knott and Gray, he had not played first-class cricket. His job was to chair the committee, which included former players and current coaches. It was a new approach that sought to give more control and more responsibility to the professionals in charge of the club's playing fortunes. Nonetheless, there were mumblings of discontent among the members at the disappointing results and these often surfaced at the annual general meeting or the mid-season members' forum. There were also rumours of pressure groups although these were less apparent than similar liaisons at some other counties.

At the end of 1998 Hampshire released Richard Dibden and Paul Whitaker while Cardigan Connor and Rajesh Maru retired. The latter was appointed as Hampshire's Community Development Coach. McLean returned for 1999 and Steve Lugsden, a pace bowler from Durham, also signed.

The English season of 1999 opened in somewhat damp weather with the World Cup. England and New Zealand both thrashed Hampshire in warm-up matches at Northlands Road where Alan Mullally, who had played once for Hampshire in 1988 before moving to Leicestershire, took 4-20. Within a year he would return permanently to Hampshire. The county played host to two qualifying matches won by West Indies and Sri Lanka.

Sadly, England had a very poor tournament under the captaincy of Alec Stewart and he was replaced by Nasser Hussain for the home series against New Zealand that followed the World Cup. England won the first Test by seven wickets despite being dismissed for 126 in their first innings but they lost the next Test at Lord's where Hussain scored 61 in the first innings but was unfit to bat again. In the third Test England were almost 300 behind on first innings but the game was drawn; then at The Oval New Zealand clinched the series. England were bowled out for 153 and 162 with a batting tail so long that Mullally was at number nine, ahead of Tufnell and Giddins. At the conclusion of the match the spectators booed the England side. In the following winter they toured South Africa, losing two and drawing two of the first four Tests. Three days were lost in the final Test, after which Cronje set England what seemed a generous task to keep the game alive. They won, scoring 251-8 in the 76th over, but it was a hollow victory. Fairly soon, the world would learn that Cronje was a corrupt match-fixer at the heart of an international betting scandal.

Smith's Hampshire side were again reasonably successful in the Championship in 1999 but they were a poor limited-overs side and were relegated from the new First Division of the National League, made no progress in the NatWest Trophy or the one-off aberration, the Super Cup. This was created to replace the Benson & Hedges Cup and to reduce the number of early season limited-overs fixtures as the authorities tinkered with the structure of English first-class cricket to seek a remedy for the failings of the national side.

These changes were the product of the lengthy discussions around the country that emanated from a document published by the Management Board of the ECB. Entitled 'Raising the Standard', it was described as a 'blueprint for the future playing structure of cricket'. It was always seen publicly as the brainchild of the Chairman Lord Maclaurin, although his board had 13 other members, including David Acfield and Roger Knight who had played county cricket. Another with first-class experience was Tim Lamb, the Chief Executive.

The key point was perhaps that the document addressed 'cricketers at every level', including schools, clubs, county sides and the Test team. In his foreword Maclaurin wrote of aiming for 'the best possible standards' at all levels, emphasising 'the England team [as] the number one priority'. This view was now a given in English cricket, transformed from 100 years earlier when there were too few good international sides to ensure regular Test cricket and the English game often centred upon county cricket and other forms. By the 21st century, international cricket was the economic lifeblood of the game worldwide and England was no exception.

Nonetheless, the document and the consultation did concern itself with cricket at all levels and led to significant changes in league and schools cricket. Maclaurin suggested that there would be no 'quick fix' but in a little over five years there was evidence of increasing numbers of children playing the game, while the

England side was becoming a major Test side again although its limited-overs performances were not yet so strong.

In terms of the key proposals of 'Raising the Standard', those for the county game have been much less easy to realise. The executive summary wish list included the following:

- Bridge the gap between recreational cricket and the First Class game and provide the opportunity for the most talented cricketers to fulfil their potential
- Give talented cricketers the opportunity to progress seamlessly through club and non-First Class representative County cricket to the First Class game
- Reduce First Class County staff sizes to allow more cricketers to progress further in the game
- Wind down the First Class Counties' 2nd XI programme
- Reduce the number of domestic First Class matches to create a better balance between match-play, recuperation and preparation
- Establish a Three-Conference County Championship with an enhanced prize money structure to increase competitiveness and intensity and raise interest levels for spectators and cricket followers.

In addition to these there was a proposal for a two-division National League implemented almost immediately and a suggestion to expand the NatWest Trophy. This happened, adding countries and cricket boards to the Minor Counties but by 2006 that experiment had been abandoned and the minor counties had vanished from the competition too.

The real non-starter was the Three-Conference Championship. Journalists joked that no one could really understand it. The document acknowledged the case for two divisions, against which it put the key arguments that sides losing England players would be penalised and that counties would depend on 'old stagers' rather than taking 'a chance on youth'. By 2005 we could see that international cricketers with Kolpak entitlements or convenient passports were supplanting these old stagers. The issue of losing Test cricketers simply vanished as their county sides effectively wrote off their centrally contracted players.

But the document had also come up with a proposal for 18 centres of excellence, including academies, housed in each of the counties, and it feared that two divisions would create some second-class counties who would not be able to sustain that vision. By the end of 1999 Hampshire faced the real prospect of being one such county for, when *Wisden* published its Championship table of the decade's results, only Durham kept them from bottom place. It is interesting that by 2005 these two counties enjoyed the most modern facilities, were supplying England with Test players and producing far better playing results on the field.

The Three-Conference proposal was for 14 four-day matches with an end-of-season play-off climax for all the sides in a round-robin format. The end-of-season proposal would have made Test players available for the final stages. The organisation was intricate, the rationale impeccable but the English counties would not have it and went for the two-divisional structure, which has certainly done very little to encourage the development of younger English cricketers. As a consequence there is little evidence of the seamless flow of players from the top club and colts sides into first-class cricket.

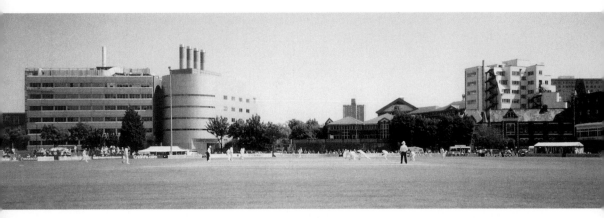

70 *US Ground Portsmouth – the university's buildings loom over the Royal Navy.*

One of the campaigns in the press was to leave county cricket fairly much as it was but to introduce an additional tier of regional representative cricket. Sadly, the ambition to 'bridge the gap between recreational cricket and the First Class game' is happening rather more in reverse as discarded county players move back into the new league systems. In recent years, former Hampshire players like Laney, Keech, Prittipaul, Kenway, Savident, Schofield, Dibden, Goldstraw and Brunnschweiler have all been seen in Southern League cricket. Very few players are making the move the other way and remaining there.

Prittipaul made his 2nd XI debut in 1998, the year following Derek Kenway's first match for the county. At the time Hampshire were unconvincing on the field, unsure of the right captain and with a succession of short-term overseas players. They were still playing at Northlands Road, Basingstoke and Portsmouth and they were still a traditional *members'* county cricket club with an elected committee and a Chief Executive. By the time their disappointingly short careers came to end in 2005, Hampshire County Cricket Club had been transformed into Hampshire Cricket plc with a board of directors, a brand new ground hosting international cricket and the world's greatest cricketer as captain. Furthermore, for the first time in 13 years they won a major trophy in a Lord's final and came within a couple of points of winning their third Championship.

7

2000–2005

LORD MACLAURIN'S proposals for a Three-Conference County Championship met with little support and, despite the reasonable warnings of reduced opportunities for young players, the counties opted instead for two divisions with promotion and relegation about thirty years after Ronnie Aird had declared his support. In both the Championship and the National League six teams every year would move either up or down – a considerable proportion – but a figure that would ensure many competitive matches through the season. In 2006 the number was reduced to two-up and two-down.

In the County Championship, the leading nine sides at the end of the 1999 season would be members of the First Division when it began in the following April. On Wednesday 15 September a round of matches began to decide the final positions. Surrey had replaced Leicestershire as Champions and those two sides and the runners-up Lancashire were secure but there was still much to play for. In the event, Somerset in fourth place finished only seven points above a place in the Second Division.

Hampshire travelled to Derbyshire needing to win to be in the top half while Derbyshire also required sufficient bonus points. Meanwhile, Warwickshire entertained Sussex on a 'sporting' Edgbaston pitch with both sides also able to qualify. In the event Warwickshire won inside two days, consigning Sussex to the Second Division but, if Derbyshire were deprived of bonus points and lost, or Hampshire failed to win, Warwickshire would be 'up'.

Nothing was resolved at Derby on the first two days, both of which had lost some overs to rain. Friday was grey with the threat of poor weather about and an autumnal Midlands chill in the air but it was not unpleasant. The cricket correspondents of the Portsmouth and Southampton newspapers, John May and Simon Parker, were both on the ground. With joint football reporting duties this was unusual at away matches in September but the question of Hampshire's divisional status was not the only attraction. On that morning Hampshire released their press statement announcing that their overseas player in 2000 would be Shane Warne. There had been rumours but the signing and announcement was such a secret that Vic Isaacs, the club's scorer, statistician and website controller, did not know officially and was grumbling that at this distance he could not announce the news to his electronic followers. The *Guardian* reported that the deal would be worth around £150,000 – a sum that neither player nor club ever

159

confirmed. They also reminded readers that during the previous winter Warne had lost his Test place in the Caribbean and appeared in 'terminal decline' (!) although this view had changed during the 1999 World Cup when Hampshire first made contact with Warne.

This was an informal approach by Hampshire's Chairman Brian Ford at a reception for all World Cup teams in Buckingham Palace. Ford insists that the informality was necessary to avoid competition but he was equally convinced that it was not his approach but the presence of Robin Smith at Hampshire that attracted Warne, because Smith is a delightful man and a hugely popular figure in world cricket. For Warne there was also the possibility of joining an ambitious club with a new ground were he to return for a second season.

But before Warne's arrival there were points to play for to ensure that he might compete in the top division of English cricket. So, on this third day, Derbyshire resumed on 143-3 chasing Hampshire's first innings of 362. They began comfortably enough but then McLean and Hartley took two wickets each while 20 runs were added. At 178-7, Derbyshire were still more than 30 runs short of saving the follow-on. This they managed, thanks to a good 50 from DeFreitas but they needed to reach 250 and extra batting points to pass Warwickshire's final position. Otherwise they would have to win the match to overtake their final points total.

Robin Smith was off the field with a groin problem that eventually required a winter operation and Udal was captaining the side. At 231 he took Derbyshire's eighth wicket (DeFreitas) but, with Derbyshire struggling, he turned to 'Chalky' White. This may have been the employment of Hampshire's only fit leg spinner to celebrate the signing of another one. Otherwise it was somewhat surprising.

In fairness, White had returned his career best figures (3-23) just up the road at Trent Bridge in May, so perhaps Udal was looking for a repeat. On the other hand, in six seasons he had bowled only 90 overs with six previous wickets. One plausible explanation was that the openers McLean and Hartley had enjoyed a good bowl and Hampshire's first-change pair Renshaw and Mascarenhas were not particularly hostile, managing just one wicket between them in the match. In the event, White took a wicket, ensuring another point for Hampshire, but he also conceded 16 runs in two overs, which took Derbyshire to a certain First Division place and great celebrations among players and supporters. Shortly afterwards they declared with a deficit of eighty-five. At this point Warwickshire, their season over, were still in the top division for next year. Hampshire now had to win.

Five sessions remained and the weather seemed tolerable. Smith struck twice for Derbyshire, reducing Hampshire to 13-2 with his namesake unlikely to bat, but a difficult prospect for Hampshire was alleviated when Cork decided to bowl his wicketkeeper Krikken and other part-time bowlers. Derbyshire sometimes fielded deliberately poorly and Hampshire were able to declare on the third afternoon at 199-5, setting Derbyshire 285 to win in almost four sessions. Paul Weaver (the *Guardian*) described the cricket as 'bizarre and sometimes disgraceful', Pat Gibson (the *Times*) suggested that it 'brought the game into disrepute', while in the *Portsmouth News,* Simon Parker believed it was 'inexcusable'.

The display was carried out to derision from the crowd and – after a brief shower – in reasonable weather. The main case for the contrived declaration was that the forecast was poor and the weather unsettled, so Hampshire had to be generous. This was by no means the first performance of this kind in county cricket but where four-day cricket was intended to prevent its necessity, promotion and relegation provided a new impetus. Indeed, this may be the first time this has happened on the *penultimate* day because of a weather *forecast*, rather than in response to actual time lost.

In addition, despite the poor bowling and fielding, Hampshire scored just 199-5 in the 35th over – no more than a good 'Sunday' performance against proper bowling and fielding. Had Derbyshire set an attacking field throughout with their 'real' bowlers, Hampshire could still have produced a decent target and the spectators could have watched a real match.

The target itself was clearly 'contrived' but that merely followed a tradition in the county game that goes way back – perhaps as far as Hampshire's match with Sussex in 1894 when Hampshire became the first team to win a match after a declaration by their opponents. On that occasion, Sussex, trailing by 109, reached 349-8 at lunch on the final day and set Hampshire 241 in three hours. Hill, Barton and Wynyard (117) took Hampshire to victory and intriguingly, in this modern context, H.S. Altham believes it was the match 'which perhaps determined the county's promotion' to first-class status the following season.

Will Kendall was dismissed for nought in the second innings before the 'joke' bowling began. In his chronicle of the season in the county's *Handbook*, he wrote:

> The captains agreed on a target of 285 … in what was effectively four sessions. Yes it was a generous target but given the weather and the desire of both sides to win, not an unreasonable one. The one session of non-competitive cricket was inevitable to set up the finish but it happens often in county cricket. Neither side has anything to hide and the umpires were happy that everything occurred properly.

Whatever had gone on behind the scenes or on the field on that Friday there is no doubt that, once Hampshire declared, the cricket was first-class. McLean dismissed Stubbings immediately and at the close of the third day with Derbyshire 109-4 Hampshire were probably favourites. On the Saturday morning, as the grey skies hovered, Hampshire took three more wickets, reducing Derbyshire to 163-7, still 122 short of their target. But then DeFreitas (61), Krikken (27) and Lacey began to score more freely against a tiring attack. The eighth wicket added 104 and at 279-8 Derbyshire needed just six runs to win.

By this point, the nonsense of the previous afternoon was forgotten and the match was played in a tense atmosphere. Tim Tremlett, deputising for Malcolm Marshall, circled the ground nervously and suffered with his team when Peter Hartley dropped what appeared to be a vital catch. The same bowler had Aldred lbw at 282 and, shortly afterwards at the same score, he held on to the caught-and-bowled chance from Lacey that gave Hampshire victory by two runs. The celebrations of the young Hampshire players made the sense of relief and excitement palpable, while Lacey who fell at last for an heroic 42 (and a broken finger) appeared devastated.

71 *Warne smiling at Southampton.*

On that Saturday evening it emerged that Warwickshire's victory over Sussex had not been sufficient and that both of those sides would begin 2000 in the Second Division. The Sussex captain Chris Adams had little sympathy for Warwickshire. He told the *Times*:

> They cannot prepare sub-standard pitches to suit themselves and then moan and groan at counties contriving a result that doesn't suit them.

By an extraordinary coincidence, Hampshire then travelled to Edgbaston for the final National League match of the season. The divisional split in this competition had first occurred a year earlier when Warwickshire, the reigning champions, had been runners-up and Hampshire in eighth place just qualified for the top division.

In 1999 Hampshire were eighth again but this time it meant relegation. Meanwhile Warwickshire came to the last match needing to win to avoid the same fate. Derby's threatened rain finally arrived in Birmingham but eventually the two sides began an 11-over match and Hemp led Warwickshire to 114-5. Laney went early and Hampshire lost wickets regularly. Giles dismissed Udal with the first ball of the 10th over at which point Hampshire were 76-6, needing 39 to win in 11 balls – an almost impossible task. But then the rain became sufficiently heavy for the umpires to halt play, which was eventually abandoned, and Warwickshire were relegated for the second time in two days. Had Giles' over been completed, Hampshire would have needed 27 in five balls or Warwickshire would have won and stayed up.

Over that weekend Dennis Amiss, Warwickshire's Chief Executive, asked the ECB to investigate the match at Derby on a claim that the two captains brought the game into disrepute. Then on the Sunday he held a press conference at which he said he was 'astonished' at the umpires' decision and their lack of 'common sense'.

In the event this tale has a happier outcome for Warwickshire and Sussex than it has for Hampshire or Derbyshire. Within five years, Sussex and then Warwickshire would be county Champions whereas the other two sides were both relegated after one season in the top division. Indeed Derbyshire have never recovered that status and are now one of the weakest of the 18 county sides. In the National League, Hampshire and Warwickshire have tended to move back and forth between the two divisions but neither have yet been Champions.

The ECB agreed to investigate the circumstances of the Derbyshire match but decided that there was no serious issue and the matter was officially over. However, the media took a slightly different view. This was not least in the context of the emerging accusations and revelations about match fixing that eventually centred upon the South African captain Hansie Cronje but also focused on other events and players around the world, including Shane Warne. In England on 16 April 2000 the *News of the World* carried the front-page headline '3 England Tests Fixed', quoting revelations from Chris Lewis.

April 2000 was, then, a momentous month with Warne due to arrive at Hampshire, the first allegations of match fixing against Cronje and the England team signing their first central contracts after some tough negotiations between the players and the ECB. In the light of the match-fixing controversies, a game between Essex and Lancashire in the early 1990s became the topic of renewed media interest. Christopher Martin-Jenkins, writing about this in the *Times* (22 April 2001) reminded his readers of the game at Derby the previous year and – specifically – the decision to bowl White. But the Derbyshire/Hampshire match soon became insignificant in the context of the revelations about worldwide corruption in international cricket and it is all but forgotten.

When Shane Warne came to Hampshire in April 2000, he came to 'Happy Hampshire' – named as such by H.L.V. Day in *Wisden* 1962, referring to his side of the 1920s. Although Hampshire had featured many fine players through its history and the county had by now won eight trophies, the name stuck. In one sense it was complimentary, suggesting that it was always a pleasure to play against such nice chaps who might, on a good day, give you an awful thumping before buying you beer (or champagne or gin and tonic). But they might on another day crumble and fall, allowing points or cup progress followed by a beer.

There was a feeling that perhaps the players did not ultimately compete and a sense that perhaps there was too much beer. Some of the younger players seemed to miss the point that if senior men like Robin Smith or Adi Aymes spent their evenings socialising, they were usually the first men in the nets the next morning. At practice, Smith was often accompanied by his father John who would feed the bowling machine, while Aymes would often persuade available supporters to do the same for him. A few of the younger men seemed to enjoy the evening socialising more than the morning practising. In the early weeks of 2000 the consequences were apparent and would be one reason why Warne's continued presence would nurture a nastier side to Hampshire in the 21st century.

Warne arrived at the beginning of the 2000 season as *Wisden* named him as one of their five cricketers of the century. The others were Bradman, Sobers, Hobbs and Richards and apart from Warne only Tendulkar (17th) of current players was even in the top twenty. During the winter, Hampshire had also re-signed Alan Mullally, the England pace bowler who had begun his county career with one season at Hampshire 12 years earlier before moving to Leicestershire. There was a feeling that Mullally and Warne would take enough wickets to bring success to Hampshire. Since their batsmen had earned more bonus points than any other side in 1999 confidence was high, although a speculative attempt to lure an out-of-contract Andrew Flintoff south was unsuccessful.

Warne arrived to a flurry of Hampshire marketing, a lively press conference and rain and he made his English county debut at Chelmsford in the Benson & Hedges Cup. The previous match at Southampton had been abandoned but Hampshire won Warne's debut by five wickets and their senior spin bowler took 2-27. He was, of course, Shaun Udal, while Warne's figures were 0-44 in

72 *2000: waiting to play – the old players' pavilion at Northlands Road: Savident, Warne, Udal, Smith, White.*

10 overs, but he took a wicket in the next game at Hove on Easter Sunday. This time Hampshire lost and their other home match in this competition was also a costly washout.

So they went to The Oval needing to beat Surrey, for whom an abandonment would suffice to get them into the quarter-finals. Once again it rained and Surrey were reluctant to play but the match began as a 10 overs each side game in the late afternoon. Hampshire scored 87-7 thanks mainly to Kenway (47) but Surrey had reached 60-3 when Warne bowled. He dismissed Thorpe and Holliake and took a remarkable 2-6 in his two overs. Surrey needed 10 to win from the final Mullally over but lost by two runs. For the first time Warne had made his presence felt and Hampshire were to visit Glamorgan in the quarter-final.

There was controversy when Mullally was called into the England training squad because he was not one of the centrally contracted players. This meant that Hampshire lost the player but did not receive the compensation that was available to the chosen players' clubs. In the event the problem vanished because Mullally suffered a recurrence of a winter side injury and played for neither side. Meanwhile, Somerset dismissed Hampshire for 126 with White carrying his bat for 78*. Hampshire lost and Warne 'bagged' his first 'pair'. Then Hampshire entertained Warwickshire in the National League, their first meeting since the controversy of the previous September and, collapsing again, lost by 97 runs.

These early batting performances did not please their new coach, the South African batting star Jimmy Cook. During 1999, Malcolm Marshall had been suffering from cancer and was not really fit to carry out his duties so Hampshire had advertised for a new coach for 2000. In November 1999, Marshall died at home in Barbados at the age of forty-one. Hampshire were represented at the island memorial service and held their own service in Southampton in the spring for this great player.

The choice of Cook was interesting. By this time, Hampshire and the associated Hampshire Cricket Board had created a major network of full and part-time coaches, most of whom were former Hampshire players, including Tremlett, Marshall,

Middleton, Maru, Garaway, Reed and Rice. Before them had come Hayward, Sainsbury, Keith, Harrison and Holt and it was 50 years since an 'outsider', Sam Staples, had coached regularly at the county. There was a strong feeling in the committee that changes were needed on the field and that this might be best achieved by bringing in fresh ideas. As a consequence Paul Terry was one of the applicants not chosen. The problem for Cook was that the same dressing room that sometimes complicated life for the outsider captain John Stephenson did not clearly welcome the new coach.

Hampshire travelled to Cardiff for their quarter-final and on a poor pitch restricted Glamorgan to 182-6 in their 50 overs. But in reply Hampshire were put out for just 69 – and that constituted a recovery from 16-5 and 38-8. Bournemouth club cricketer Owen Parkin took 3-16 for the Welsh side.

Hampshire's awful early season batting excited some concern in the press. Robin Smith described that Cardiff week as 'easily the worst' in his time with Hampshire and local news reports quoted former players who generally sympathised with the 2000 side. Richard Gilliat suggested that 'it doesn't take much for results to change', Kevan James worried that perhaps they had 'played above themselves' in the previous year, while Mark Nicholas recalled that sometimes 'the harder you try ... the worse it becomes'.

If they did try harder in the next match, a Championship game at Headingley, it certainly did get worse as they lost by an innings, with Warne recording his fourth consecutive Championship 'duck'. Only Will Kendall with 78 passed 25 in either innings and throughout that season he was the one consistent batsman, exceeding 1,000 runs at an average above forty. Only Prittipaul with the promise

73   *2000: Alan Mullally and Shane Warne receive their county caps from captain Robin Smith, David Robinson (Cricket Chairman) and Brian Ford (Chairman).*

74 *Summer 2000 – the first match between the 2nd XIs of Hampshire and Sussex. Captains Greenfield and Savident toss.*

75 *The first pitch at the Rose Bowl.*

of an end-of-season debut had a better average and no other batsman came close to 1,000 runs or an average of thirty. With Smith and Laney averaging around twenty and Stephenson 6.40 in his last season it was unsurprising that Hampshire were relegated.

When fit, Mullally returned impressive first-class figures and, despite bowling for a side under pressure, Warne took 70 wickets at 23.14. No other bowler managed more than 30 wickets. Hampshire also endured one of their worst ever league seasons, finishing next-to-bottom of the Second Division. Warne and Mullally again bowled well with good support from Mascarenhas while Kendall and Smith were the leading batsmen. Smith's notable performances as batsman and captain were in the NatWest Trophy. Despite the general disappointment of the season, Hampshire reached the semi-final, beating the Kent County Board, Durham and Middlesex. In each match their opponents batted first and failed to reach 150. For the semi-final they had another meeting with a vengeful Warwickshire. While Shane Warne was absent, representing Australia against South Africa, Alan Donald escaped and played for Warwickshire. Knight and Singh opened with a partnership of 185, Warwickshire set a target of 263 and, despite a fine half century from Smith who opened, Hampshire lost by 19 runs.

The 2nd XI finished in 11th place, although there were some promising performances from Andrew Sexton, Lawrence Prittipaul, Zac Morris, Jimmy Adams and James Hamblin. They also reached the Aon Trophy final where a strong side captained by Udal lost to Leicestershire. Their most notable moment however came on D-Day, 6 June, when Hampshire-born Jimmy Adams, opening the batting, faced a ball from Hampshire-born Billy Taylor of Sussex in the first match at the Rose Bowl. The game was played on the Nursery Ground with considerable media attention and a good crowd but despite a first innings total of 328, Hampshire lost by an innings and Will House made the first century on the ground. Taylor, who would later rejoin his native county, took 7-34. For Hampshire Zac Morris made their first Rose Bowl half-century and the captain Lee Savident was the first bowler to take five wickets in an innings.

Two weeks later in a space bereft of seating or a pavilion, the 2nd XI played the first-ever match on

76 *Basingstoke – the final match versus Durham.*

the main ground and beat Glamorgan by nine wickets. Lawrence Prittipaul was
the first centurion (132) and opening bowler John Moss in his only appearance
for Hampshire 2nd XI took 4-63 and 5-54.

While the 2nd XI christened the Rose Bowl's two grounds, the first team
still struggled in the Championship, although Barry Richards felt the team was
sometimes 'unlucky'. An example was at The Oval where, after fine bowling from
Warne and Mullally, Hampshire chased 266 to win. Once again the batsmen failed
although Warne scored fifty. But at 173-9 the match seemed over when Simon
Francis joined Mascarenhas. The latter played superbly with good support and at
tea an incredible victory was close with only five runs needed. In the first two
overs Mascarenhas took two singles and then trying to finish the match gave a
return catch to Tudor and Hampshire lost again.

From mid-June the team embarked on a farewell tour of the county's traditional
grounds at Basingstoke, Portsmouth and Southampton and the first venue,
Basingstoke, provided Hampshire's first Championship victory. Their total of 340
did not include a single half-century but there was a promising 36 from debutant
opener Sexton. Durham failed to reach 100 in either innings and Warne had

77 *Handshakes
between Hampshire
and Kent at the
conclusion of
Portsmouth's final
Championship
match.*

78 *Portsmouth's final Sunday – Udal, Shackleton and Warne.*

match figures of 8-56. The game finished a day early and then in bright sunshine Hampshire said goodbye to May's Bounty with a rare Sunday League victory.

This was not the sign of better things as Surrey came to Northlands Road and won easily, before in early July at Taunton Kendall made the season's first century to rescue Hampshire. On 12 July Chris Tremlett, making his first-class debut against New Zealand 'A' at Portsmouth, dismissed Mark Richardson with his first ball but Hampshire lost the match as the visitors successfully chased 337 to win.

Hampshire remained in Portsmouth with their final Championship match on the Naval ground against Kent – a match that was memorable for two performances by Warne. In the first innings he scored 69 in 62 balls and seemed poised for his first first-class century when Patel bowled him. Then on the second afternoon he dismissed Key, Masters and Alan Wells cheaply before embarking on a remarkable duel with Rahul Dravid. In the end Dravid was able to master the variety of wrist spin with a beautiful display, scoring 137 of Kent's 252 all out. It was an example of everything that is best about cricket, marvelled at by a crowd that included Kent's President Colin Cowdrey on what turned out to be his last visit to a county ground. It was the antithesis of Derby in the previous year where the game had been sacrificed to the result. Here the game was everything and while Derby has faded from memories there are still many supporters who will speak of that magical afternoon.

White again carried his bat (80*) but Hampshire sacrificed a lead of 68 to lose again, by six wickets, despite the efforts of Udal (4-42). They lost too on the Sunday to Middlesex, a last-over defeat by four wickets after an injured Robin Smith was run out for forty-two. The result was closer than it might have been and the occasion was perhaps more notable for the last Pompey streaker.

Hampshire then went back to Derby on Wednesday 2 August where Mullally became one of a select band of Hampshire bowlers to take nine wickets in an innings. His 9-93 was thwarted mainly by a century from Matthew Dowman that helped Derbyshire to pass 300 and by the second evening Hampshire were 141-5 with Kenway and Mascarenhas the not-out batsmen.

A few weeks earlier, Warne's English season had been interrupted unpleasantly by a lurid front-page story in the *Mirror* (10 June 2000) 'Shame Warne: Married cricket legend harasses a mum for sex with obscene phonecalls.' Around Hampshire there was an unofficial feeling that Warne might try to avoid such situations given his high profile, but no official position was adopted since that would merely add credence to a nasty story. It would also be naïve to suppose that Warne was the first Hampshire cricketer to find himself in a temporary relationship with a young woman during an away trip. He was merely the first to be exposed on the front page of an English tabloid. For those interested in pursuing the personal consequences of the tale, Warne wrote about it in his autobiography.

While Hampshire took a mature arm's-length view of the events, there were significant implications from the story for Warne's Test career. During the match at Derby Hampshire were in a hotel north of the city on the next M1 exit. On the Friday morning Warne was late for breakfast. During the night, news had emerged from Australia that he had been stripped of the vice-captain's position in the national side. When he arrived in the hotel foyer he was visibly shattered. Meanwhile, most of his teammates were at breakfast or in reception having finished eating. As he appeared, he was surrounded by other 'guests' who, it quickly transpired, were actually representing the Australian media. There were enough Hampshire people present to rescue Warne who agreed to give interviews at the ground once he had batted.

The incident was surprising since it suggested that the young increasingly republican country was far more ostentatiously moralistic than Britain where such exposés seem a daily occurrence. From England's point of view it was a significant moment since it perhaps ensured that Australia's finest available captain would never get the position. Had he done so, 2005 may have been very different.

At this point in the 2000 season, Kendall's century at Taunton was Hampshire's only three-figure Championship innings. Kenway (50*) and Mascarenhas (4*) resumed knowing that Warne would bat next, after which he would face his inquisitors. They were ranged at the long-on boundary, with recorders, notebooks and cameras at the ready but became increasingly bored as Kenway and Mascarenhas batted through the morning. Kenway batted on and on for over six hours, passing

79 *Warne avoiding the bored Australian journalists at Derby.*

80   *Late summer 2000 – the crowd wait for the last ever day at Northlands Road.*

his century and going on to 136 before falling to the previous year's hero Lacey. Mascarenhas too reached a century, his first in the Championship and the pair added 187 – an Australian 'devil' number. Those photographers who were still awake finally got shots of Warne in mid-afternoon as he contributed to Hampshire's lead of eighty-four. Then it was time for him to bowl although Mullally was again among the wickets as Derbyshire slipped to 66-4. Warne finally granted his interviews after the close of play and on the next day Derbyshire battled to a draw.

Hampshire lost to Kent and Leicestershire, and won in a soggy contrivance at Durham as Kendall made another century. He repeated the feat in the next home game against Derbyshire where Prittipaul made his stunning first century in his third match and Hampshire won by an innings. So in mid-September, they came to the last-ever matches at Northlands Road.

On Sunday 10 September they lost in the league to Derbyshire after seeming in control of a target of 196. Kenway made 90 but the tail crumbled and Tremlett, needing to hit a six to win the game, was bowled by the last ball. On Wednesday 13 September they began the final Championship match against Yorkshire on a wicket that helped the spin bowlers throughout. Warne took 5-92 to dismiss

81   *2000 at Northlands Road v Yorkshire, the final Championship match.*

Yorkshire for 205, Hampshire managed just eight more (Middlebrook 6-82) but Lehmann (92) helped to set a target of 258. Hampshire reached 65-1 and 113-2, before Middlebrook (4-88) and Fisher (3-40) instigated a collapse. The final over was bowled by Fisher to Alex Morris with his fellow Yorkshireman Peter Hartley at the non-striker's end. The only 'Hampshire' men present were the two umpires Trevor Jesty and John Holder. Morris survived five balls but edged the sixth to slip and Hampshire had lost by 72 runs. At the close, in an act of extreme bureaucratic officiousness, the ECB's pitch inspectors, led by Mike Denness, imposed a penalty of eight points on a ground that would never be used again. It had no impact on the Championship table but left a sour taste, as well over a century of cricket history came to an end.

On the Sunday, Notts Outlaws scored 234-8 in 45 overs (Afzaal 95*) and Kendall (63) and Prittipaul (61) led the reply. Morris needed to score 13 in the final over but for the third time in eight days Hampshire fell short in the final over and lost by three runs. Prittipaul, who had scored the first century on the main Rose Bowl ground for Hampshire 2nd XI, could add to that record the last Championship century and the last limited-overs half-century at Northlands Road.

At the end of this nostalgic but equally disappointing season, Peter Hartley retired after giving brief but excellent service to his third county and Simon Renshaw and Lee Savident both left Hampshire. Savident had suffered from persistent back injuries that prevented him from realising his considerable potential. Jimmy Gray, Cricket Chairman when Savident had arrived from Guernsey, thought him as talented as any of his contemporaries. For his part, Savident felt that he had not always had sufficient opportunities to prove his worth.

From 2001 he would play with Portsmouth – Prittipaul's club – in the Southern League. Portsmouth, originally South Hants Cricket Club, had been one of the leading club sides in the south-east of the county since the Southern League had begun in 1969. The first winners, Trojans and then Old Tauntonians, were both from Southampton, which was then the strongest area for club cricket. In 1973 the Hampshire League was established and while the Southern League was still the strongest competition, the Hampshire League involved many clubs. A few like Hambledon resisted the wholesale change to league cricket, which in truth had existed in pockets in the South even before the war. But the traditionalists found their Saturday fixtures seriously affected and soon most clubs joined the leagues.

There had also been increasing competitions for village sides and national knock-out competitions. Among the Hampshire sides who appeared at Lord's were Longparish, Hambledon and Gosport and it is a sad thought that Longparish are perhaps only the most eminent of a number of once successful teams no longer in existence. But while changes to village life have led to the demise of some clubs, in the cities there tended to be amalgamations with the stronger clubs often fielding four or five sides. The Southern League also included sides from outside the county, notably Bournemouth and South Wiltshire (Salisbury).

'Raising the Standard' had a significant impact upon league cricket in the county. From 2000, clubs were scrutinised thoroughly for the quality of their pitches, other playing facilities and a successful colts structure. They had to be able to demonstrate a high-quality organisation to qualify for Gold Standard cricket. Sadly, for a variety of reasons, inner-city cricket in Hampshire struggled to match these criteria and, when the streamlined Southern League began, Winchester, Southampton and Portsmouth were all under-represented. In the ensuing six years only Portsmouth have resolved the issue with its major club moving grounds to meet the criteria while attracting a number of former or younger fringe county cricketers including Raj Maru, Lee Savident, Lawrence Prittipaul, Matthew Keech, Derek Kenway, James Schofield, Michael Barnes and James Manning.

One of the innovations in Gold Standard league cricket was the all-day match, played at the height of summer. With travel often lengthy across central Southern England these were not always popular with the players but more seriously, in Hampshire at least, these innovations have coincided with a period when the transition from club and league cricket to the county side seems harder than ever – the complete opposite of the intentions expressed in 'Raising the Standard'. Indeed it seems often that county cricket provides the training for a decent league club career rather than the other way round. Apart from Portsmouth Cricket Club, the Southern League has provided opportunities to watch a number of players who have been on Hampshire's staff including Jason Laney, Richard Dibden, Ian Turner, Glyn Treagus, Dan Goldstraw, Ian Brunnschweiler, Andrew Sexton and Matthew Swarbrick. At least one of those has commented that he has never missed four-day cricket since turning his back on professional county cricket.

Meanwhile the Hampshire Cricket Board has been working energetically with schools and clubs to encourage more young people – boys and girls – to take up the game. National League matches at the Rose Bowl are usually preceded by games of 'Kwik Cricket' and the coaches tour the county working to train more coaches in the regions. The academy under Tony Middleton now receives a substantial grant from the ECB and is ever more a Centre of Excellence for an elite squad, which in 2005 included a promising girl. The academy side competes in the Southern League Premier Division, usually in mid-table as it provides opportunities for younger players. In recent years, David Griffiths, Kevin Latouf, Chris Morgan and Mitchell Stokes have followed Udal and Tremlett from Hampshire sides to representative honours.

The magnificent coaching facilities at the Rose Bowl are central to Hampshire's involvement in the national network of centres of excellence, which includes the county academies and the new university centres. The Rose Bowl can offer a dedicated nursery ground, outdoor nets and an indoor academy with full-length run-ups and modern technology to support young cricketers. The dressing rooms are luxurious and there are good treatment facilities for injured players. From the early planning days this was always a part of the vision for the new ground and yet it so nearly led to disaster, not luxury.

In 1986, accountant Tony Baker, who had once captained Old Tauntonians to the Southern League title, moved from the post of Honorary Treasurer to become Hampshire's first Chief Executive. He succeeded Jimmy James, who had followed Desmond Eagar as Secretary in 1978. In 1987 Baker sought advice about developing Northlands Road but it was obvious that neither the ground nor that area of Southampton was large enough to allow the development of a modern ground. The advice was to move out of the city.

So Baker, Bill Hughes, who would become vice-chairman of the committee, and a local property developer turned their attention to the green spaces alongside the M27, which ran across the north side of Southampton, linking the edge of the New Forest to Portsmouth. In January 1988 the *Southern Evening Echo* ran the headline 'To move or not to move' suggesting that the debate might become 'heated'. Tony Baker pointed out that the first step was no more than a feasibility study, David Turner offered support to the idea, pointing out the poor facilities at Northlands Road, Neville Rogers accepted the necessity of the idea despite his 'many memories' but Jim Bailey, player and committee member, suggested it was a 'diabolical' idea, warning against the loss of many members.

Hampshire spent that winter canvassing the opinions of their members before further discussion at the AGM in March. There was a question about the wisdom of recent developments at Northlands Road given the possibility of a move but Baker pointed out that this would not happen for at least five years. In the event it took thirteen.

With membership approval, the search continued and they identified an unused area owned by Queen's College, Oxford, which the owners were willing to make available on a 999-year lease. The agreement would require first-class cricket to be played on the ground but other developments were possible and Hampshire began planning. Property prices were good enough to hope for up to £10 million for the Northlands Road site and by February 1990 the club set a target of 1995 for the new ground. But property prices crashed and the value of Northlands Road was suddenly insufficient for the project, which seemed to have stalled. In 1993, Hampshire no longer played at Bournemouth, while spectators found new plastic seats at Northlands Road. The club announced that these could be removed to the new ground.

Then in October 1994 the lease was signed and the club appointed their architects, Michael Hopkins and Partners, who had designed the new Mound Stand at Lord's. In addition Britain had a sudden source of public funds for such projects through the National Lottery and Hampshire made an application, as well as launching a centenary appeal to mark 100 years in the Championship. As they did so, Brian Ford replaced Donald Rich, who had been Chairman for the previous nine years.

The National Lottery Sports Fund took some time to respond but, after further forms and meetings, on the 'glorious' 12 August 1996, Hampshire were granted the sum of £7,176,728. Mark Nicholas, who had always had some input into the project, later identified Bill Hughes as the key figure in the visionary project and Nicholas, Robin Smith and Shaun Udal had their photograph taken with a resident horse on the sloping rough land that would become Hampshire's new home.

There was a ceremony to dig out the first turf in 1997 with a new target of 2001. The *Hampshire Handbook*, published in the spring of 1998, showed an aerial photograph of the new ground with its two ovals and the two squares clearly visible. The accompanying article identified the sum of £16 million to complete

82   *Building work at the Rose Bowl – Kendall, Robin Smith, Udal and White swap helmets for hard hats (IM).*

the project. Members had their first visit to the site in the autumn of that year but while building was in progress there remained a funding shortfall. Now the club had to organise the sale of Northlands Road.

The freehold was sold to Berkeley Homes for an index-linked sum that eventually reached £5,735,000. But all the while building costs were rising and in 1999 the main contractors went into liquidation and the project was halted. Hampshire employed fund-raisers who had little success in raising any major sums and there were no signs yet that they might emulate Surrey's Foster's Oval with a major ground sponsorship.

During 1999, early reports from Portsmouth suggested that their pitch was in poor condition and, with a place in the new First Division at stake, Hampshire could not afford to lose penalty points. They switched the proposed Portsmouth matches to Northlands Road and while they returned to Portsmouth for the final time in 2000 it was clear that the future of cricket in Hampshire would centre on the new ground. Basingstoke members and supporters remained optimistic about retaining their 'week' but the financial implications made this improbable.

The Rose Bowl's nine-hole golf course opened towards the end of the 1999 cricket season and in the following year the first 2nd XI matches were played on both squares. The estimated cost was now around £19 million, leaving a shortfall of £5 million with no sign of a major sponsor. By this time, work had begun on the main pavilion, atrium and cricket academy. It was due to be completed by March 2001, but bad weather and building problems delayed the completion and the first season at the Rose Bowl began with the pavilion boarded up and the players changing in one of the pods around the berm.

The 2000 season had ended with Hampshire in poor shape on the field. Shane Warne had been their outstanding player but he had only come in the first instance for the year. Robin Smith had struggled with his own form and had given clear indications that he was not particularly enjoying captaining a weak side. In September, the club organised a huge farewell dinner in a marquee on the Northlands Road ground. It was attended by all the living captains and was a fine final gesture. Within days the bulldozers moved in and the pavilions were no more.

However, by this point the expected cost of the Rose Bowl had risen to well above £20 million with only half that amount covered by the lottery grant and the sale of Northlands Road. It was no exaggeration to suggest that there was a Rose Bowl crisis and, in the winter of 2000–1, this precipitated the most radical changes in the running of county cricket in Hampshire since the members' club had been formed in 1863. In June 2000 Charles Randall wrote about the new project in the *Daily Telegraph* and quoted Tony Baker, saying 'we are not going to go bust spending money we haven't got'. In the event that is very nearly what did happen.

The Hampshire Committee in the late 1990s comprised mainly Hampshire men. One or two had grown up elsewhere but even they had spent decades in the county. The Chairman Brian Ford was a third-generation member of the committee, his vice president Bill Hughes had captained Holt's colts in the 1960s. They were all professional men – in one or two cases retired but mostly still working. Many had played local cricket to a reasonably high standard and there was still one county cricketer, Barry Reed, as a member. The other professions and businesses included computing, solicitors, accountants, a High Court judge, a journalist, a university lecturer, a dentist and general practitioners. The President, Wilfred Weld, and the club's officers Tony Baker, Brian Osman and Mike Taylor attended committee meetings.

During this period, uncertainties about the new ground and poor performances on the field created the Hampshire form of a pressure group. This cannot be compared with the ructions at other clubs such as Yorkshire, Lancashire and more recently Sussex but there were rumours, awkward questions and on one occasion media coverage of critical speeches at a members' forum. There were suggestions that an attempt might be made to replace the committee and it was sometimes suggested that this might involve a wealthy local businessman Rod Bransgrove. These rumours remained merely that.

Bransgrove was not a Hampshire man, having grown up supporting Surrey, but he now lived in the county. He was very wealthy, having made his money in chemicals and ran an entertainment company. He was also a friend of a number of cricketers and had an involvement in a business with Robin Smith. Committee members, by contrast, would sometimes be on good terms with players but two areas, across the boundary rope and inside the dressing room, were worlds inhabited by players, coaches and physiotherapists – not committee members. Relationships were friendlier and less hierarchical than they might have been in, say, some of the difficult times of the late 1970s but the traditional committee member and the players had a fairly clear if implicit relationship.

Bransgrove had a different approach. He clearly enjoyed a lively and friendly relationship with players and this was reciprocated. Shane Warne, in his autobiography (2001) mentioned Bransgrove and his wife Mandy as becoming 'really good friends' during his year at Hampshire. But Bransgrove's friendship with cricketers was not his only, nor indeed his major, difference. He brought to Hampshire cricket a tough, modern business approach, although initially only as one member of the committee, having been elected in 2000. It was not clear that he was always in full support of the committee's activities but for their part he appeared to offer the kind of expertise – and perhaps the finance – they needed.

Moving towards Christmas 2000, Northlands Road had gone, there were no plans to return to Basingstoke or Portsmouth but the Rose Bowl project was taking more and more time and causing increasing anxieties. While Bill Hughes was able to devote professional hours to the project because his company was involved, Brian Ford, the Chairman, in his early fifties and still running his own business, found the demands and the pressure too much. He offered his resignation as Chairman, which was accepted, and in the swiftest elevation in Hampshire's history, Rod Bransgrove replaced him.

But things did not get easier. There was no sign of the major sponsor or the additional funding required to complete the design. Early in the New Year the committee was called to a special meeting in one of the portakabins on the ground that now housed the club's administration. Once there, Malcolm Le Bas, one of their number but also the club's Hon. Solicitor, informed them that Hampshire County Cricket Club had reached crisis point. To date, the 'club' had acted with sufficient responsibility that its committee and members would not be found liable for debts. This was no longer the case and Le Bas advised that trading must cease on the following Monday morning to establish responsibility and avoid personal liability. Then he offered the one alternative.

This was that the new Chairman would underwrite sufficient elements of the whole project to allow it to continue and a loan agreement would be drawn up (February 2001). For the committee there was no choice. In the sense that there would be the funds to complete essential parts of the project it was indeed good news. But it also signalled the beginning of the end for the traditional model of a members' club, electing its own committee and operating in an ostensibly democratic manner. Not too much should be made of the Hampshire version of that. There was no real history of election campaigns or hard-fought issues – most members were really supporters purchasing a fairly cheap way of watching county cricket on a regular basis with special access to certain areas and tickets for major matches. Nonetheless, membership at Hampshire – despite the retention of the name – would now offer much the same rights as a season-ticket holder at one of the local football clubs.

Bransgrove took control of the finances and the project and in May 2001 wrote to the Executive Committee, identifying the need for further financial support, which would only be forthcoming, 'Within a legal, financial, fiscal, and commercial framework for the Rose Bowl that is *viable* (as and when determined by myself, after appropriate professional advice).' Whatever the sums, at this point he informed them that his commitment would not exceed £4 million. In this respect Bransgrove had now become the third funding source so urgently needed during the development of the project in the late 1990s. What was different was the extent to which he identified a certain model of Hampshire cricket and one that was certainly informed in some key respects by his relationships with the leading players at Hampshire and elsewhere.

By the end of May 2001 Bransgrove had appointed Graham Walker as the Senior Executive at the Rose Bowl. He had previously been at the Millennium Stadium project in Cardiff and while he was not a cricket man he knew about sporting projects of this size. Bransgrove required all members of all committees within Hampshire County Cricket Club Limited to resign prior to the next AGM, although they were all entitled to stand again, and some did, as the committee was reduced to 12 members. Meanwhile Mike Taylor and Tony Baker planned their retirements although Baker would remain in a part-time capacity until October 2005, associated especially with match days at the Rose Bowl. The new organisation was changing dramatically but Bransgrove was happy to reassure committee members that, I remain personally committed to helping to safeguard the future of the Rose Bowl and especially the playing of first-class cricket there by Hampshire County Cricket Club.' Over the next five years, Bransgrove more than demonstrated that commitment except in one pedantic respect. As the members' club became less relevant he rebranded Hampshire County Cricket Club 'Hampshire Cricket' – not merely as a plc but as the side that takes the field on behalf of Hampshire. After about 140 years, Hampshire County Cricket Club was no more. In respect of the protection of cricket at the Rose Bowl, this was enshrined in the agreement with Queen's College, Oxford, and also in the issue of a golden share.

Despite all the problems, a Hampshire side did take the field at the Rose Bowl led by Robin Smith and watched by their new Chairman. Although its windows and doors were boarded up, the pavilion's elevated roof appeared to float unaided above the long rectangular building – appropriate enough in 2001. Behind this futurist symbol, the hill and trees confirmed Hampshire's move from inner city to a particularly rural suburbia and from the top tier of the pavilion it was possible to look across the fields beyond Fareham towards Hambledon.

Hampshire had newly designed caps but these were replaced by woolly hats on the first day of the season at Edgbaston. Knight and Ostler made centuries and Hampshire followed on nearly 300 behind. It seemed that on the field little had changed although a welcome century from Smith saved the game. Incredibly, it was his first in the Championship since August 1998.

Hampshire moved to The Parks, where they divided their time between watching the rain and playing football, then to Canterbury where after four overs the match was abandoned. Their Rose Bowl debut was on 2 May 2001 in the Benson & Hedges Cup. Essex were their scheduled opponents but not a ball was bowled. Two days later they finally played an uninterrupted game at the ground and Mascarenhas bowled the first ball to Mark Butcher. But Hampshire, having confined Surrey to 194 all out, lost their new overseas player Neil Johnson for nought and were defeated by 23 runs. As a taste of things to come at the Rose Bowl no batsman on either side passed thirty-five. On the other hand things improved for Johnson. Having turned his back on Test cricket he was an ideal

83   *The first Championship match at the Rose Bowl: Smith, Udal, Aymes and Kendall (IM).*

overseas signing since he was available for the whole season. By the end of 2001 he was the only batsman to pass 1,000 first-class runs (at almost forty-five), was the leading limited-overs run scorer, had taken 23 first-class and 13 limited-overs wickets and had been an outstanding slip fielder.

At the Rose Bowl, the first Championship match was against Worcestershire. As in the previous year, the batsmen failed but from 79-6 Hampshire were rescued when Mascarenhas recorded the ground's maiden first-class century. Hick replied in kind but all the other batsmen struggled and Hampshire won this first match by 124 runs. Although batting was difficult on the ground, Hampshire supporters who had become over familiar with drawn games on the Northlands Road surface enjoyed results on the new ground and even the draws were exciting. Against Gloucestershire, Kenway and Smith made centuries but the rain deprived the two sides of about 130 overs. On the last afternoon Gloucestershire battled well enough to leave Hampshire a target of 56 in 10 overs. They panicked, lost wickets regularly and finishing on 55-6 had to settle for six extra points with the scores level.

There was one uncharacteristically high-scoring draw as Sussex became the first side to reach 500 on the ground (Goodwin 195) and Hampshire were just 63 short of their score (White 141), but this draw was a dull exception. In mid-season Hampshire won successive home matches against Durham, Derbyshire and Nottinghamshire before entertaining the touring Australians, who included Warne.

The first morning was extraordinary. Hayden took a single in Mullally's first over, then debutant Schofield's first ball had him caught at slip. Langer scored two and Katich three, Noffke was top scorer with just 28 and the tourists were dismissed for 97, days after their total of 401 had taken them to an easy victory over England at Lord's. It remained the lowest total on the ground in its first five seasons. Mullally took 5-18 and Schofield 3-25.

White and Kendall both went for nought but Kenway scored 70 and Robin Smith enjoyed one of his last great days with 113 against Lee, Gillespie, Warne and the others. Johnson's 88 took Hampshire to a lead of 257. In their second innings Australia reached 389-9 (Hayden 142) when Waugh declared, challenging Hampshire to score 133 in 26 overs. They chased furiously and while Warne took four wickets they cost six runs an over. Brunnschweiler and Schofield were together when the winning runs came with nine balls and two wickets left.

Many older supporters, remembering when the tourist match was the highlight of the season, believed this to be a major achievement. In truth, tourist games no longer warrant the same attention and Waugh's generous declaration was untypical of the man whose ruthless side won the first three Tests to retain the Ashes. The match featured no fewer than 14 Hampshire cricketers but it is a salutary thought that within four years only four of them would still be playing for Hampshire's first team: Udal, Mascarenhas and two 'Aussies', Warne and Katich.

If this victory was less important than it might once have been, this was partly because Hampshire spent the season challenging for promotion from the Second Division of both the Championship and the National League. In the event they missed success in the league by two points, having lost three consecutive matches in the late season, but in the Championship they were more successful. After the good run that culminated with the victory over Australia, they won only one of the next four but then met Middlesex at the Rose Bowl in the penultimate match. On the first day Mascarenhas, still enjoying the new ground, took 6-26 but Hampshire were reduced to 63-7, still 38 behind. Udal and Aymes effected a rescue operation, were not out overnight and added 102 to ensure a useful lead. The promising Andrew Strauss followed his first innings 56 with a century but Middlesex slipped from 233-5 to 253 all out, leaving Hampshire 164 to win.

At 27-3 they were struggling but Kendall (38), Johnson (74) and debutant John Francis (29*) ensured a victory that left them needing just three points from the last match at Trent Bridge. Despite regular interruptions for rain they managed this and secured second place as Mullally took 5-74 and Johnson and White scored centuries. A young Nottinghamshire batsman in his first English season, Kevin Pietersen, scored 87 against 'joke' bowling in the second innings before he was stumped by White off the bowling of Kenway.

At the end of the season Shaun Udal was awarded the Players' Player of the Year and he, Mullally and Alex Morris all passed 50 first-class wickets. There was more good news when the 2nd XI won their title, having been in front for most of the season. Prittipaul led the batting averages while Laney, Sexton and Francis all passed 500 runs. Wicketkeeper Brunnschweiler had a good all-round season as did Hamblin, who was the leading wicket-taker. Most of these players had come through the colts and Hampshire Board sides that had enjoyed success in recent years and they looked very promising. Disappointingly, of the regular players in that 2nd XI, within four years only two remained, James Adams and James Tomlinson, and neither was firmly established in the first team. The saddest figure was the spin bowler Charlie van der Gucht. In July he suffered serious leg injuries in a road accident in London and while he eventually recovered to play again he was never fit enough for first-class cricket. Laney and Stephenson

84   *Five of the six debut centurions, Baldry,*
Hayward, Crawley, Watson and Bichel.

shared the captaincy and at the end of the season the latter returned to Essex after a fairly unhappy period with Hampshire.

2002 was another yo-yo year for Hampshire as they were relegated in the Championship and in mid-August the coach Jimmy Cook was sacked and replaced temporarily by Tim Tremlett. They made no progress in either of the knock-out cups and finished in the bottom three of the Second Division in the National League. It was to be Robin Smith's last year as captain although he would remain as a player. Clearly it was not a very happy season. Neil Johnson was less successful than in 2001 and only Udal took over 50 wickets. Chris Tremlett continued to show promise and Hampshire gave opportunities to wicketkeeper Nic Pothas, a South African limited-overs international, eligible to play on a Greek passport. It signalled the end of Adi Aymes's very fine career.

It looked initially as though Hampshire's other new signing would make a huge impact. During the winter John Crawley left Lancashire under somewhat unhappy circumstances and joined Hampshire, where he made an immediate impact in becoming the third player in their history to score a century on first-class debut. But this was no mere century. At Canterbury in late April, Kent declared on 577-7 and Hampshire replied with 671. Johnson scored 117 and Crawley 272. The match was drawn. Bizarrely, neither player scored another first-class century for the county during the season and only Robin Smith (twice) reached three figures.

Meanwhile Hampshire struggled through the season, winning just two County Championship matches although both were at the Rose Bowl. The wickets seemed increasingly unreliable and in two matches caused real problems. Against India the tourists declared their second innings on 139-4 rather than risk their leading batsmen but were still able to win by 66 runs. No Hampshire player reached fifty. Three days later they began a match against Lancashire from which they lost eight points from the pitch inspector. Sadly they were also outplayed and ended up with minus five points as Lancashire, all out for 183 and 187, still won by 111 runs. A young and clearly promising bowler called James Anderson took 6-23 and 3-27.

Nonetheless, the season ended with a Rose Bowl match that produced the second highest aggregate in Hampshire's history. Saqlain took 0-100 in 16 overs but Surrey won by 123 runs. Hampshire and Middlesex then complied with an ECB request to stage two matches under the 20 overs per side format that would replace the Benson & Hedges Cup in 2003. Will Kendall observed that while 'it will be a bit mad at first ... fast entertainment is guaranteed'.

Hampshire had won the Benson & Hedges Cup twice in 1988 and 1992 and they won their last-ever match in the competition by three runs in what was to be Angus Fraser's farewell appearance. Crawley with 103* was Hampshire's final centurion but it was not enough to take them to the quarter-finals.

In February 2003 Charlie Knott died at the age of eighty-eight. From 1938–54 he became Hampshire's finest amateur bowler and one of their best of any kind. Then, during the 1970s and 1980s, he was central in the fashioning of two different teams that won major trophies. Even after his retirement as Cricket Chairman he remained actively involved in the club's Heritage Committee and he watched regularly until the county left Northlands Road.

Early in the New Year, England took part in the World Cup in South Africa. It was not a particularly happy tournament for them or indeed more generally with too many matches, especially dull ones. There were also two forfeitures when England refused to play Zimbabwe and New Zealand would not play Kenya. Accounts ranged from politically neutral cricketers fearing for their security to governments objecting to sporting links with repressive regimes. England failed to qualify for the Super Six part of this overlong tournament and when New Zealand were knocked out those two sides retained the unhappy record of competing in every World Cup since it began in 1975 without ever winning it.

The Australians were worthy Champions again. In the final, their score of 359-2 overwhelmed India (234) even without the assistance of Shane Warne. During Hampshire's winter Rod Bransgrove replaced Jimmy Cook with Paul Terry – to be known as manager – and, having said goodbye to Neil Johnson, re-signed Shane Warne as his new captain. He described the pairing as his 'dream team' but it turned into a nightmare as Warne was sent home from the World Cup for drug abuse and banned for a year. Estimates put the personal cost to Warne at approaching £1 million and the Australian Cricket Board's judgement included their refusal to 'accept that he was entirely truthful'.

Hampshire considered signing Shoaib Ahktar as a bowling replacement but left it late to announce the signing of Wasim Akram, now 36, adding that Crawley would captain the side. During the winter, Will Kendall had been reappointed to be vice-captain for the third year but this role was suddenly abolished with deputies appointed on a match-by-match basis. Kendall was not delighted by the news.

Counties were now allowed to sign two overseas players, so Australian Simon Katich joined Akram but almost immediately he was called into the Australia 'A' side and missed the opening weeks of the season. Another new signing was pace bowler Ed Giddins, formerly of England, Surrey, Warwickshire and Sussex, whence he had departed in shame after a ban for the use of recreational drugs.

In the County Championship, Hampshire and perhaps even more their supporters endured a diabolical season in which only Derbyshire kept them from last place. They won just two matches although one of them has claims to be the greatest victory in their history.

The Championship season began with a maiden century from Nic Pothas and occasional appearances by Tomlinson and Bruce as Giddens struggled with injury. At Oxford, Thorburn and Clapp, two trialists, played for Hampshire and promptly disappeared, having 'earned' their place on the Rose Bowl board of first-

85   *2003: Rod Bransgrove displays the brand new Twenty20 trophy before the first ever match at the Rose Bowl. Hampshire beat Sussex but have yet to win the cup.*

class cricketers. In early June Hampshire were unlucky in a rain-affected match against Durham when the visitors followed on and were still behind with nine second-innings wickets down at the close. Katich recorded his first century for the county.

Sussex were the visitors on Friday 13 June as English cricket rejected all superstition and launched their latest competition, the Twenty20 Cup. The first major match in this format anywhere in the world was at the Rose Bowl, arranged partly for the benefit of Sky Sports viewers.

In the *Guardian*, Mike Selvey wrote of this as an antidote to 'plummeting' attendances, although in truth Hampshire's membership and gate receipts were fairly steady. He suggested further that the competition was aimed specifically at people who do not normally attend cricket, such as 'women, kids, men in the laddish late-teens-to-thirtysomething bracket and almost by definition families'. In some respects this was an obvious and common comment, as was Will Kendall's view that it was 'frenetic and action packed'. In fact, many regular cricket watchers watched this competition so that the audience was expanded rather than replaced and many regular watchers were pleasantly surprised by the visible skill required and by the sense (if not the sound) of spectacle. After the match there was a concert by Mis-Teeq and D-Side, which a small proportion of mainly younger spectators appeared to enjoy but which was otherwise somewhat redundant.

There was a sell-out crowd of 9,000 at the Rose Bowl to watch James Kirtley bowl the first ball to James Hamblin. He and Kenway both passed 30 in an opening stand of 66 but Hampshire were surprisingly all out with two balls left for 153. Sussex struggled but needed 22 from the last two overs and ten from Giddins' final six balls. He denied them and so Hampshire won this first match in the new competition. It did not last. In the next match Andrew Symonds hammered them at Beckenham and they lost the next three matches against Essex, Middlesex and Surrey to go out at the group stage.

They did at least win promotion in the National League, even though they stumbled through the final stages, losing their last four matches. They were helped as much by the failure of their rivals as by their own efforts although Crawley and Katich batted consistently and Mascarenhas had an outstanding season with

237 runs and 34 wickets. During an August heatwave they recorded their highest ever League score of 335-6 at Taunton as Katich made 106, Crawley 92 and John Francis fifty. Shortly after this, Somerset began an eventually successful move to lure Francis from Hampshire. In the C&G Trophy they lost their first match from a relatively comfortable position as Chris Adams launched an astonishing assault on Wasim, taking 20 from one over and winning the game.

The most remarkable match of this and most other years came at the Rose Bowl in mid-July when Glamorgan were the visitors. Will Kendall was omitted for the first time in almost five years, Alan Mullally and Shaun Udal were injured, Giddins was in discussions, which led to his retirement, and Wasim retired through ill health on the eve of the match. Crawley led a side with Katich and only two other men, Kenway and Mascarenhas, with county caps. Otherwise the eleven included Adams, John Francis, Pothas, Tremlett, Bruce, Tomlinson and Richard Hindley, a Southern League cricketer from Havant. He had played for the 2nd XI but was not on the staff and offered Crawley an off spin option in the absence of Udal.

On the first day his nine overs cost 46 runs as Dale and Maynard hit centuries. Glamorgan were dismissed for 437 with Katich taking 3-87 but no Hampshire player reached 30 and they followed on 252 behind. Katich made 53 but wickets fell regularly and at 194-5 they were still in arrears. Then came an extraordinary change in fortunes. Pothas scored another century (121) and enjoyed excellent support from Hindley, who batted with two broken bones in his hand to make 68 not out. Mascarenhas scored 75 and Bruce 10 and Hampshire's final total left Glamorgan a target of 198.

Tremlett and Bruce struck on the third evening and Glamorgan were in difficulty at 33-3. On the following morning wickets fell early and regularly and Tremlett (6-51) and Bruce (3-42) bowled Hampshire to victory by 93 runs. They did so with Hindley in hospital; he missed the remainder of that season and never played county cricket again.

It was only the third occasion that Hampshire had won after following on – the other two being their first ever Championship match at Taunton in 1895 and Edgbaston in 1922, which Frank Keating had selected as the best county match of the 20th century – perhaps this would be the best of the next century? In the context of the season of 2003 and the problems of that particular week, the victory against Glamorgan was perhaps even more remarkable than that against Warwickshire in 1922. But it did not signal a general improvement in fortunes.

Otherwise they won only at Derby in mid-September, avoiding the wooden spoon. Katich made another century but the hero was Hamblin with 96 and 6-93. These were his best two first-class performances but he never appeared in the Championship again and left the club 12 months later.

By the time of the Derby visit, Robin Smith had played his last match for Hampshire. He had been troubled by a hamstring injury for some weeks but returned to the side at Taunton in the last week of August. On the first day Kenway made a century but Smith had to retire hurt before returning with seven wickets down. On the second morning, batting with a runner, he went from seven not out to 56 not out and Hampshire reached 395 before 19-year-old Neil Edwards

86   *Robin Smith's final appearance (at Taunton) flanked by his runner Jimmy Adams and last man James Tomlinson.*

scored 160 in an eventual Somerset total of 705-9 declared. On the following day he gained the headlines while Smith was ignored completely by the *Times* and the *Daily Telegraph*. In the *Guardian* Paul Weaver commented on the 'hobbling' Smith, adding 'but the day belonged to the young and fit'.

Some departures are like that. Robin Smith played for England many more times than any other Hampshire player and left Test cricket with an average just below forty-four. In limited overs internationals he averaged slightly below forty and his 167* against Australia remains the highest in that form of the game for England. For Hampshire he scored around nineteen thousand first-class runs at an average of 42.09 and his limited-overs average was similar. He scored 49 centuries for Hampshire and 12 in other first-class matches and the manner of his batting always brought great pleasure to spectators. It was not certain that Taunton would be his final appearance but it seemed very probable and this was confirmed just a few weeks later. He deserved a more public tribute. Alex Morris, who never overcame his injury problems, and reserve wicketkeeper Ian Brunnschweiler also retired from first-class cricket. The latter must have hoped to succeed Aymes, also recently retired, but Hampshire opted instead for the batting ability of Pothas. The retirement of Aymes marked a point of interesting comparisons of Hampshire's wicketkeepers:

Dates	Wicketkeeper	Dismissals	Stumpings	Stumpings %
1895–1906	C. Robson	202	37	18%
1900–1914	J. Stone	474	113	24%
1913–1929	W. Livsey	629	254	40%
1932–1951	N. McCorkell	690	176	26%
1939–1966	L. Harrison	666	99	15%
1959–1968	B. Timms	462	60	13%
1969–1980	G.R. Stephenson	645	75	12%
1980–1992	R. Parks	700	70 (10%)	10%
1987–2002	A. Aymes	560	44	8%

This shows that from the end of the First World War Hampshire's wicketkeepers have successively taken a higher percentage of catches and fewer stumpings because they have come to rely increasingly on pace bowlers in first-class cricket, where spin bowlers are less effective on covered wickets, with fielding restrictions and against increasingly heavy bats. Four-day cricket has disappointed in that wickets have not often turned on the third and fourth days and only unorthodox or great wrist spinners can now bowl sides out regularly. Consider this table of Hampshire's leading spin bowlers, paying particular attention to their career average (to the end of 2004):

Dates	Bowler	Wkts	Avge	Dates	Bowler	Wkts	Avge
1906–30	J. Newman	1946	24.82	1957–66	A. Wassell	317	27.04
1921–39	S. Boyes	1415	23.68				
1927–52	J. Bailey	467	26.97	1974–89	N. Cowley	425	32.89
1932–54	G. Hill	617	29.92	1975–83	J. Southern	412	29.81
1938–54	C. Knott	647	23.53	1984–98	R. Maru	504	33.62
1953–63	M. Burden	481	26.11	1989–	S. Udal	635	32.75
1954–76	P. Sainsbury	1,245	24.14	2000–	S. Warne	121	23.56

Newman bowled seam and spin but we can see that of modern spin bowlers (from Cowley) only the great wristspinner Warne has an average to compare with most of the men who bowled regularly on uncovered wickets. Of course, recent county scores were generally higher than those of the mid-century but nonetheless, Hampshire's leading pace bowlers of the recent past like Marshall (18.64), Tim (23.44) and Chris Tremlett, McLean and Mascarenhas average under thirty.

It is interesting also to note certain statistics that indicate significant changes in performances since the introduction of four-day Championship matches in 1988. The pitches became increasingly predictable and although the weather in 1988 was mediocre, the two following summers were among the driest and hottest in the century. In 1990, Gooch, Cook and Hick averaged over ninety, Moody over eighty, Atherton and Hardie over seventy and 10 others over sixty. But hardly any bowlers averaged under twenty-five, and only one under twenty – the incredible Malcolm Marshall with 72 wickets at 19.18. At the end of that season Marshall was the only bowler registered for county cricket with a career average below twenty (18.22). Yet at the end of the damp 1958 season and uncovered wickets, 17 county bowlers including Derek Shackleton, had career averages below twenty.

Six of those men, Laker and Lock, Hilton and Tattersall (Lancashire), Slade (Worcestershire) and McConnon of Glamorgan were spin bowlers.

A survey of high and low scoring throughout Hampshire's history is equally revealing. If we consider the 40 highest totals by Hampshire, 20 of them occurred between 1895–1929 and 18 more since 1990. The other two were in the 1930s but at the lower end of that group and none between 1946–90. Similarly, 23 of the highest 40 against Hampshire came before 1930 and 11 since 1990 with only one in the first 45 post-war seasons – that famous innings by the 1950 West Indians. By contrast, 13 of Hampshire's lowest scores came between 1946–89 and 17 of the lowest 40 against them were in the same period. Not one of the lowest 40 scores for or against has occurred since 1990. In such ways county cricket has changed dramatically in the past 60 years.

Despite this era of generally high scoring, during 2003, Katich was the only batsman to reach 1,000 runs, although Pothas passed 800 and averaged around forty-five. Crawley struggled as he had always done when captaining a side although he does not believe that the two things are linked. He was more broadly very unlucky to lose his England place after coming south. His opportunity came after he scored 272 on his Hampshire debut at Canterbury in April 2002 – the highest score by a Hampshire player since R.H. Moore's record 316 against Warwickshire 65 years before. Crawley made half-centuries in his next four Championship appearances and by July he was back in the England side, scoring 64 and 100* v India at Lord's. He finished that shared series with an average of 47.4 and ahead of Butcher, Thorpe and Key.

Crawley went to Australia later that year. England lost the series but Crawley began it with 69*, was run out without scoring and then missed two matches. He returned with scores of 17, 33, 35* and eight and a series average of 40.5 – ahead of Hussain, Butcher, Trescothick and Key. Despite his Test average of well over 40 while a Hampshire player, he was never selected for England again whereas each of those players who had been below him in those series continued to play.

Udal and Mascarenhas were the only bowlers to exceed 40 wickets but both averaged over thirty and it was clear that Hampshire needed a stronger attack. Chaminda Vaas joined for a few weeks in late season but to little effect.

Once again the 2nd XI did well, finishing third in the Championship and for the first time winning their limited-overs competition after beating Warwickshire by eight wickets. In the final, their key performers were Adams with 97*, Kendall the captain with 46, Bruce with 3-22 and Lamb with 3-35. Within two years Lamb and Latouf would collect winners' medals against the same county in their Lord's final, by which time five of their team-mates had left Hampshire.

The other major event of the summer was the first international fixture staged at the Rose Bowl when, on 10 July, South Africa easily defeated Zimbabwe in the triangular tournament. Again there was a full house and, apart from difficulties of transport access, the day was a considerable success and another step on the way towards the transformation of this once-modest county. However, this was not unproblematic as the finances continued to give cause for comment if not concern. In mid-season Rose Bowl plc announced an operating loss for the year to October 2002 of just over £1 million, with an overall loss including depreciation exceeding £4 million.

The *Daily Echo*'s Business of Sport columnist Peter Sharkey commented, however, that Hampshire looked reasonably healthy, commending their variety of 'revenue streams', which comprised, 'A golf club, a health and fitness centre, pop concerts and conference and banqueting facilities in addition to the cricket ground'.

Sharkey pointed out that counties had become increasingly reliant upon the ECB grant and that it was far better for them to develop diverse incomes. While the new Twenty20 competition was helping to create an additional audience for cricket, county cricket was still poorly attended by comparison with other sports like rugby and football. For example, research by Deloitte & Touche found that the average attendance over a four-day Championship match in 2001 was 3,400, with the overall figure in decline over the previous three years. While this might be unsurprising since it includes midweek morning attendances, even in the evening or Sunday for a National League match the average attendance was just under 2,500, down again, and lower than most Football League matches. In Hampshire the news was worse because their attendances were below the average. The bonus for counties was the increase in income from the ECB, now exceeding £1 million per year.

In 2003, attendances at Test Matches were again satisfactory. The year began with two innings victories for England over Zimbabwe, who were captained by Heath Streak and included an unsuccessful Sean Ervine. The main business of the summer came in the series against South Africa, who began with 594-5 declared in the drawn first Test. Their captain Graeme Smith hit successive double centuries and when the visitors won the second Test by an innings it appeared that England faced another difficult summer, despite a magnificent century from Flintoff. But then a century from Butcher and effective bowling by Anderson and Kirtley took them to a victory at Nottingham. South Africa won the Leeds Test and an intriguing series finished square when England won at The Oval by nine wickets after a double century from Trescothick. Before Christmas England lost in Sri Lanka by one match to nil but they were showing steady signs of improvement and a spring tour to the Caribbean brought the riches of a 3-0 series win.

On the eve of that tour, in an interview in the *Sunday Times,* Michael Vaughan told Simon Wilde that while every England captain for 20 years had sought change in county cricket 'nothing seems to happen'. In fact, in 1983 county cricket had been one competition with no promotion or relegation played over three days and 24 matches. Now it was in two divisions with 16 four-day matches. Then there were two knock-out cups of 55 and 60 overs, by 2003 there was one of 50 overs. The single-division Sunday League, played over 40 overs, was now a two-division 45-over contest and the period had seen the introduction of Twenty20 cricket and the use of floodlights. Vaughan's comment was absurd but put him firmly in line with former England captains like Willis and Atherton who, having disliked county cricket themselves, now took every media opportunity to rubbish it. One strong thread was that since the South Africans and Australians were better than England we should model our domestic game on theirs, particularly by reducing the number of counties. The proposal ignored or misunderstood the social, geographical and political differences in the three countries but within two

87   *In charge: Warne (captain) and Tremlett (Director of Cricket).*

years, as England won Test series against both sides, the suggestion seemed to fade away. No one had the courage in 2005 to suggest to Australia and South Africa that the way back was to *increase* their number of first-class sides to eighteen.

In July 2003 the *Portsmouth News* reported a move from Liberal Democrat and Conservative councillors in Portsmouth to persuade Hampshire to bring cricket back to the city. It was an odd initiative that took no account of the economic need to focus on the Rose Bowl and ignored the deterioration in the ground and pitch, which was now tended by a franchised company rather than a full-time groundsman. Unsurprisingly, the tale soon petered out. Meanwhile the Rose Bowl hosted a pop concert featuring Darius and Blue as well as a performance by the Royal Philharmonic Orchestra. They went ahead despite local objections and criticisms from Eastleigh Borough Council.

During the winter, the members' bar at the Rose Bowl was named in honour of Derek Shackleton and there was a delightful ceremony presided over by his former captain Colin Ingleby-Mackenzie, now President, and many of his former team-mates. Meanwhile, pace bowler Billy Taylor moved from Sussex to Hampshire. Taylor was born in Winchester and played for Hampshire 2nd XI but was never offered a contract. He had played in the Sussex side that won their first ever Championship title in 2003 but as a local man he expressed himself delighted to be returning to his native county. Another bowler to announce his return was Shane Warne who, having served his suspension, was available to start 2004 as Hampshire's captain – their 100th season of Championship cricket. In response, membership increased significantly during the winter despite the poor results of the previous summer.

Warne returned to Test cricket against Sri Lanka in March, took 10 wickets in the match and became the first bowler to pass 500 wickets in Test cricket. He arrived in Hampshire with fellow Australian Michael Clarke, a promising young batsman who had previously played in the Lancashire League. Prittipaul, still struggling to establish himself, commented on the marked change in the dressing room with the return of Warne and on the first day of the season at the Rose Bowl Hampshire dismissed Durham for 128 and replied with 195-5, including a stunning debut innings from Clarke. Hampshire, 165-2, collapsed to 221 all out and, chasing 109 to win, were 52-7 before Kendall and Mascarenhas carried them to victory. It seemed that the Rose Bowl surface still posed problems to the batsmen and Clarke was unable to sustain his promising start, finishing with an average of 35.45 thanks to three centuries, all away from home, including two in the match at Trent Bridge. Even that effort was eclipsed by John Crawley who scored 301* in the same match – his only first-class century of the season and just 15 short of R.H. Moore's Hampshire record.

Nottinghamshire were progressing towards the Second Division title and beat Hampshire at the Rose Bowl later in the season. Richard Logan took 4-56 and 4-34, while Pietersen's 49 was higher than any Hampshire score. Within a few months both players moved to Hampshire. The return at Trent Bridge was a high-scoring dull draw. Hampshire declared on 641-4 and Nottinghamshire replied with 612. Crawley's triple century was only the third in Hampshire's history. The game petered out with Hampshire on 295-6.

Although Crawley made only that one century he topped the averages but in some respects the most impressive performers were Pothas, who averaged 40, and Michael Brown, the new opener from Middlesex, who played in every match scoring 838 runs at 32.23. There were two double centuries at the Rose Bowl by visiting batsmen – Yorkshire's Phil Jacques and Will Jefferson of Essex. His side won by 384 runs, the largest run-margin defeat in Hampshire's history. There was an odd event against Glamorgan as Darren Thomas scored a century but was then replaced by Simon Jones, who had been released by England.

Mascarenhas had a fine season, taking 56 first-class wickets at 18.67. Warne, Tremlett and Udal all enjoyed good seasons and Billy Taylor's 33 wickets offered good support. Hampshire's good bowling kept them in the leading positions and they finished second, winning promotion. Another impressive performance came from the Australian Shane Watson, who replaced for Clarke while the latter was playing for his country. Against Somerset at the Rose Bowl he scored 112* on his county debut – the fifth player to achieve that feat for Hampshire and the first to do so with a runner! At one point he shared a stand with Mascarenhas who also had a runner, so mid-pitch conferences involved four Hampshire 'batsmen'. Simon Francis took four wickets in each innings but his former county won easily.

The Twenty20 competition remained a huge commercial success. Total attendances were about fifty per cent of those for the whole of the Championship in addition to the income generated by television coverage. Watson was instrumental in getting Hampshire into the quarter-finals. They began by losing to Essex and Surrey before a televised floodlit match at Hove. Mascarenhas took 5-14, including the competition's first hat-trick but, chasing just 68 to win Hampshire stumbled to victory by three wickets. Back at the Rose Bowl, they beat Middlesex and brought a crowd of 9,000 to their final match against Kent. Watson hit 97* and Bruce, Tremlett and Mascarenhas reduced Kent to 20-4. They did not recover. Warne returned from overseas and replaced Watson for the quarter-final against Lancashire but, batting at number three, he was dismissed for nought. Hampshire could not defend their 120 all out and another sell-out crowd saw them lose by nine wickets in the 17th over.

Warne's figures were 0-22 but this was one of the few matches in which his inspirational leadership did not lead to success. The other notable failure came at Bristol in the C&G Trophy, where he chose to bat on a green wicket and was one of three casualties as Hampshire fell to 4–3. Mascarenhas took them to 154 and Warne took 4–23 but Gloucestershire triumphed and eventually won the cup again. Australian Michael Dighton played in this match and Katich appeared a few times in late season, making a total of five Australians selected. Throughout the English season more than a quarter of players in the domestic game had been raised abroad – a situation that encouraged the ECB to develop a procedure for rewarding financially counties who developed English players. At Hampshire, the five Australians and two Southern Africans contributed to Hampshire's new 'nasty' image as the English umpires' marks consigned them to bottom place in the 'fair play' league.

Hampshire made what seemed an annual autumnal trip to Derby where Benham (74) and Lamb (94) made impressive debuts. They had earned their opportunity with some good performances in the 2nd XI who had an average season. Jono McLean, a South African in his mid-20s, was the most promising of the new players and was given a contract for 2005, while local opening batsman Damian Shirazi, who had broken batting records on the MCC ground staff, was their leading scorer. For whatever reason he never did enough to win a contract and is now just another Southern League cricketer.

Hampshire played their September matches away from home because, along with Edgbaston and The Oval, the Rose Bowl was chosen to host the ICC Champions Trophy. This seemed a misconceived commercial venture, which to some extent was disrupted by rain as one might expect at the end of the English season. The Rose Bowl looked magnificent for the various games but there were serious transport problems that the press seized on eagerly. Spectators were also subjected to the pedantic requirements of the sponsors and the difficulties were exacerbated by other major events, including local football and the Southampton Boat Show.

The matches were dull, one-sided affairs. India beat Kenya by 98 runs, Australia beat the USA by nine wickets in the eighth over, the West Indies beat Bangladesh by 138 runs and Pakistan by seven wickets and, under Duckworth-Lewis calculations, England beat Sri Lanka by 49 runs. Rod Bransgrove acknowledged the problems and failings at the ground and promised no repeat. Things did improve considerably in the following year. Meanwhile England seemed certain to win the final against the West Indies but managed to make a mess of things as they failed to solve their limited-overs problems. At Hampshire there was incredulity when Mascarenhas failed to make the initial squad of 30 players, although he represented England in the Hong Kong six-a-side competition. Chris Tremlett did make the England squad but did not play. He enjoyed a happier season after a hip operation in the previous winter, although still suffered some difficulties with his feet.

Despite their limited-overs disappointments, England won three of the four Tests in the Caribbean pre-season, beat New Zealand by three Tests to nil and then the return series with the West Indies four-nil – 10 victories and just one draw.

Hampshire finished third in the First Division of the National League and, while they never threatened to thwart the champions Glamorgan, their good season ensured that in 2005 Hampshire would play in the top divisions of both competitions for the first time.

They would do so without Will Kendall and James Hamblin, who both retired, realising that their opportunities were increasingly limited. For a time

Kendall had seemed likely to become Hampshire's captain and he had enjoyed some very good seasons without perhaps ever fulfilling his promise. Hamblin was a pace bowler who became a batsman but never developed consistently in either mode. In their place Hampshire signed Kevin Pietersen, who brought a somewhat difficult reputation from Nottinghamshire. He was clearly attracted by the prospect of playing under Warne but then during the winter produced some very impressive performances for England in their otherwise frustrating limited-overs series in South Africa. It appeared possible that he would not play much for his new county. His good friend Richard Logan, reputedly the fastest bowler available, came with him and Sean Ervine, who had played Test cricket for Zimbabwe, signed on a British passport. David Griffiths also signed a contract but, touring with England under-19 in the winter, injured his back and missed the whole season.

Warne and Katich signed as the two overseas players, although both would be missing for the Ashes tour and Katich for the limited-overs series that preceded it. This part of the tour began with the first international Twenty20 match in England at the Rose Bowl, and a capacity crowd filling the temporary stands cheered England to a huge victory in this form of the game by 100 runs, Pietersen impressing with 34 and three catches. As the 50-over series began, he also scored a magnificent 91* at Bristol as England beat Australia and English supporters began to wonder whether they could regain the Ashes. Tremlett made his international debut and was robbed of a hat-trick against Bangladesh as the ball hit the bails but failed dislodge them after he had taken two wickets in two balls.

Hampshire began their season with Championship victories at the Rose Bowl over Gloucestershire, Middlesex and Glamorgan, which took them to the top of the First Division, but they then lost in two days to the reigning Champions at Stratford. They won a remarkable victory at Trent Bridge when, after rain, Warne challenged Nottinghamshire to score 276 to win. At 250-4 the home side looked comfortable but Tremlett took a hat-trick, six wickets fell for 11 runs and Hampshire won to go back to the top after seven matches with Nottinghamshire 12 points behind.

They were less successful in the National League, despite beating Lancashire twice and registering their record score at Lord's. At the end of the season they were relegated as they kept losing vital matches but the daftest conclusion in their history came at Trent Bridge. Hampshire scored 240 and Nottinghamshire reached the final over on 238-9. The crowd were enthralled but the umpires ruled that Hampshire were one minute behind the set time to begin their last over, awarded six runs to Nottinghamshire and the exciting finish never materialised.

This match came just two days after an astonishing victory in the C&G Trophy at The Oval. Hampshire began the competition by beating Shropshire as Logan and Warne took three wickets and Pietersen scored seventy-six. They beat Glamorgan at Cardiff by six wickets as Ervine took 5-50 and Pietersen scored 69*. Hampshire's hero was Pothas, who opened and scored 114*. They were drawn away to Surrey in the quarter-final, where their former 2nd XI player Jon Batty scored a century in Surrey's 358-6. Opener Greg Lamb went for nought and, although Hampshire battled, at 279-7 they seemed to be losing. But Watson set a remarkable record,

88   *Rod Bransgrove and Shaun Udal celebrate the C&G triumph (SM).*

following his Championship debut century with one in this competition. He scored 132 and with 40 from Crawley, Udal and MacMillan, Hampshire won by two wickets with two overs to spare. Their 359-8 was the highest score by any county chasing and winning a match in this competition.

New Zealander MacMillan had joined in mid-season with little success. He returned to international cricket as Australian pace bowler Andy Bichel arrived in time for the home semi-final against Yorkshire. The Northern side were hampered by having to travel from Old Trafford on the evening before the game but made a complete mess of their travel arrangements and the start was delayed. It did not help them as Hampshire fielded superbly and took wickets regularly enough to restrict Yorkshire to 197-9. Crawley went early but Pothas anchored Hampshire with 73* and Ervine scored a superb century as Hampshire won by eight wickets with 10 overs to spare. In the meantime, Bichel became the sixth Hampshire debutant to record a first-class century.

The semi-final victory was a tremendous result for Hampshire, who continued to press in the Championship. Their supporters and local media responded to the cup fever and many packed coaches converged on Lord's where Hampshire, starved of success for 13 years, dominated the day in the stands and much of it on the pitch. Ervine emulated Worcestershire's Solanki 12 months earlier by scoring centuries in the semi-final and final, Crawley, Pothas and Watson all batted well and Hampshire set Warwickshire 291 to win. It often looked likely to be more but they lost late, cheap wickets.

Warwickshire began superbly. Carter, savaging Tremlett, hit a furious 32 before Ervine ran him out with a direct throw. Even so, Bell and Knight took Warwickshire to 166 but Bell, struggling with cramp, was dismissed by Watson and wickets began falling as Bichel encouraged the supporters and bowled a superb second spell. Knight made a century, but not quite quickly enough, and even six penalty runs for another slow over rate left Warwickshire 18 runs short as Tremlett took the final wicket and the celebrations began. Shaun Udal, deputising for Warne, led Hampshire to their ninth trophy and was the first Hampshire-born player to do so. Sean Ervine won the Man of the Match award.

Meanwhile, in mid-season in the Championship, Surrey, struggling after many successful years, nonetheless won easily at the Rose Bowl. It was a bad time for Warne ahead of the Ashes tour as he once again appeared on the front pages of the tabloids accused of more sexual indiscretions. He had bought a home in Hampshire but his wife and children returned to Australia, announcing a trial separation, which clearly distressed Warne. He disappeared for two weeks as the Twenty20 started, although the rain had a greater impact on Hampshire's progress and finances.

Oasis starred at the Rose Bowl as Warne returned to score a century at Southgate just two months after the first of his career at Canterbury. He then departed to join the Australians and he and McGrath bowled Australia to an easy victory in the first Test at Lord's. Then McGrath was injured at Edgbaston, Ponting invited England to bat and Trescothick and Strauss scored 112. England dominated throughout, almost lost and clinched an incredible finish by just two runs. The balance of power had shifted and when Pietersen scored 158 on the last day at The Oval the Ashes came home. Pietersen, in his debut series, was England's leading batsman with 473 runs at 52.55 while Australia included four men who had played for Hampshire: Hayden, Clarke, Katich and the outstanding Warne. He scored 249 runs at 27.66 and took 40 wickets at 19.92. He also held five catches but incredibly dropped Pietersen on that crucial last day. Tremlett was selected in the 12 for the first four Tests but never played, and with Jones injured he was discarded at The Oval. In fairness, his form had declined significantly and he was again struggling with injury – this time to his knee. He was encouraged to be selected for England's tour of Pakistan along with Udal and Pietersen. Sadly, Tremlett was not fit and withdrew. Instead he had an operation and spent the winter recuperating in Australia.

Hampshire stayed in contention in the Championship and with two matches left were 24 points behind Nottinghamshire, who they would play at the Rose Bowl in the final match. Their Director of Cricket, Mike Newell, announced that they would be happy 'if it rains now for two weeks'.

Nottinghamshire went next to Canterbury where it did indeed rain. Kent had to win to keep their remote chances of the title alive and allowed themselves to be tempted by a huge last-day target of 420. With rumours of dissent in their dressing room, Kent batted very poorly and by mid-afternoon Nottinghamshire had won by 214 runs and Nottinghamshire were Champions. Warne was publicly furious with Kent's captain David Fulton, who resigned the captaincy a few weeks later. Warne led Hampshire to victory in the penultimate match at Cardiff and Hampshire hammered Nottinghamshire in the final match to clinch second place, as they achieved in 1958, 1974 and 1985.

Having won the title, Nottinghamshire relaxed and celebrated. They made three changes on Wednesday at the Rose Bowl, including a second match for Mark Footit, a fast left-arm bowler who coincidentally on the same morning was one of three promising young English pace bowlers profiled and pictured in an article in the *Guardian*. In the years of single-division cricket, promising youngsters like Footit would have had more opportunities to learn about first-class cricket but in 2005 about half the county sides were still involved in battles for or against titles, relegation and promotion at the beginning of September and they had to keep picking their strongest sides.

During 2005, the Rose Bowl wickets were becoming much easier for batsmen. In the previous match against Warwickshire, Shane Watson had made a double century and Hampshire posted the highest total ever at the ground. It was a surprise, therefore, when Stephen Fleming won the toss and chose to bowl although, even during the day, the Nottinghamshire bowlers confirmed that there was something in the wicket.

89   *Autumn looms: runners-up Hampshire beat Champions Nottinghamshire at the end of the season.*

They had an early success dismissing Ervine, but Katich and Adams made half-centuries while John Crawley, on his 34th birthday, reached 65 to become the first English player to pass 1,000 runs for Hampshire since their move to the new ground. Pothas gave Crawley good support but fell just short of his 1,000 on the second morning. By this time Crawley had gone past his century and 150 and, joined by Mascarenhas, took advantage of some tired bowlers and fielders.

Shortly before lunch, three byes took the Hampshire score beyond 672, which had been for 106 years the highest total in the county's history. At lunch-time Hampshire were just short of 700, Crawley approaching 300 and Mascarenhas was in the 90s. Knowing that cricketers generally claim to be unsentimental about records and personal achievements, many supporters believed that Warne would declare but he did not. After lunch, Hampshire reached 700 for the first time in their history and shortly after Crawley passed 300 as he had done against the same opponents at Trent Bridge in the previous season.

On that occasion Warne had declared with Crawley 301*. This placed him third in the list of highest scorers for Hampshire behind Dick Moore (316) against Warwickshire at Bournemouth in 1937 and 304 by R.M. Poore in the match at Taunton in 1899 when they had amassed the 672-7 declared. In 2004, the Hampshire statistician Vic Isaacs told them that Crawley had just missed the record but they did not seem bothered then and had probably forgotten by 2005.

On this occasion, however, it seemed that once they had batted on after lunch there was no reason for him not to pass Moore's record. By this time the Nottinghamshire opening bowler Smith had reverted to vulnerable slow left-arm and Crawley reached 311 while Mascarenhas was still in the 90s. Then Crawley patted back two balls of Smith's over before Mascarenhas reached his century. Crawley took the run and continued to the pavilion.

Those who knew about the record were surprised. The argument seems simple. In cricketing terms there was no case for batting on after lunch. If Hampshire could not win from a score of 692 they were unlikely to do so with 714. So, the decision to bat on was surely sentimental in the sense that it was for the sake of the individuals. But why would that be? Crawley had already scored a triple century and over forty first-class hundreds and Mascarenhas had made first-class centuries before in tougher circumstances. If 700 was the target why not declare then?

But Hampshire went on and in the report on the following day the *Southern Daily Echo* ran a headline quote from Crawley 'Warney was right to call me in – it was more important Dimi got his ton than I got a record.' In the interview Crawley was also quoted as saying that 'things' like records 'don't bother me' but he did not explain why it was 'more important' for Mascarenhas to reach a century but not for him to break an all-time record, and neither did he say precisely for whom it was more important. One assumes it was an unselfish gesture by a very nice man, in support of a younger teammate.

Vic Isaacs confirmed that he had told the team of the target during the lunch interval although in the Portsmouth *News* Crawley said he did not know the figure. The key then is whether the team knew, and it is fairly clear that they did. In the *Guardian*, Rob Smyth wrote:

> In the list of archetypal Australian ideals, superfluous sentiment lies somewhere between warm beer, cold weather and Chris Tavaré, and Shane Warne fitted the hard-hearted profile yesterday by declaring on John Crawley.

It is the obvious reading of the situation *except* that the superfluous sentiment had already manifested itself in the batting on after lunch, which is only explicable in terms of personal achievement. Furthermore, Crawley claimed that the declaration had been proved correct because Hampshire had dismissed Nottinghamshire by the end of the day in a match that they needed to win to finish second and earn £40,000. But that would have been more possible by declaring at lunch-time and anyway, why did he not try to score six runs from the two balls before Mascarenhas made his century? Even if he did not know about the record, the team did and the declaration could have been delayed slightly.

Is this examination over-detailed? David Robinson, formerly Hampshire's Cricket Chairman, asked legitimately whether the record would have been that meaningful given the quality of the bowling and fielding on the second day. Poor young Footit, for example, returned figures of 17-0-153-1. But that argument, like those of the cricketers (although flawed in this instance), is not the whole point.

On a beautiful late September day a crowd of around fifteen hundred were enjoying the achievements of their batsmen in a season and on a ground where they had often not performed very well. It was fascinating to watch spectators consulting their *Playfair Cricket Annuals* as the records approached. They had been pleased to applaud Crawley past his thousand for the season and his various staging posts on the way to 300. Just past 250 one supporter began regaling his neighbours with memories of Gordon Greenidge against Sussex at Southampton in 1975 and others nodded in remembrance. Mike Taylor, who had played in that game, was present and told one or two more detailed stories of that match, which were fascinating for those who only watch beyond the boundary rope.

In the telling, hearing and re-telling of such tales spectators redefine themselves as supporters and 'fine tune' the degree of their passion. Only a few weeks earlier thousands of Hampshire 'fans' had made the trip to Lord's to be a part of a cup-winning triumph. Such experiences mark out and transform the business of being a spectator, a supporter or a fan and a failure to understand such differences can have both a cultural and an economic impact on the health and well-being of sporting organisations.

In other fields, for example popular music or film, serious and extensive research has been done on fans and consumers. This is sometimes academic rather than applied, but it can be very useful as a way of informing the industries what they are dealing with. One simple example is that work on fans' use of the internet has coincided with the film industry marketing their products extensively through that new technology.

In English sport, the main research has been done in football, although the ECB does analyse fairly carefully the audience for Test cricket. But the question of Crawley's 'record' is about a more complex aspect of the consumer/spectator/ fan/supporter issue. It has economic implications in the simplest sense because such events create marketing opportunities, but that is a fairly crude reason to bother with a record. It is more significant in the long term as a cultural issue, in the sense that being a supporter of Hampshire cricket is a cultural activity and cultures need to be nurtured.

So, in simple terms, everyone who was at the Rose Bowl on Thursday 22 September 2005 will be able to recount those tales in future years of Hampshire's record score and (perhaps) of Crawley's nearly record innings. But to say 'I was there' when, after 101 years of Hampshire county cricket, a man finally scored 317 (or more) is a tale that helps a spectator, or fan to become a supporter with all the implications of commitment that is carried with that.

Of course, in an ideal world it would be much more interesting to have people engaged in lengthier comparative discussions about players' techniques, captaincy in the modern age, the changing nature of first-class pitches or the optimum length of the limited-overs match. And of course such discussions do take place but they are often more esoteric and not necessarily an essential element of being a *county* supporter. That is often far more dependent on recalling for example the importance of 1961 at Bournemouth or 1988 at Lord's. Perhaps it will be Richards' century against Lancashire in the 1972 Gillette Cup or 'Butch' White's hat-trick at Portsmouth.

To doubt this is to forget Richie Benaud's tale that, since the first tied Test match in 1960, he has met so many people who were 'there' that the ground might have been filled five times. Now it may be that Crawley will say that he does not care about records or that the captain will argue the need for the declaration and – to reiterate – had Warne declared at lunchtime that would have made perfect sense. But when Crawley or Warne chose not to be bothered about a record that was there for the making, they betrayed a lack of awareness of what it is to be(come) a supporter of a sporting team, of the sense of identity, of the significance of the major moments.

Yet on that occasion a few weeks earlier at Lord's, as Hampshire struggled to break the partnership between Knight and Bell that could take the cup to

Warwickshire, Andy Bichel on the field began urging the Hampshire fans to roar their support. They did, the team reciprocated and the cup was won. It was Hampshire's cup and everyone had been a part of it. In the same way, while it was or was not Crawley's record, those Hampshire supporters on the ground had, or did not have, a part of it too. Because of the declaration they can only say – as anyone can on any day – I was there when Moore's record was *not* broken.

Hampshire's victory clinched second place and it was Chris Adams's turn to be furious with Nottinghamshire. They beat Kent in their final match and would have been second had Hampshire not beaten Nottinghamshire. Adams was astonished that they had invited Hampshire to bat and suggested that they had not tried very hard. One explanation was that Nottinghamshire's attention was focused on the Sunday, when the two winners of Hampshire v Nottinghamshire and Worcestershire v Lancashire would stay in the National League First Division at the expense of their opponents. It may be that Nottinghamshire, with an eye on that game, invited Hampshire to bat so that they might spend the previous day in the field and be less fresh for Sunday. In the event the match finished in three days but the day off was no use to Hampshire who were relegated with Worcestershire. It was a rather flat and rather damp end to an extraordinary season.

While Warne's presence clearly had a huge impact on Hampshire's performances it is worth pointing out that they won the C&G Trophy without him and never lost a Championship match when he was not playing. It was as if he had helped his refashioned side to believe more consistently in their own abilities.

As the season drew to a close, the local newspapers suggested that Hampshire were hoping to sign the Lancashire opening batsman Ian Sutcliffe and South African pace bowler Nantie Hayward as a 'Kolpak' player. Then it was reported that Warne might not return to honour his three-year contract, preferring to settle his domestic life in Australia. A few days later in his column in the *Times,* he denied this. Off the field, Hampshire's parent company reported that their hopes of a first profit had been over-optimistic and it was suggested that Rod Bransgrove had vetoed any further signings. On a number of occasions, media reports suggested that Hampshire were one of a number of wealthy clubs able to sign players to strengthen the squad, but the reality at the Rose Bowl was somewhat different. A few weeks before the end of the season an interview with Rod Bransgrove in the *Financial Times* suggested that he might welcome a partnership with venture capitalists, who would be unlikely to replicate his enthusiasm for cricket in general and Hampshire cricket in particular. The ECB were also due to introduce financial inducements to field English-qualified players from 2006 with estimates that, in the first instance, the Hampshire side of 2005 would have lost around £20,000 for their various 'foreigners'. If that looks manageable, then by 2007 that figure would rise to a loss of around £70,000, so there was clear pressure on Hampshire to field more Englishmen. It was a salutary thought that after some years of encouraging local players with little success, Durham enjoyed their best ever season after importing a number of players. By contrast, Gloucestershire and Glamorgan fielded the largest number of home-grown players and were both relegated by some distance from the First Division of the Championship. Despite the achievements of the 2005 season, the future for Hampshire cricket was as uncertain as it had ever been.

8

TO THE FUTURE

'Ever since I played, they always said cricket has no future but it's still here.'

Bryan Timms

ON THURSDAY 29 June 2006 during the midsummer heat wave, St Paul's Cathedral was the location of the 'Service of Thanksgiving for the Life of Colin Ingleby-Mackenzie'. The event was attended by many of the personalities of English cricket including Ted Dexter, Christopher Martin-Jenkins and Mark Nicholas, who offered a splendid appreciation, part reproduced subsequently in the *Daily Telegraph* (3 July 2006). In it, Nicholas described Colin Ingleby-Mackenzie as

> An amateur in the true and best sense. His light touch and extraordinary enthusiasm made him a force for good without compare … Gateman and groundstaff were treated as equals and all of them, from each corner of his rich tapestry, were seduced.

Also in attendance were a number of personalities from British acting and television, including Edward Fox, Peter O'Toole, John Standing and Ronnie Corbett, Hampshire's Chairman Rod Bransgrove, Patron Wilfred Weld, Robin Smith and members of the committee and vice-presidents. Most importantly, Hampshire County Cricket Club was represented by most of the surviving members of their Champions of 1961 including, in probable batting order, Jimmy Gray, Mike Barnard, Peter Sainsbury, Leo Harrison, 'Butch' White and Malcolm Heath. Of those six men, only White was born outside the county and he played in Hampshire sides from Club and Ground to the county Champions over a period of some 15 seasons.

Later that afternoon, Hampshire's current side offered their own tribute, thrashing Middlesex by 59 runs in one of the new Twenty20 matches. Hampshire's new signing Michael Carberry (via Surrey and Kent) top-scored with 90 and their latest Australian Dominic Thornely gave a good all-round performance with 50* and 3-30. Of their local players, the young Mitchell Stokes from Basingstoke scored 62, Chris Benham could not get to the wicket and Tremlett and Taylor took two wickets apiece. Since the side was captained by Udal there was a significant local presence in the side and in the Championship of 2006 both James Bruce and James Adams also made a significant impact. Adams in particular, after some years of unfulfilled promise, passed 1,000 Championship runs, formed a fine opening partnership with Michael Carberry and was capped, along with Bruce and Billy Taylor. While Bruce was born in London and Benham in Surrey both

90   *Ingleby–Mackenzie's memorial ceremony at St Paul's Cathedral and 50 years of Hampshire cricket: Tim Tremlett, 'Butch' White, Neil Trestrail (committee), Robin Smith, Jimmy Gray and Peter Sainsbury.*

they and the Hampshire-born players had come through the county's junior and 2nd XI sides.

Only two years earlier, commentator Bob Willis had noted in a Sky Sports commentary from Canterbury that 'a lot of young players have been given a lot of opportunities at Hampshire and none of them have really delivered the goods.' While this has been a significant problem for the county for some years it may be that 2006 did indicate a shift in Hampshire's team-building. Adams, Benham, Bruce, Taylor and Tremlett all appeared fairly regularly in the first team while there were opportunities for members of the next generation including Stokes, Tomlinson, Latouf and wicketkeeper Burrows. In addition, Hampshire employed only two overseas players throughout the year in comparison with five in 2005.

Hampshire's increasing use of their own players may have been partly in view of the impending financial rewards for playing English-qualified cricketers. But perhaps it also reflected not merely the will to develop young Hampshire cricketers but the success of the refined Academy system with its investment in junior and colts cricket in Hampshire. By 2005, Hampshire had their own infrastructure with representative sides at every age from under-10 to under-17 plus the colts, academy and 2nd XI teams as a route to county cricket. Their team photograph included Tim Tremlett the Director of Cricket, Manager Paul Terry and coaches Tony Middleton and Bruce Reid, and there were other coaches at the Rose Bowl including Raj Maru and Giles White, as well as the part-time contributions of Barry Reed, John Rice and others. By comparison, when Colin Ingleby-Mackenzie had first appeared in the Easter nets of 1946 he was coached by the senior professional Jim Bailey, because Hampshire only

91   *2006: Warne bowls to Compton as Strauss looks on.*

ever employed one man as their coach (then, Sam Staples). Nonetheless, when Ingleby-Mackenzie first captained Hampshire 12 years later he led a squad that included 11 Hampshire-born players: Jimmy Gray, Peter Sainsbury, Leo Harrison, Mervyn Burden, Malcolm Heath, Mike Barnard, Vic Cannings, Ray Flood, Ray Pitman, Alan Wassell and Bryan Timms. That immediate post-war period was remarkable in the county's history in terms of on-field achievements and the development of players but it would be a perfect tribute to the memory of Colin Ingleby-Mackenzie, Desmond Eagar, Arthur Holt and Harry Altham if the county were able to translate the current level of investment in junior cricket into a successful *Hampshire* side.

But this book has stressed that the 1950s were atypical for a county that has rarely produced major cricketers. For example, a best XI of Hampshire-born players from those who played in the trophy years from 1961-2005 might be: Gray, Middleton, Rice, Jesty, Barnard, Sainsbury, Ayling, Harrison or Aymes, Udal, Chris Tremlett, Malcolm Heath. It is not a bad XI but compare that with a side of men born overseas who represented Hampshire in the same period: Richards, Greenidge, Hayden, Roy Marshall, Robin Smith, Pietersen, Pothas, Warne, Streak, Malcolm Marshall, Roberts – and some useful cricketers have been overlooked. Another strong side could also be assembled from cricketers born in England but outside the county. Nonetheless, if there is to be any point in the investment in regional cricket, academies, coaches and representative sides, then Hampshire must produce more of their own cricketers in future.

Of course, one of the great difficulties for those charged with coaching, developing and managing first-class county sides is the expectation of success. While a side like Leicestershire currently languishes in the lower reaches of the Second Divisions they won their second Twenty20 trophy in 2006. There have been a number of different Championship winners in recent years and, after some years of success, Gloucestershire's grip on Lord's finals has been loosened with Hampshire and Sussex as the recent winners.

Hampshire won the C&G Trophy in 2005 and were runners-up to Nottinghamshire in the County Championship. Given his approach to the game it was perhaps no surprise when captain Shane Warne informed the members' AGM that he saw no reason why Hampshire should not win all four major trophies in 2006. The season had been revamped yet again with an unpopular 'league' version of the knock-out trophy, in which Hampshire were never consistent enough to prevent Sussex from heading the Southern group. Sussex met Lancashire in the final and these two sides also dominated the Championship, while Hampshire flattered to deceive. They beat Yorkshire twice in a season for the first time in their history, with Jimmy Adams scoring the winning runs on both occasions, but they also suffered a number of bad defeats, not least at the Rose Bowl to Sussex, Durham and Warwickshire.

They met Warwickshire on Wednesday 16 August, exactly 45 years to the day after the same fixture at Northlands Road, and on both occasions Warwickshire batted first and posted over three hundred. In 1961 Mike Barnard replied with a century and he was on the ground in 2006 commentating for local hospital radio. Sadly no one replicated his feat, Hampshire followed on, appeared to have salvaged a four-point draw and then lost from the final ball. What they lacked was the equivalent of Derek Shackleton, who had bowled them to victory in 1961 – the first of four consecutive victories that brought them the title.

In some respects, Dimitri Mascarenhas is the bowler who most resembles Shackleton, although the conditions and circumstances of contemporary cricket do not compare with 'Shack's' time. The wicket-taking role should be – indeed sometimes is – Chris Tremlett's. Had he remained fit he would almost certainly have become that elusive first Hampshire-born, Hampshire cricketer to represent his country in a home Test match. But he has not stayed fit and during 2006 he produced a number of fine performances, but also missed seven of the 16 Championship matches. Incredibly he was rested from Hampshire's last Pro40 match at Headingley, came on as substitute, broke a finger and missed the end of the season. It is the kind of occurrence that makes one believe in bad luck.

Tremlett had been one of three Hampshire players selected for England's tour of the subcontinent during the previous winter – the first occasion that three Hampshire players were selected together for more than eighty years. Sadly, in mid-October the newspapers reported that he had withdrawn with hamstring tendonitis behind his right knee. David Graveney made sympathetic noises but Angus Fraser (*Independent*) suggested that Tremlett's 'ongoing' injuries 'are becoming a worry'. Since his debut in 2000 he had suffered from broken bones in his feet, had undergone a hip operation and now had this knee problem. He had never completed a full English season although at 24 he was still young enough to overcome those difficulties. Fraser added that 'injury prone is a tag no young fast bowler wants', while Christopher Martin-Jenkins (*Times*) noted that he had been 'dogged by injury for much of his short career'.

In 2000 he was still a student when he made his debut against New Zealand 'A' at Portsmouth. Ironically he was not permitted to bowl long spells in that match – by rules designed to protect the fitness of young bowlers. That was his only first-class match in 2000 but in 2001 he played in five league matches and joined the staff full time while still nineteen. He played fairly regularly in the National League side that year and began playing more regularly in the Championship. In 2002 and 2003 he spent his winters with the England Academy. Despite this early promise and progress he missed almost forty per cent of Hampshire's matches in his first five years and bowled only 300-400 overs in a season – hundreds fewer than might have been expected 40 years earlier.

His father Tim was neither as tall nor as fast as Chris but he will point out that, by the age of 24 in 1980, he had bowled just 178 Championship overs and 50 in the Sunday League, so that there may have been too many early expectations of Chris. In that very difficult season for the county Tim was not a regular player in the opening weeks and was also sometimes played mainly as a batsman. Similarly Tony Middleton, who has been involved in coaching Chris, points out that, whereas supporters and critics were once excited if the young bowler took, say, 2-40 or 3-70, their expectations have risen with his increased publicity and selection for England squads.

Perhaps at Hampshire, the most apposite comparison is with Bob Cottam, who was also less quick but somewhat similar to Chris Tremlett. He was 24 in 1969 and coincidentally he had just returned from Pakistan, where he made his Test debut. Although he took nine wickets in his first two Tests he was then discarded by England. In the 1969 season he bowled 933 Championship overs as well as 117 in the first year of the Sunday League. Even if Chris reaches full fitness he will not bowl anything approaching 1,000 overs in any English season.

Cottam's two partners during the 1960s also bowled a considerable number of overs at the age of 24 – in both cases their first full seasons in first-class cricket. Derek Shackleton had made his debut the year before and in 1949 he bowled 941 overs in the Championship. 'Butch' White made his debut in 1957 and in 1960, when 24, he bowled 830 overs.

It appears then that these older players were able to retain their fitness in a way that has eluded Tremlett. One simple explanation for this is that Tremlett is lucky to be that talented but also unlucky to struggle with fitness. If that is the case, if it is a particular and individual case, then all that remains is to hope that Tremlett overcomes these problems and fulfils his undoubted promise to the advantage of Hampshire and England.

But what if this 'case' is indicative of something more significant in modern cricket? It invites us to ask whether pace bowlers were fitter 40 or 50 years ago than they are today? In some senses it is not difficult to measure by considering how many matches players missed then. In the case of Derek Shackleton the answer is so few between 24 and his early 40s as to make research unnecessary. But we know that Shackleton was not really a *fast* bowler and was easy on his feet. 'Butch' White, on the other hand, carried a large upper body and was in temperament and actuality completely a fast bowler, putting huge strain on his fitness with every delivery. In his biography of Fred Trueman, John Arlott suggested that after Tyson's retirement only White could challenge Trueman as the fastest bowler in English cricket. He too made it to Test matches in Pakistan following Hampshire's title success in 1961 and it precipitated the one major fitness problem of his career, but even with the injuries that he suffered in 1962 and 1963 he was a regular member of the side. Between the ages of 24 (1960) and 30 (1966) he played in 190 first-class matches for Hampshire in seven seasons – around ninety per cent of the total – and he continued to play regularly for some years after that. If Tremlett matches that record over the next seven years it should be hugely to the advantage of Hampshire and perhaps England.

While White was a big man with a very physical action, he had the advantage in this period of only playing a few Gillette Cup matches. It may be that the extra demands of the various limited-overs competitions have a negative impact on the fitness of young bowlers in the 21st century. Another key point is that White generally bowled on uncovered wickets, which, in wet summers, meant his front foot landing on a relatively soft, giving surface. Despite his successes at Portsmouth and its reputation as a fast bowler's wicket, 'Butch' will recount how by the end of the August 'Pompey week' his body would ache from bowling on that harder ground. For Tremlett, most pitches are like this. In addition, Tremlett has not enjoyed opening the bowling with someone like Shackleton – nor has he handed over to Bob Cottam as first change. In essence these men were able to bowl themselves to fitness together through the season.

Throughout the 1990s and early 21st century, it seemed that every analysis of the latest defeat of the Test side would be accompanied by the claim that the cricketers, and especially the bowlers, were working too hard, yet everyone knows that the workload is not comparable with that which bowlers accepted decades ago. For example, in the beautiful summer of 1959 Derek Shackleton bowled over 1,300 overs and opening bowlers like Jackson (Derbyshire), Smith (Gloucestershire), Halfyard (Kent), Higgs (Lancashire) and Thomson of Sussex all bowled more than 1,000, all taking over 100 wickets. A number of other pace bowlers passed 900 overs, spinners regularly went past the 1,000 mark and every county had at least one bowler who bowled 800 overs. Even the England bowlers got through many overs, despite missing county matches when selected and despite their Indian opponents being a weak batting side. For example, Fred Trueman bowled 980 overs for England and Yorkshire and, if you add his 39 overs for the Players against the Gentlemen, he too bowled beyond the 1,000 and then went off to the West Indies for the winter. But, as Arlott once noted, Trueman 'rarely missed a match through injury or unfitness over twenty years'.

By comparison, in 2002, just four bowlers exceeded 600 first-class overs (Udal, Sheriyar, Croft and Batty) and 14 men bowled more than 500 overs. Udal bowled most – 627 – plus 104 in National League and 69 in the two knock-out cups – a total of 800. Yet in 1959, 38 men bowled more than Udal's 800 overs.

Similarly in 2005, 11 bowlers exceeded 500 overs in first-class cricket and again, as in 1959 and 2002, the leading figure was a Hampshire bowler in his 30s, although during that season Shane Warne also bowled for the touring Australians. Mushtaq Ahmed (Sussex) and off spinner Brown (Northamptonshire) were the two others to pass 600 while both Test sides were affected at crucial moments by injuries to leading pace bowlers, Jones for England and McGrath for Australia. The only pace bowler in 2002 to pass 600 overs, Alamgir Sheriyar, had virtually disappeared by 2005 although still only 31 and, at the end of the season, Kent released him. In 2005 the leading pace bowler was the South African Gideon Kruis at Yorkshire, who was 15 overs short of six hundred. During the winter, Jones and Tremlett were selected for the England tour but both withdrew injured, while Harmison returned home early with injury and England's injury problems continued in 2006, affecting Flintoff, Vaughan and Giles as well as most of the reserve pace bowlers.

During the winter of 2005–6, while the veteran Shaun Udal was enjoying his Test matches, Chris Tremlett and Sean Ervine both had major operations. In late March, Hampshire's local newspapers reported that the players had returned for their pre-season training and that Tremlett, Ervine, Tomlinson and Griffiths, all pace bowlers, were struggling to be fit for the new season. During 2006, England suffered serious problems with injured players and Pakistan too lost members of their pace attack.

One of the dafter comments about the issue of bowlers' fitness came from Kevin Shine, the former Hampshire opening bowler. After his appointment as England's bowling coach he answered readers' questions in the *Guardian* and commented that, 'We're only interested in facts about injuries not in hearsay or conjecture and now we can analyse the angles and forces involved in fast bowling'.

Had Shine been better read, he might have been aware of Dickens's parody of the schoolmaster Gradgrind and his obsession with facts. But if Shine insists on facts then they are that, after England won the Ashes in 2005, the only bowler who stayed free from injury was Matthew Hoggard, until exactly one year later even he was withdrawn from Yorkshire's final matches. At Shine's old county, by contrast, the only major pace bowler to suffer serious injury problems in almost fifty post-war years to the departure of Malcolm Marshall was Malcolm Heath. By contrast, Lofty Herman, George Heath, Shackleton, Cannings, White, Cottam, Bob Herman, Mottram, Roberts, Stevenson, Marshall and Connor generally enjoyed injury-free careers. Those are 'facts' of the kind that make Shine's interest in 'angles and forces' less significant. Contemporary pace bowlers are less free from injury than they used to be – fact!

Meanwhile, off the field the press carried a number of reports of economic problems at counties like Derbyshire, who lost £215,000 in 2005, Kent (£310,000), Sussex (£631,000) and Leicestershire (£84,000). While these counties welcomed the payout from the Ashes Test series they still recorded financial problems reminiscent of the early 1960s and, at the end of 2006, Glamorgan, in rapid decline on the field, announced they could not afford any overseas players for 2007. The non-Test counties drew particular attention to the increasing gap between counties with international venues and those like themselves who could not operate at that level. For example, in the same period Warwickshire recorded profits of £750,000, Lancashire £500,000 and Nottinghamshire, the county Champions, £100,000. In July 2006, Leicestershire won the Twenty20 trophy at which point their Chairman Neil Davidson claimed that the ECB's distribution of income from the competition would leave the winners with no more than £2,000 while estimating that the hosts Nottinghamshire could expect around £300,000. Nottinghamshire disagreed, suggesting around £50,000, but nonetheless the implication was that the counties with international venues were increasingly privileged over those without, regardless of on-field success. As a consequence more and more counties, including Hampshire, were seeking to join that international club.

The major international venues in England remained those at Lord's and in the five counties of Lancashire, Nottinghamshire, Surrey, Warwickshire and Yorkshire. But in the early 21st century Durham, Glamorgan, Gloucestershire and Hampshire were increasingly hosting international fixtures and, while Hampshire met some difficulties with spectator access, the modern facilities and excellent attendances created real competition for fixtures.

But establishing a new Test venue is not straightforward, since it implies other counties losing those fixtures. In February 2006 Ivo Tennant in the *Times* revealed that Rod Bransgrove was 'threatening to give up' funding the Rose Bowl if Test status was not confirmed. This was in the context of Rose Bowl plc reporting a trading loss of £750,000 and subsequent cutbacks including the closure of the Connor's fitness centre. Tennant added that if Bransgrove does choose to withdraw his support 'the future of the club will be in doubt'.

One month later the English Cricket Board visited the Rose Bowl again to consider the ground for Test status, having turned down applications in 2004 and 2005. By then, there were six new permanent floodlights in anticipation of two limited-overs international matches during the season, with England scheduled to play Sri Lanka and Pakistan and a scheme promising investment of £35m. It was all a long way from senior players coaching schoolboys on the old Northlands Road ground in 1946 while Hampshire held fund-raising whist drives and regretted that they could not afford to offer a contract to Vic Cannings.

Sadly, only weeks later Hampshire heard that Cardiff had been the preferred venue. One explanation was that Hampshire could not request 'conditional' approval on their pitch improvement, yet Cardiff's plans for necessary developments had not even received planning permission and were meeting local opposition. Hampshire were not the only disappointed county, as Old Trafford was dropped for the Ashes series of 2009, and Durham were also overlooked but Bransgrove was again quoted as 'considering his Hampshire future'. In the *Wisden Cricketer* (June 2006) Bransgrove pointed out that Lin Tatham, who had been an executive for the Welsh Sports Council for 15 years, had chaired the ECB's Inspection Team while the ECB Chairman David Morgan is also from Glamorgan. More specifically, Bransgrove wondered whether his regular disappointments at the hands of ECB reflected a suspicion 'of new grounds that had been backed by private money'. If so, this may have significant implications for the future of the English

92 *High summer, cricket on the grass and soccer on the screen.*

domestic game, which is struggling to survive through the old members' clubs model. He concluded, We have the overheads of an international ground, have provided a world class venue ... but have little international cricket to pay the bills'. Nonetheless, in November 2006 Bransgrove announced plans to increase the ground's capacity to 23,000, accompanied by other improvements to create a leading Test ground. Shortly after this, the ECB finally awarded the Rose Bowl Test Status from 2010 onwards and Bransgrove declared himself 'very happy'.

One way of paying at least some of the bills was examined by Andrew Culf in the *Guardian* (4 May) who asked whether live concerts by Elton John and others might be the 'saviour of county cricket?' Kent, over £300,000 in debt at the end of 2005, expected their largest-ever crowd for a concert by Elton John to address their 'fragile finances'. Hampshire's Chief Executive Glen Delve told the members' AGM that they were considering taking cricket back to Basingstoke or Bournemouth in 2007 to allow more free time for concerts and international fixtures at the Rose Bowl and in 2006 they scheduled two events – Billy Joel, an American Elton John equivalent and operatic tenor Luciano Pavarotti. In the event Joel, having sold out concerts elsewhere in England, attracted no more than a third of the Rose Bowl's capacity while Pavarotti's disappointing ticket sales were relieved by his illness and withdrawal.

Hampshire's new floodlights were christened on a fine day at the Rose Bowl. A capacity crowd enjoyed a friendly match between various veterans and current Hampshire players, then watched the tea-time World Cup soccer match between England and Trinidad & Tobago before a thrilling final-over Twenty20 victory for Sri Lanka against England. Sadly, not for the first time, the late finish was exacerbated for many with another set of problems in getting spectators away. Many were still queuing for 'park & ride' buses past midnight.

There were no such problems for Hampshire's floodlit Pro40 match against Surrey in late August because the match was abandoned with no play. During that week there was also the doubt about England's 50-over match against Pakistan caused by the ball-tampering controversy but in the end the extraordinary revelations about Umpire Hair relieved some of the pressure and the game went ahead on a beautiful day, with a crowd of 20,000 coming to and leaving the ground with no problems. It seemed that the Rose Bowl's lessons had been learned and the solutions found.

In the furore about ball-tampering a number of former cricketers revealed interesting tales to confirm that it had been a regular problem in the game for some time, and former players including Bob Woolmer and Mike Selvey suggested that ball manipulation using natural resources should be permitted. It is a powerful argument since it helps the balance between bat and ball and demands improved techniques and improvisatory skills.

Of course, in England there was a lingering suspicion that Pakistan may have been 'guilty', partly because for some years they have been demonised in the media and by popular opinion. They have not always helped themselves with their arrogant responses to accusation – usually characterised sentimentally as 'proud' – and Mark Nicholas revealed that, at Taunton in 1991, Hampshire's young Pakistan pace bowler Aqib Javed had been 'caught' by umpire David Shepherd changing the ball's condition. A friendly word was sufficient to stop the

93 *The floodlights shine for the first time.*

94 *Part of the 20,000 Rose Bowl crowd to watch Pietersen and Bell batting for England v Pakistan, 2006.*

95 *Kevin Pietersen.*

mischief although stories still circulate around Hampshire of how Aqib the likeable teammate of 1991 turned into an aggressive opponent as one of Javed Miandad's visitors to Northland Road the following summer. That year was a low point in on-field relationships between England and Pakistan cricketers but by 2006 the relationships often seemed cordial.

But Pakistan cricketers did not invent ball tampering. Charlie Knott retired in 1954, the year that their new nation first toured England. He once revealed how in a game in Gloucestershire he received the ball at the end of his run and was very surprised by its condition. As a young player, he said nothing about it but he always had his suspicions about the culprit in the days when Hampshire generally fielded an entirely English side. One of the least-balanced responses to the incident came from those press reports suggesting that the game would be changed irrevocably, whereas in truth it has survived previous tampering incidents, W.G. Grace, bodyline, Cronje's match-fixing, Lever's vaseline and all kinds of crises, as it will survive this one.

By the time Pakistan came to the Rose Bowl in 2006, Hampshire had been to Hove where, on the Friday afternoon, a small group of Hampshire supporters opened a bottle of champagne at 4.08p.m. to drink a toast to the men who, exactly 45 years earlier, had brought that first title to the county. Colin Ingleby-Mackenzie and Roy Marshall were no longer around to share the memories and Derek Shackleton was not well enough to recall the day, but the memory of that event was still strong in their adopted county.

But the match at Hove was drawn as Sussex, with the best-balanced side and

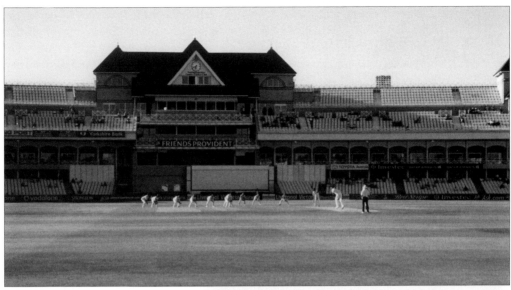

96   *Trent Bridge 2006 and Warne sets 10 slips and gullies.*

97   *Benham acknowledges his century v Glamorgan in the 2006 Play-Off.*

almost no international calls, went to a well-deserved second title. Three weeks later Hampshire entertained Lancashire at the Rose Bowl with an outside chance of overtaking the Northern county to finish second. In the event Lancashire outplayed them for two days, secured second place and then wrecked the final day by batting throughout. The Hampshire bowlers, as frustrated as the crowd, served up lobs, bowled from their 'wrong' hand and Warne deliberately threw – the first Hampshire bowler to be 'called' since 'Butch' White in 1960. By comparison, on the following day Hampshire met Glamorgan at the Rose Bowl in the first-ever English 'play-off' for a place in the First Division of the Pro40. Thanks mainly to a magnificent 150 from Chris Benham and some hostile out-cricket they had some revenge on the Welsh to conclude 2006, and promotion was secured.

But by the end of 2006, a top-three Championship place and promotion was insufficient to alleviate a sense of disappointment in the season. By comparison, the players of 1955 had been fêted for months for achieving the county's first-ever third place. This different reaction was a measure of the extent to which in the ensuing decades Hampshire cricket and the expectations of its followers had been transformed. As a consequence of its off-field and international ambitions it still faces uncertain but ambitious times. The hope remains that, if they continue to entertain, they will not perish.

BIBLIOGRAPHY

Allen, D., Jenkinson, N., Renshaw, A., *Hampshire County Cricket Club* (2000)

Allen, D., Jenkinson, N., Ricquier, B., *100 Greats: Hampshire County Cricket Club* (2003)

Altham, H.S., Arlott, J., Eagar, E.D.R., Webber, R., *Hampshire County Cricket – the Official History* (1957)

Ashley-Cooper, F.S., *Hampshire County Cricket* (1924)

Barker, J.S., *Summer Spectacular: West Indies v England* (1963)

Bird, D., *White Cap and Bails* (2000)

Birley, D., *A Social History of English Cricket* (1999)

Brooke, R., *A History of the County Cricket Championship* (1991)

Eagar, E.D.R., *Purely Personal* (1953)

Gannaway, N., *A History of Cricket in Hampshire* (1990)

Greenidge, C.G., *The Man in the Middle* (1980)

Hayes, D., *Famous Cricketers of Hampshire* (1993)

Hill, A., *Brian Close: Cricket's Lionheart* (2003)

Ingleby-Mackenzie, A.C.D., *Many A Slip* (1962)

Isaacs, V., *Hampshire CCC First Class Records 1864-1992* (1993)

Marshall, M., *Gentlemen and Players: Conversations with Cricketers* (1987)

Marshall, M.D., *Marshall Arts* (1987)

Marshall, R., *Test Outcast* (1970)

Martin-Jenkins, C.J., *Twenty Years On: Cricket's Years of Change* (1984)

Marwick, A., *The Sixties: Cultural Revolution in Britain, France, Italy & the United States c. 1958-c. 1974* (1998)

Matthews, D., *On the Spot: Derek Shackleton* (1998)

Mote, A. (editor), *John Nyren's The Cricketers of my Time* (1998)

Murphy, R., *Sixties British Cinema* (1982)

Oborne, P., *Basil D'Oliveira – Cricket and Conspiracy: the Untold Story* (2004)

Richards, B.A., *The Barry Richards Story* (1978)

Robinson, M., *Football League Tables 1888-2002* (2002)

Ross, G., *The Gillette Cup 1963 to 1980* (1981)

Saunders, S., *Cricket in Hampshire: a Bibliography* (1997)

Smallbone, K., *Farewell to May's Bounty* (2000)

Tennyson, L.H., *Sticky Wickets* (1950)

Trueman, F. and Mosey, D., *Cricket Statistics Year by Year 1946-1987* (1988)

Westcott, C., *Class of '59* (2000)

Wynne-Thomas, P., *The History of Hampshire County Cricket Club*, 1988

Hampshire Handbook (various)

Playfair Cricket Annual (various)

Wisden Cricketers' Almanac (various)

Articles

Arlott, J., 'Ain't Half a Bloody Game', first published in the magazine *Lilliput*

Solan, J., 'Through the Crystal Ball' in *Wisden* (1963)

INDEX

Page numbers printed in bold type refer to illustrations.

216